Life
in the
Pueblo

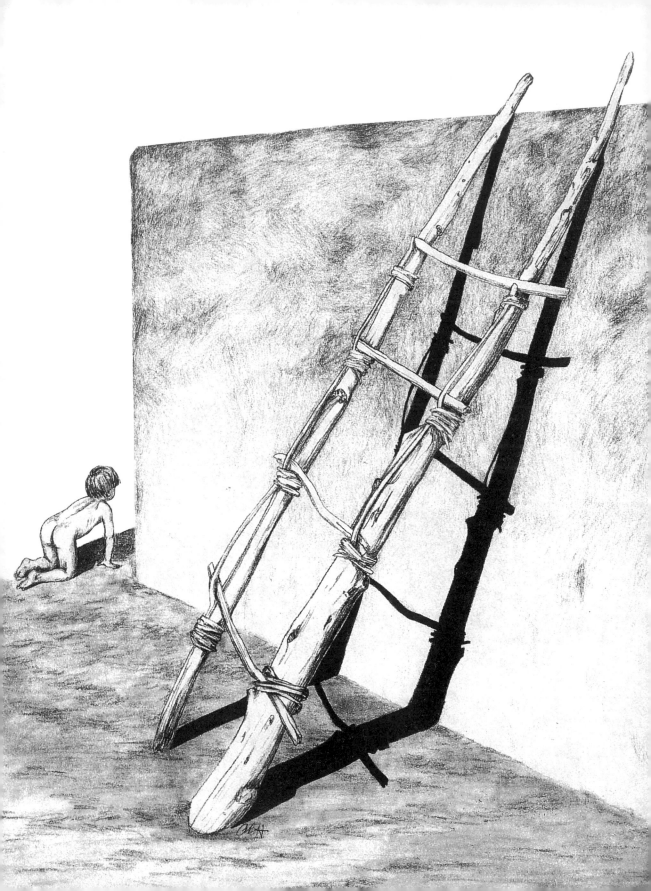

Life
in the
Pueblo

Understanding the Past
Through Archaeology

KATHRYN KAMP
Grinnell College

Illustrations by
Amy Henderson

WAVELAND

PRESS, INC.

Prospect Heights, Illinois

For information about this book, write or call:
Waveland Press, Inc.
P.O. Box 400
Prospect Heights, Illinois 60070
847/634-0081

Contents

Preface

There are many stories of the past, as many tales as there are tellers. Even within a single family, each individual experiences the same events from a different perspective. If we could magically transport ourselves to the Flagstaff, Arizona region in the eleventh or twelfth century A.D. and interview the inhabitants, we would without a doubt find a diversity of experiences and opinions. To an extent, these differences would be idiosyncratic, depending on personality and life history. To an extent, they would be patterned, depending on generation, gender, ethnicity, and other sociocultural variables. Overall, however, the beliefs of individuals would cluster around a core of consensus about basic cultural patterns, and their experiences would reflect the social realities of the time and place.

My aim is to shed light on the lives of the residents of a small prehistoric hamlet, Lizard Man Village, to tell the stories of individuals now long dead, and to determine what their culture was like. The task is made difficult by the variability mentioned above. It is further complicated by the fact that the village was occupied for almost two hundred years, roughly between A.D. 1070 and 1250. Thus, the changes that took place during the span of several generations must be considered. We must add to this challenge the fact that it is impossible to talk to the occupants of Lizard Man Village. Nor did they leave any written accounts to aid us in our queries. The only evidence of their existence long ago consists of the remains in archaeological sites like Lizard Man Village and in the stories of a remote past recounted by their distant descendants. It is from this heritage that a past must be reconstructed.

When the past is viewed from the perspective of the present, the variability in viewpoints becomes even greater. The past is of necessity perceived through the filter of the present. Thus, the cultural and political realities of the present inevitably influence the questions asked, the types of answers sought, and the nature of the evidence considered. I will present three interwoven narratives, each with its own perspectives and contributions.

First, stories and ethnographic information from modern Puebloan groups, the descendants of the village's inhabitants, provide a link between the present and the past. To an extent, most interpretations of prehistoric Puebloan groups are based on what we know of their historic or modern descendants and of human behavior in general. In addition, however, because archaeological cultures like the Sinagua and villages like Lizard Man Village are part of the ancestral heritage of existing individuals, they potentially have current social, religious, and political meanings. Interpretations of the past may provide a means for social integration, a verification of religious ideology, or a focus for political action.

Second, archaeological research provides reconstructions of the lifeways at Lizard Man Village and similar contemporary sites. Since I am by profession an archaeologist, it is this perspective that will be emphasized. One of the goals of this book is to give some insight into current techniques of archaeological discovery and analysis. Here it is certainly worth noting that, although there is some consensus about archaeological technique, there is rarely unanimity about the details of archaeological interpretations. The archaeologist provides another story of the past, one with its own rules of evidence and logic.

The third story, which is really, as mentioned earlier, a multiplicity of stories, is that of the actual individuals who lived at Lizard Man Village. We will never really know these stories, but I have used the accumulated evidence and my imagination to speculate about what one of them might be like. This fictional reconstruction, presented in chapter 5, is as consistent with the data from Lizard Man Village as I could make it (test this out as you read), but, of necessity, goes beyond the boundaries of what archaeology can tell us about the past in order to portray the detail that is necessary for any complete depiction.

While these three perspectives together only claim to provide an initial insight into the lives of the occupants of Lizard Man Village, it is my hope that together they will raise questions, spark interest, and inspire the desire for more knowledge.

Acknowledgments

The research at Lizard Man Village and the writing of this book has involved a vast number of people and organizations. I am sure that I will inadvertently forget someone, and I beg their forgiveness. My husband, John Whittaker, has been a full partner in all aspects of the Lizard Man Village excavations as well as providing encouragement and advice for this volume. I can never thank him enough. As I thank others, however, I speak for him as well in acknowledging everyone who has aided our efforts to investigate Lizard Man Village and hopefully, in the process, to teach students a love of the past and of the investigative process.

Of greatest importance to me are the Grinnell students and colleagues with whom I have interacted over the years. They are the ones who inspired me to attempt to write about our excavations at Lizard Man Village in a manner accessible to a wider audience than just professional archaeologists. Of special note are Ralph Luebben and his wife Jan, who conducted a field school for Grinnell in the 1960s and 1970s and who were extremely gracious about helping me integrate into the department.

A number of students participated in field schools at Lizard Man Village, working with John and me, and living with us and our daughter April. They often provided great cuisine and wonderful companionship in addition to copious amounts of labor. I thank: (1984) Steve Boyd, Robert Brubaker, Barbara Cardell, June Krell, Melinda Lopes, Steve Nash, Rexford Osae, Kevin Rhodes, and Anneke Walker; (1985) Elizabeth Apel, Sara Bruins, Lisa Piedescalsi, Jackie Jendras, Gwen Johnson, Sandra Raimondo, Hiliary Thompson, Neil Weintraub, and Michael Williams; (1986) Sara Bruins (field assistant), Heather Barthell, Deanna Bickford, Karen Brockman, John Campos, Romy Coberly, Sara Croft, Mary Novotny, Kirsten Pogue, Jonathon Till, and Jennifer Wright; and (1988) Paula Briggs, Sara Deichman, Danja Foss, Steven Hingtgen, Colleen Mahar, Rebecca Matthews, Amy Naughton, Dana Robson, Suzanna Smith, and Richard Wallace.

A number of students also worked analyzing the Lizard Man Village collections or entering data from them into the cataloguing system at the Museum of Northern Arizona. These include: Heather Barthell, Sara Bruins, Barbara Cardell, Jon Cook, Sara Gottschalk, Jules Graybill, Matt Hedman, Melinda Lopes, Colleen Mahar, Ayse Mallinder, Janet Matthews, Vickie Michner, Leslie Morlock, Lisa Piedescalzi, Sandra Raimondo, Katya Ricketts, Gerrit Saylor, Jonathon Till, Jonathon Van Hoose, Rebecca Wallace, Anneke Walker, and Neil Weintraub.

Quite a few professional anthropologists and friends have helped us with our field school over the years, by volunteering their time to provide lectures, field trips, and excavation labor. These include: Rick Ahlstrom, Bruce Anderson, Ann Baldwin, Mary Bernard, Mike Bremer, Sarah DeLong, Chris Downum, Lee Fratt, Kelly Hayes, Amy Henderson, Eric Henderson, Dennis Gilpin, Dave Greenwald, Dawn Greenwald, Nancy Parezo, Peter Pilles, Jane Rosenthal, Chet Shaw, Kay Simpson, Alice Schlegel, Gretchen Schwager, Jon Till, Neil Weintraub, David Wilcox, and Steve Williams. Elaine Hughes and Bridget Sullivan are particularly to be thanked for their assistance in excavating and conserving the fiber armband mentioned in the text. Richard Ciolek-Torrello taught John Whittaker how to take archaeomagnetic samples, and Peter Pilles coached John and Kathy on ceramic typology as well as providing lectures, field trips, and advice. Lee Fratt assisted Kathy in learning how to do usewear analysis. Steve Williams provided chemical analysis of pigments and worked stone, and Sharon Urban identified a sample of representative shells.

Both the Museum of Northern Arizona and the Coconino National Forest personnel have been indispensable to the success of both our field schools and our research. Peter Pilles and Linda Farnsworth of the Coconino National Forest have given unstintingly of their time to help us obtain excavation permits, arrange housing, and even to provide funding. David Wilcox and Don Weaver of the Museum of Northern Arizona arranged curation permits and acted as valued colleagues in many other ways. During a sabbatical, when I spent much time working in the collections area of the museum, looking at comparative artifactual material and at site records, Dawn Greenwald and Elaine Hughes made my stay a joy.

Grants to support the Lizard Man Village Field School have been provided by the Agnese Lindley Foundation, the Coconino National Forest, and Grinnell College Faculty Grant Board. The administration of Grinnell College has provided funding to ensure that the field school is able to operate and has frequently provided aid to students to help them attend, irrespective of financial need. A National Science Foundation ILI grant purchased the Electronic Distance Meter mentioned in the text.

Comments on all or parts of this manuscript were provided by Michael Adler, Jonathon Andelson, Amy Henderson, Ralph Luebben, Betty Moffett, Kay Simpson, Jon Till, Neil Weintraub, and John Whittaker. Amy Henderson labored to produce fabulous illustrations. Robyn Wingerter and many others provided secretarial assistance.

Finally, I would like to thank my daughter, April Kamp-Whittaker, who began her field training at just over one year old. Despite the disadvantages of giving over most of her summers to archaeology and sharing her parents with a large "family" of college students, she has generally remained good humored and understanding.

Photo Credits

Chapter 1 1.2 Courtesy of Museum of Northern Arizona Photo Archives, Neg. No. 10280 **Chapter 2** Opener, 2.1, 2.2, 2.7, 2.8 and 2.9 John Whittaker 2.6 Kathryn Kamp **Chapter 3** 3.1* and 3.4 John Whittaker 3.6 and 3.7 Kathryn Kamp† **Chapter 4** 4.2, 4.3, 4.5, 4.6, 4.8. 4.9, 4.10 and 4.14 John Whittaker 4.12 Kathryn Kamp **Chapter 6** 6.5, 6.8 and 6.10 John Whittaker 6.9 Amy Henderson 6.11 Arizona State Museum, University of Arizona, E. B. Sayles, Photographer **Chapter 7** 7.3 Courtesy of Museum of Northern Arizona Photo Archives, Neg. No. 64.887 7.5 Courtesy of Museum of Northern Arizona Photo Archives, Neg. No. MS101–2–44 **Chapter 8** 8.1 Amy Henderson 8.3 The Field Museum, #2343, Chicago 8.6 Amy Henderson 8.8 Smithsonian Institution, Neg. No. 2263B 8.15 Courtesy of Museum of New Mexico, Neg. No. 21540 8.17 Cline Library, Leo Crane Collection, Northern Arizona University, NAU.PH.658.220 **Chapter 9** 9.2 Kathryn Kamp 9.3 and 9.4 John Whittaker **Chapter 11** 11.1 John Whittaker

*First published in *The Kiva*, 1992.
†First published in *The Kiva*, 1995.

Illustration Credits

All text illustrations by Amy Henderson unless otherwise noted.

1.5 Redrawn from McGregor 1943 with permission of the American Philosophical Society.
4.13 Drawn after Paleopole plot by Jeff Eighmy.
6.1 Redrawn from Brothwell 1972: 59, Figure 24 with permission of the author.
7.2 Frank Cushing's drawing from Cushing 1920: Plate V.
7.4 Frank Cushing's drawing from Cushing 1920: Plate IV.
8.9 Composite illustration courtesy of University of Texas Press, from Whittaker 1995, Figures 2.2 and 2.3.
10.1 Drawn using Hohman 1992, Figures 46, 47, 48, and 51.

Chapter 1

INTRODUCTION

In about A.D. 1064 and for several years thereafter a volcano erupted to the northeast of modern-day Flagstaff, emitting gasses, extruding lava, and spewing volcanic cinders and ash over some eight hundred square miles. It is within the ashfall of this volcano, now called Sunset Crater, that a small group of people founded Lizard Man Village (figure 1.1). The eruption of Sunset Crater must have been terrifying, and its ecological consequences for the immediate surround were certainly profound. Not unexpectedly, information about the event has survived in local traditions. The Hopi tell the following story about the creation of Sunset Crater.

A Hopi Story of the Eruption of Sunset Crater*

Long, long ago the beautiful daughter of the headman of the village of Mishongnovi was wooed by a handsome and mysterious stranger, who presented her with gifts of food such as fresh roasted sweet corn out of season, watermelon, and dried meat. Ultimately she agreed to marry him.

The two went west to meet the groom's family. At first they journeyed on foot. Then the young man took a rainbow out of his pouch, saying that since they had far to go to his village, that would be a more efficient means of travel. The girl was frightened but climbed aboard and was whisked away on the rainbow. During a short stop on the journey, Spider Woman, a supernatural helper and teacher of the Hopi, informed the young woman that her fiancé was actually a supernatural spirit, a Ka'nas *katsina* (figure 1.2). Spider Woman offered to accompany the bride on her journey and help her succeed in the trials that awaited.

The girl, with Spider Woman riding hidden behind her ear, was taken to a *kiva*, a subterranean ceremonial room, somewhere on a peak in the San Francisco Mountains. In the kiva were many katsinas and, following a sumptuous feast, the groom appeared in his true guise as a Ka'nas katsina.

The next morning before dawn Hahay'iwuuti, mother of the katsinas, led the girl to the grinding bins and gave her some chunks of ice with instructions

---

* The following story has been summarized primarily from Malotki (1987). Other versions were also recorded by Colton (1932) and Voth (1905).

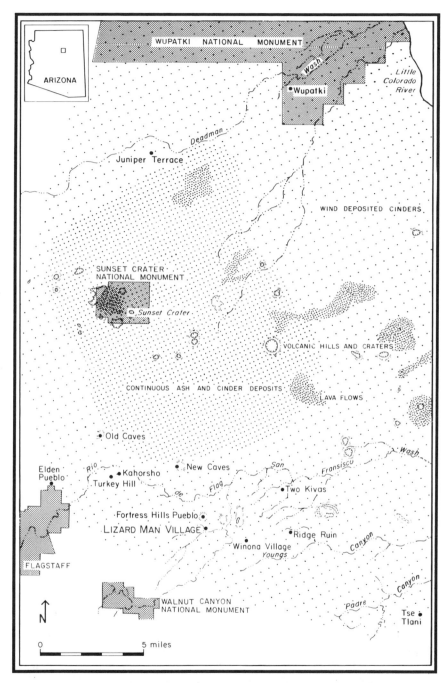

Figure 1.1 *Map of Northern Sinagua sites showing the location of Lizard Man Village and some of the other sites and physical features mentioned in the text. The densely stippled areas are lava flows; the moderately stippled areas continuous ash and cinder deposits, and the lightly stippled areas wind-deposited ash.*

to grind them. The ice was impossible to crush and the girl was extremely cold. Just as she was despairing, Spider Woman laid a turkey feather across her mano to warm it, allowing the maiden to grind the ice by melting it. When she had finished, Hahay'iwuuti came in and collected the water.

Figure 1.2 *Doll showing the characteristics of the Ka'nas Katsina. The face of this katsina is blue and yellow. He wears a rabbit-skin kilt and an embroidered sash and carries corn in his hand and over his shoulder. The carving is by Jim Kewanwytewa of Oraibi.*

That night the bride was put in a room inhabited by a fierce, frigid wind, but Spider Woman presented her with a mattress of four turkey feathers and a blanket composed of another four to keep her from freezing to death. The next two days the girl was again forced to grind icy substances, first icicles, then hail. Only through Spider Woman's intervention and her own strength of character did the young woman survive and succeed in her tasks.

At last the girl's ordeals were over. She had proven herself a worthy bride and could return home. The katsinas all accompanied the newly married couple to Mishongnovi, the bride's village. There they danced and provided a feast for the whole village. The villagers in turn blessed the katsinas with cornmeal and presented each with a prayer feather. Rain poured down on the village, not ceasing even as the katsinas departed. Indeed, it was to provide this rain and rains for the years to come that the girl had ground so much ice into water.

For many years the Ka'nas husband and his human wife lived at Mishongnovi. The rains came, the crops flourished, and the village prospered. The katsina youth was especially prosperous but shared freely with his less fortunate neighbors. Nevertheless, some of the villagers were jealous. They decided to trick the young man's wife. While the Ka'nas husband was visiting his relatives, one of the villagers disguised himself as a Ka'nas, pretended to be the katsina returning early from his visit, and slept with the Ka'nas' wife. When her husband returned, she realized that she must have been deceived and confessed as much to her husband.

Because her husband understood that she had not intentionally deceived him, he was not angry with her. Nevertheless, he returned to his katsina home in the San Francisco Mountains, refusing to allow the evildoers in the village to benefit by his presence. Before leaving Mishongnovi, the Ka'nas explained to his wife and her father his need to leave, but he suggested that her father find him a spot near the village which he might inhabit and where they might worship him. On a mesa north of the village they constructed a shrine. The Ka'nas instructed his wife's father in the proper manufacture of prayer sticks and told him to come to the shrine to pray for rain and for successful crops. He then presented his father-in-law with a piece of corn cob, which the katsina told him to place at the bottom of his corn stack to ensure his food supply.

Once home, the Ka'nas katsina became angrier and angrier. Finally he decided to punish the villagers for their treachery and to put fear in their hearts. With the advice of the katsina elders and the help of a great whirlwind, he created an enormous fire that burrowed into the mountain, turning it into a huge volcano that spewed out fire and vast streams of lava. The villagers were terrified and repented their past actions toward the Ka'nas youth and his wife. Luckily the Ka'nas katsina had only intended to frighten the villagers, not destroy them entirely. Finally he directed the wind to blow away from the village and stopped the lava flow, saving the inhabitants.

Still the punishment of the villagers was not at an end. For four consecutive years droughts and hail plagued the village's crops. Famine ensued. Some were forced to leave the area; others were reduced to the most meager living gleaned primarily from gathering scarcely edible plant foods; others (but only the evil ones) died. Through all the famine, however, the Ka'nas' wife and her family did not go hungry.

Finally, the Ka'nas katsina felt the village had suffered enough. He pleaded with the elder katsinas to end the drought. They agreed and the katsinas returned to Mishongnovi, bearing gifts of food after their long absence. After feasting and watching the katsinas dance, the villagers were reluctant to allow them to return to the San Francisco peaks and pleaded with the katsinas to remain with them forever. They refused to do this, but before departing they presented the villagers with baked corn to place at the bottom of their stored corn to ensure that supplies be sufficient, and showed them the location of the shrine constructed by the Ka'nas wife and father-in-law. Thus, the Hopi resumed their ceremonial cycle and continued to pursue normal, prosperous lives after being punished for their betrayal of the Ka'nas katsina.

An Archaeological Perspective

Archaeologists relate these events in slightly different terms. According to them, at the time of the eruption the area around Sunset Crater was occupied primarily by a group they have dubbed the "Sinagua," from the Spanish *sin* and *agua* meaning without water, since the region has very few permanent water sources. Neighboring named groups (figure 1.3) have been designated

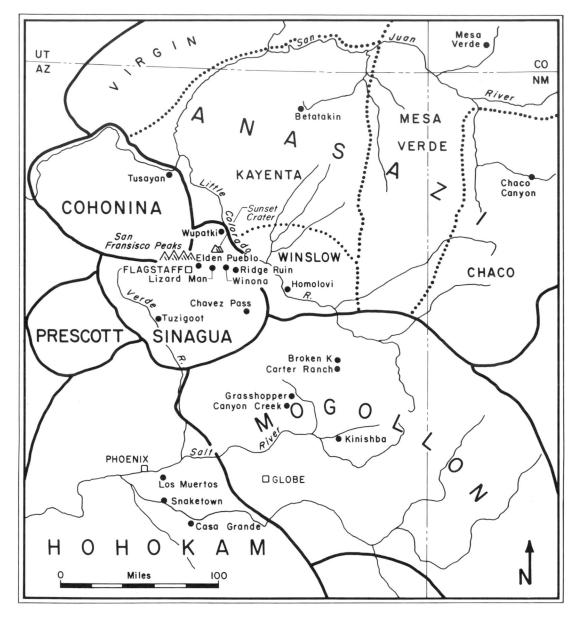

Figure 1.3 *Map of prehistoric Southwest showing the major archaeological culture areas and sites.*

as archaeological cultures on the basis of regional similarities in the style of pottery, stone tools, architecture, burials and other traits. The Sinagua themselves are divided into a northern branch located primarily to the east of modern Flagstaff, and a southern branch living in the Verde Valley.

Controversy surrounding the use of one these terms illustrates one of the ways that the past has meaning for modern groups. Archaeologists have traditionally used the term "Anasazi" to denote the prehistoric peoples who inhabited the mesas and canyon lands of the four-corners area where Arizona, Colorado, New Mexico, and Utah meet. Many of these peoples are probably the ancestors of the modern Hopi. The Anasazi are then subdivided into smaller cultural groups, such as the Winslow Anasazi and the Kayenta Anasazi. Unfortunately, the word "Anasazi" means "enemy forefathers" in Navajo. The reason for this nomenclature is historic. Early explorers were directed to the ruins by Navajo and were told that "Anasazi" had inhabited them. Today, the Hopi object to the word as derogatory. They refer to all of their prehistoric ancestors as "*Hisatsinom*," meaning "ancient people." This designation is more inclusive than Anasazi, encompassing groups like the Sinagua as well as their neighbors to the north and east, thus it does not exactly fill the terminological gap. In deference to Hopi wishes, I will attempt to avoid the use of Anasazi in favor of more specific group designations like Kayenta or Winslow, when possible, or by referring to the Puebloan groups to the north or of the four corners area when a broader reference is required.

Archaeologists divide the Sinagua occupation of the Flagstaff area into a series of temporal phases, each characterized by distinctive styles of dwellings, ceramics, and other cultural traditions. In the Northern Sinagua area, the eruption of Sunset Crater is seen as particularly significant, and the phases before its eruption, the Cinder Park Phase (A.D. 600–700), the Sunset Phase (A.D. 700–900) and the Rio de Flag Phase (A.D. 900–1064) are referred to as the pre-eruptive period. Those following—the Angell-Winona (A.D. 1064–1100), Padre (A.D. 1100–1150), Elden (A.D. 1150–1250), Turkey Hill (A.D. 1250–1300), and Clear Creek (A.D. 1300–1400) Phases—obviously constitute the post-eruption period.

The archaeological story emphasizes the Sinagua's adaptation to their changing environment, the movement of populations through time, the development of technology and crafts, internal social integration, and the relationships of the Sinagua with neighboring populations.

According to archaeologists, the Sinagua first arrived in the Flagstaff area around A.D. 600, initially building pithouses in the transitional zone between the Ponderosa pine uplands and the lower pinyon-juniper areas. This location allowed them to take advantage of both ecozones, raising corn, squash, and beans in the lower elevations and hunting and gathering wild resources at both the higher and lower altitudes. While these villages were fairly small, a vigorous trade was maintained, particularly with the Hohokam to the south, the Cohonina to the northwest, and the Puebloan groups to the north and east (figure 1.3). Although at this time there are not discernable specialized religious structures, a rich ceremonial life is almost certain.

By the 900s the climate became somewhat drier and the Sinagua changed the locations of their settlements in response, generally moving to somewhat higher elevations on the lower slopes of the San Francisco Peaks where there was a bit more rainfall. There they continued hunting and gathering and farmed in favorable locations, especially in and near the open park areas.

In A.D. 1064 Sunset Crater erupted for the first time; subsequent eruptions occurred in 1066, 1067, and perhaps sporadically until around 1250. The initial eruptions must have had a profound effect on the inhabitants. While it seems likely that they had forewarnings of impending disaster and were able to evacuate the area, probably even dismantling their pithouses and salvaging the valuable roofing timbers, the devastation of the local environment would have been impressive. Lava flows, ash and cinder fall, fires, poisonous gases, and acid rain totally destroyed a radius of some two miles around the volcano. Farther away the devastation would have been somewhat less, but still local environments would have been changed for some time to come.

The effect of Sunset Crater's eruption on the Sinagua has traditionally been a major concern of archaeologists studying the region. In the 1930s and 1940s Harold Colton (1960), one of the pioneer archaeologists in the Flagstaff area, suggested that volcanic ash from the eruptions acted as a mulching agent, retarding the rate of evaporation of soil moisture and hence improving farming conditions. He believed that the consequences of the eruption precipitated a prehistoric "land rush." Migrants came from surrounding areas, bringing with them not only increased population but also goods and ideas. Sinagua culture experienced a period of rapid growth and change.

Recently, this notion has been challenged. Present interpretations of the archaeological evidence suggest that most of the new traits were probably introduced via trade rather than migration, that population increase was not dramatic, and that increases in precipitation occurring in the entire Southwest as well as in the Flagstaff area probably explain the increased emphasis on farming and the expansion of areas devoted to cultivation.

A second archaeological controversy for the post-eruptive period in Sinagua prehistory concerns the complexity of the social and economic organization of the Sinagua. One model, which assumes reasonably strong leaders and a fair amount of social inequality, suggests that the Sinagua were hierarchically organized, relying on larger central villages to coordinate exchange, religion, and politics for smaller outlying settlements. An alternative model argues that the Sinagua were more egalitarian. According to this scenario, many small villages would be integrated via kinship, local exchange and mutual ceremonial visits, but no villages would be viewed as paramount. Obviously, as in all societies, some individuals would be more intelligent, prolific, or socially adept, yet none would have much power over others, except perhaps within the sphere of intrafamilial relations. As we explore the current archaeological debates, we will concentrate on examining the ways that the archaeological evidence for the post-eruptive Sinagua is analyzed and models of prehistory are constructed.

Modern Descendants

Currently, tracing the exact ties between the prehistoric Sinagua and any single modern group is not possible, although there are some distinct links to the Hopi that make most scholars view them as the likely descendants. In the seventh through thirteenth centuries A.D. Puebloan groups were widely distributed over the Southwest, occurring in much of central and northern Arizona, southern Utah and Colorado, and eastern New Mexico. By the time of Spanish contact, however, the settlements had contracted and coalesced, presumably into the most favorable locations in what are today Arizona and New Mexico (figure 1.4). Anthropologists usually refer to Puebloan tribes as belonging to either eastern (Rio Grande) or Western traditions. These are somewhat arbitrary divisions. Many continuities and gradations in language, culture, and social organization occur within and between the two groups.

Both Rio Grande and Western pueblos traditionally relied on a combination of agriculture and hunting and gathering for subsistence. Both lived in compact villages, often with plaza areas for ceremonials and other communal activities. Both had religions emphasizing rain, corn, nature, and animals like deer, bison, and antelope. Specialized religious rooms (like the kiva referred to in the Hopi story of the eruption of Sunset Crater) and village plazas were the arenas for much of the religious activity in both. Nevertheless there is considerable linguistic and cultural diversity, probably due both to prehistoric variability and to historic differences. The greater intensity of occupation of the Rio Grande area by early Spanish, in particular, must be taken into account.

The modern Western Pueblo groups, the Zuni and, particularly, the Hopi, are probably the closest living relatives of the prehistoric Sinagua. Their

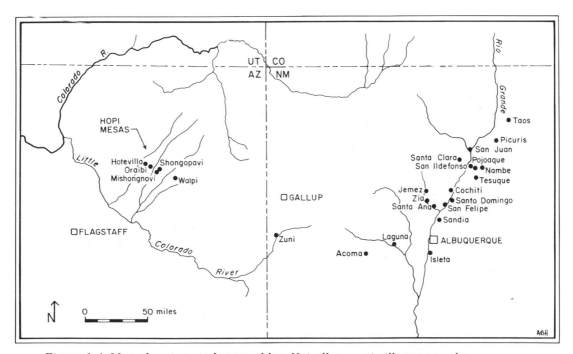

Figure 1.4 *Map showing modern pueblos. Not all current villages are shown.*

traditional lifestyles are similar in many ways to those of the Sinagua. Not only do much of the early historic pueblo architecture and subsistence resemble their counterparts found in prehistoric sites, there are probably even some similarities in religion.

Perhaps the most dramatic illustration of cultural continuity occurred in 1939 when John McGregor (1943) discovered a particularly rich burial at the Sinagua site of Ridge Ruin (figure 1.1). The body of a man, tall for Sinagua populations (about 173 cm, 5' 8") and some thirty-five to forty years of age, had either been wrapped in matting or placed between two mats and set in a one-meter (three-foot) deep pit dug into the floor of a room that had possibly been a kiva or ceremonial room. With him were over six hundred burial offerings including twenty-five whole pots, fragments of eight baskets, 420 arrowheads, numerous pieces of jewelry made of shell, turquoise, argillite, and lac, pigments, and several wooden wands and other objects that McGregor felt were probably ceremonial (figure 1.5).

When McGregor interviewed several Hopi about the burial, they agreed that many of the artifacts were ceremonial in nature and suggested to McGregor that the honored individual was a religious leader. One man from the village of Mishongnovi identified him as a *Moochiwimi* or *Nasot wimi* (stick swallower); another from Oraibi suggested that he was a *Ka-leh-ta-ka* (leader); they and others proposed several different potential clan affiliations. Despite some disagreement about a possible title and clan identity, there was general agreement that the ceremonial in which he would have engaged involved various kinds of magic and the use of wands in a ritual involving something akin to sword swallowing. The ceremony was intended to strengthen the group, and war leaders were often chosen from among its participants. Fierce animals such as the mountain lion and bear played an important part in the symbolism of the ceremony, and eight mountain lion claws and a pair of painted and drilled canine teeth were among the burial offerings. Even more intriguing was the fact that a Shungopovi man, when shown only a portion of the assemblage, described several other items that ought to have been included in a burial of this type. In fact, they were present but had not yet been shown to him.

Obviously, this suggests some clear cultural continuities. It should be pointed out, however, that despite presumed cultural similarities between modern and prehistoric Puebloan groups, it is not wise to rely too much on ethnographic analogies. All cultures are constantly changing. Puebloan cultures are no more static than Western ones. Britain in 1900 and Britain in 1300 have certain similarities, due to a continuity of tradition. Nevertheless, no one would consider using only information about recent Britain to describe Britain in the Middle Ages. Written records, as well as the archaeological evidence, clearly show that numerous changes have occurred. The same is true for the prehistoric Pueblo peoples. The primary available information in this case is archaeological, although legend and ethnohistory help, particularly for reconstruction of the fairly recent past.

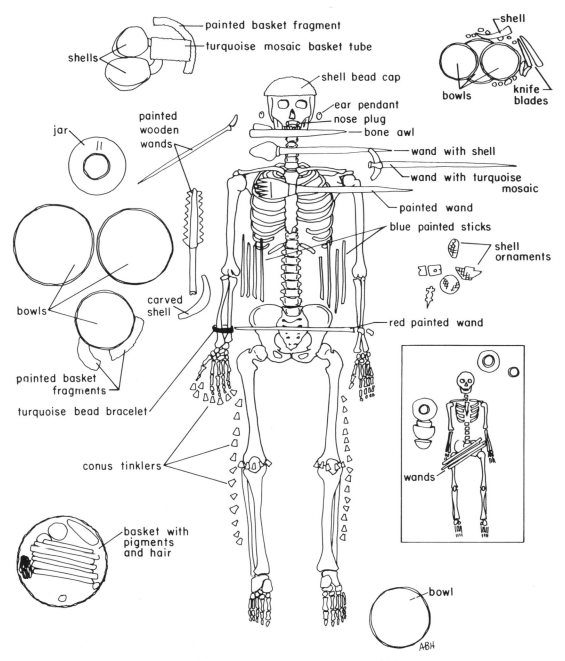

Figure 1.5 *Burial of the "magician," showing the location and type of major offerings. Over four hundred projectile points were also found with the body but are not shown here. They were found primarily in groups of eight to twelve, perhaps representing clusters of arrows, some ten inches to two feet above the body, mixed with the rotting wood of the grave covering.*

Archaeological Data Sources

There are two major sources of archaeological information: survey and excavation. Archaeological sites are found in many ways; often sites are initially discovered and reported by non-archaeologists. In each state the Office of the State Archaeologist and the State Historic Preservation Office maintain maps and files of known archaeological sites. Systematic foot survey is one means for discovering sites. Trained personnel walk over an entire area, positioned closely enough together that the terrain will be well covered. When visibility is high, this method assures that even small, unspectacular sites will be seen and provides information about where sites are not located as well as where they are to be found. In many areas of the Southwest archaeologists are very lucky. Sparse ground cover and a very slow pace of soil deposition make it possible to discover most sites just by examining the surface. Elsewhere systematic sampling with soil cores and small test pits may augment the survey procedure in an effort to discover buried sites. The archaeological survey team records the exact location of sites, visible architectural remains (if any), artifacts found on the surface, and information about the geographical and ecological surroundings. Survey data can be used to show patterns in site size and distributions that may be due to subsistence requirements, trade routes, special resource distributions, and/or religious or social needs.

Excavation provides a closer look at individual sites. Ideally, rooms and other areas within an excavated site can be securely dated to insure a rough contemporaneity. Artifact types and patterns of artifact distribution can then aid in interpreting behavior patterns, suggesting what people did in different parts of the site, allowing deductions to be made about subsistence activities, diet, health, living accommodations, social organization, and religion—a spectrum of cultural and social activities. Ideally, excavation data, especially when combined with survey information and interpreted in the light of appropriate ethnographic analogy, can allow a detailed anthropological description similar to those for existing social groups.

Goals and Organization of the Book

This volume explores Sinagua life in one community, Lizard Man Village. The village was occupied from shortly after the eruption of Sunset Crater until the middle of the thirteenth century, during the Angell-Winona (A.D. 1064–1100), Padre (A.D. 1100–1150), and Elden (A.D. 1150–1250) Phases. The approach used here is descriptive and comparative, relying on archaeological data interpreted in light of ethnographic comparisons to modern Puebloan groups. While survey data and published information from previously excavated sites will not be ignored, the primary data base is material from four summers of excavation at Lizard Man Village, named after a petroglyph located at the site (see the sketch at the beginning of the chapter).

I attempt to do three things: (1) describe a prehistoric Sinagua village,

(2) discuss in some detail the processes of excavation and analysis on which this description is based, and (3) present my interpretation of Lizard Man Village as one of several possible readings of the past. It is my goal to make the inhabitants of Lizard Man Village come alive for the reader as much as possible. For this reason, and to give voice to alternative Native American interpretations, Hopi and Zuni myths and ethnographic details from more recent Puebloan groups are often juxtaposed with archaeological data and interpretations. Obviously this is not meant to imply that the ancient Sinagua were identical to modern Hopi or any other modern group. Ultimately, only the relics of the past can directly testify to the lives of the ancient Sinagua.

A discussion of data collection and interpretation will be presented first, followed by more specific descriptions of the inhabitants of the village. Chapter 2 describes the excavation process, including site selection, obtaining a permit, basic excavation routines and initial laboratory processing of artifacts. Chapter 3 discusses techniques that archaeologists use to interpret what went on at an archaeological site. Included here are descriptions of site formation processes, artifact analysis, experimental archaeology, and the importance of context. Chapter 4 explains some of the techniques archaeologists use for determining when events occurred as well as our frustrations in applying these to a detailed analysis of Lizard Man Village. As part of the attempt to reconstruct the lives of the inhabitants of Lizard Man Village, I have included a brief fictional portrayal in chapter 5. I would suggest that you read this story twice, once as you encounter it in the text, and a second time after you have finished reading about the evidence for the Sinagua's lifestyle. This will allow you to think about and evaluate the reconstruction that the tale proposes. Chapter 6 discusses Lizard Man Village and its inhabitants, including information about demography and health, personal appearance, and dress. Chapter 7 considers subsistence strategies, chapter 8 describes manufacturing activities on the site, and chapter 9 discusses social organization, trade and other interconnections within and between villages. Probably the largest controversy currently surrounding the details of reconstructing Sinagua culture at the time Lizard Man Village was occupied is a debate over whether it was egalitarian or stratified. Chapter 10 probes this issue, laying out the arguments used by both sides but supporting the thesis that the Sinagua were, indeed, fairly egalitarian. Thus chapters 2 through 10 provide much of the basic descriptive data from Lizard Man Village and show how it has been interpreted to provide a picture of the village. Finally, chapter 11 provides one explanation (mine) for both the success of the Sinagua adaptation during the occupation of Lizard Man Village and contemporary communities and for the region's abandonment in the period shortly after. This interpretation combines a cultural ecological emphasis with a realization of the importance of social and political action for shaping events. Finally, research prospects for the future are discussed.

It must be emphasized that all of the archaeological interpretations are continually subject to reanalysis and revision. The story of Sinagua archaeology will never be finished as long as there is one archaeologist working in the area. New discoveries, new techniques of analysis, and new perspectives on ways of interpreting existing data make periodic reassessment vital. Furthermore, the archaeological record is so rich that the analytic potential is never really exhausted. Even for excavations at a single site like Lizard Man Village, the existing analyses usually suggest more questions than answers and inspire a multitude of projects for future research. Some can be done with existing museum collections; others will require new excavations. There is no lack of opportunities or excitement for researchers of the future.

.

Chapter 2

UNCOVERING THE PAST
Excavation

Today as you sit on the low basalt ridge to the south of Lizard Man Village, you can see the San Francisco Peaks to the west, covered with snow in the winter and often capped with white until mid-summer. It is these peaks that are the abode of the Hopi katsinas. To the north is Sunset Crater, the most recent volcano in an area characterized by many extinct cones. It is this volcano whose eruption is presumably described by the Hopi tale of the Ka'nas bridegroom. The ground in the Lizard Man Village area is covered with fine black volcanic ash from the eruption. To the south is a ravine, now traversed by the Atchison, Topeka, and Santa Fe Railway tracks, but prehistorically a wash that would have held moisture and provided possible field areas for the prehistoric inhabitants of the site. Surrounding the ridge are pinyon-juniper forests. These arid woodlands would have nourished deer, rabbit, and many small rodents and birds, as well as providing wild plants for the inhabitants of the village.

In the winter the area is cold, often covered with snow. In the summer its relatively high elevation (about 1,800 meters, or 6,000 feet) means moderate temperatures. The rainy season starts in the early part of July, providing short but sometimes intense afternoon rains. Information from prehistoric pollens found in the area indicates that the plant species during the Sinagua occupation were similar to those of today. This implies that the climate would have been fairly similar as well, although during the two hundred years that Lizard Man Village was occupied, there was some climatic variability. Bones from waterfowl and seeds from species that require standing water have been found in some Sinagua sites, which suggests that there may have been more standing water in the area than at the present time. In general, the weather may have been a bit moister during the initial occupation of the village, but somewhat cooler and drier toward the end. In a climate so marginal for agricultural activity, this minor change could have significantly reduced agricultural productivity and may have had a large impact on subsistence activities.

Directly to the east of the ridge is the site of Lizard Man Village. It is identifiable on the surface as a site because of the litter of broken pottery pieces, small chips of stone which are debris from the manufacture of stone tools, and occasional other artifacts—shell jewelry, ground stone, and bone. Two low mounds of rock are the surface remains of masonry room blocks. Scattered depressions indicate abandoned and filled-in *pithouses*. On the basalt ridge are petroglyphs, patterns pecked into the basalt outcrop, perhaps as a part of prehistoric ceremonials. These include spirals, geometrics, animals, and the petroglyph for which the site is named, a human figure with a long tail, of the type often referred to as a "lizard man."

The site of Lizard Man Village is not unique. Foot surveys in the area have discovered several similar sites within easy walking distance. When the area was occupied, the smoke from one village would have been easily visible from the others, and neighbors would have been easy to visit. Slightly larger sites such as Ridge Ruin, Winona, and New Caves are also an easy walk (figure 1.1). At a leisurely pace, a walker can reach even the lush and fairly densely occupied Walnut Canyon area in less than a day. Scattered throughout the area, some as close as across the wash, are tiny one- or two-room sites, usually referred to as *field houses*, where families probably spent time during the agricultural season.

The Choice of Lizard Man Village

In the spring of 1983 the Anthropology Department of Grinnell College requested that my husband, John Whittaker, and I conduct an archaeological field school the next summer. My chosen area of specialization was the Middle East and my previous research was in Syria, but the logistics of working abroad are daunting. It is time consuming and expensive to acquire the requisite permits, establish a residential base camp, and bring over both students and necessary equipment. Furthermore, both John and I had immediate nightmares when confronted with the idea of teaching a group of undergraduate students to cope with the cultural differences of that area of the world while they were learning archaeology. At one instant we would envision local outrage caused by some young woman's disregard of our advice about appropriate dress; the next we would imagine an entire crew with dysentery or the outbreak of a war. Added to our innate conservatism was concern over our baby daughter born that April. Probably, all would have gone well had we negotiated a Middle Eastern dig, but we decided to excavate in the American Southwest, John's specialty area, instead.

The first task was choosing a region in which to work. We decided on the Flagstaff area for a combination of professional and personal reasons. Professionally, the Flagstaff area was interesting because both the local prehistoric cultures, the Cohonina and Sinagua, are less well-known than many of the other prehistoric groups of the Southwest. Most of the significant work in the Flagstaff area had been done in the 1930s and 1940s, and relatively little had been published since then. Personally, the area seemed ideal because of the good things we had heard about Peter Pilles, the Coconino Forest Service archaeologist, with whom we would be working. Additionally, the scenery in the area is beautiful, the climate is relatively cool in summer, and it is close to both modern Pueblos and numerous prehistoric sites which would provide additional learning opportunities for students.

We contacted Peter Pilles to help us select a site for excavation. Archaeologists choose particular sites to excavate for a variety of reasons. Today much archaeological research is driven by the demands of impending construction activities. Strip mining, the building of dams and the consequent flooding of many acres of land, logging, road construction, the erection of power lines, the expansion of urban areas, and many other projects threaten the natural and cultural resources of thousands of acres annually. Environmental protection laws require that any project using federal lands or relying on federal funding must assess possible detrimental effects on the environment—cultural as well as natural.

In addition to various state laws, there are several important federal laws that protect archaeological sites. The earliest is the Antiquities Act of 1906, which made it a criminal offense to damage or destroy historic or prehistoric sites located on federal lands, established a permitting system to allow scientific investigation of these resources, and authorized the designation of National Monuments. Subsequently, this has been augmented by federal legislation, including the Historic Sites Act of 1935, the National Historic Preservation Act of 1966 with amendments in 1976 and 1980, the National Environmental Policy Act of 1969 (NEPA), the Archaeological and Historic Preservation Act of 1974, the Archaeological Resources Protection Act of 1979 (ARPA), and the Native American Graves Protection and Repatriation Act of 1990 (NAGPRA).

The National Historic Preservation Act established a National Register of Historic Places and authorized a President's Advisory Council on Historic Preservation to comment on plans by federal agencies or on federal lands that might affect cultural resources. It also determined the criteria for the inclusion of sites to the National Register. These specified that archaeological sites as well as buildings, other structures, and even whole districts could be nominated to the Register based on their significance, which is defined to include an association with specific notable persons or events, high artistic merit, the possession of distinctive characteristics for a period or type, or simply the possibility for yielding information about history or prehistory.

NEPA is a general law requiring federal agencies to consider environmental effects as a part of any planning activities on federal lands or using federal funds. As a part of the planning process, an environmental impact statement which includes an assessment of the affects on cultural resources must be prepared. The Archaeological and Historic Preservation Act of 1974 provides specific mechanisms for dealing with cases where an environmental impact statement determines that significant cultural resources will be destroyed or damaged, and allocates up to 1 percent of project funds for this purpose. Significance can be determined by referring to the criteria set by the National Historic Preservation Act. ARPA, which is the major federal legislation dealing specifically with archaeological sites, is essentially a tightening of the 1906 Antiquities Act. It was a direct response to a 1974 case (*U.S. vs. Diaz*) in which a looter got off because the Ninth Circuit Court of Appeals found the Antiquities Act too vague. ARPA required a permit for excavation on public or Indian lands, increased penalties for looting sites, and prohibited interstate traffic in illegal antiquities.

Archaeological projects generated by the need to fulfill the specifications of federal and state laws range from tiny half-day efforts to huge multiyear, million-dollar endeavors, employ many archaeologists, and produce much of our modern information about the historic and prehistoric past. Our research, as academics, did not directly fall into this professional realm, which is referred to as "cultural resource management" (CRM). Nevertheless, we were interested in helping the Forest Service with some of its conservation efforts. Many archaeological sites are located near towns or roads and are so accessible that they can be readily visited. While most of the visitors are simply interested in the past and cause no intentional damage to sites, others collect artifacts or dig illegally, hoping to find interesting and perhaps even saleable artifacts. Removing artifacts from an archaeological site that is located on government-owned land is, as mentioned above, illegal, and violators are subject to prosecution. Unfortunately, it is very hard to monitor the numerous cultural resources adequately, so damage to sites, especially those that are fairly accessible, is a continuing problem.

We were interested in selecting a site for excavation that, in addition to meeting our research needs, was in potential danger of destruction, but for which no research funds were currently available. Lizard Man Village was one of many such sites. Located on a dirt road just off a major secondary highway only fifteen minutes from Flagstaff proper, the site appeared to have already experienced some minor looting, as shown by a few small excavation depressions visible on the surface. Nevertheless, basically the site was still in pretty good condition. Given the encroachment of settlement into the area, this might not be true for long. Furthermore, Lizard Man Village was located on land slated for possible exchange. The Forest Service negotiates the exchange of pieces of private land located well within National Forest boundaries for those on peripheries or surrounded by other private holdings. These exchanges consolidate Forest Service-owned lands, making policing easier and ultimately aiding in the protection of resources. Exchanges cannot occur, however, as long as there are significant cultural resources on the property to be exchanged. Thus, an excavation of Lizard Man Village would ultimately allow the Forest Service to exchange the parcel of land on which it was located for a more remote, privately-owned parcel.

Our research interests were also well-served by Lizard Man Village. Since much of the interpretation of social organization for the Angell-Winona through Elden Phase Sinagua (A.D. 1064–1250) has been made on the basis of surface survey data and excavation data from the larger sites, we were interested in obtaining comparative excavated material from one of the numerous small village sites. Furthermore, the selection of a small site would allow even a fairly tiny project such as ours to do a complete excavation of all structures and a good sampling of nonstructural areas in a reasonable number of summer seasons. The existence of both above-ground pueblo habitations and pithouses at the same site that were at least fairly contemporary in time was also intriguing.

Obtaining Permission to Excavate

Before any collection or excavation of cultural remains is done on public lands, permission to conduct research must be obtained from the appropriate governmental agencies. Unfortunately, as you may have noticed in the section on legislation, with the exception of burials, archaeological resources located on private land are not legally protected. Archaeological resources located on private land are viewed as the property of the land owner rather than as part of a national or ethnic heritage. In this respect the United States lags behind many other countries, where the cultural heritage of the past is seen as belonging to all humanity, and the remains of the past are protected by law irrespective of where they are located.

Permission to collect artifacts and/or to excavate on government property can be granted to qualified individuals for specific purposes. Since Lizard Man Village is on National Forest Service land, the permit application must be approved by both the Forest Service and ultimately authorities at the Smithsonian Institution. Applications include a research design that describes the questions the investigators hope to answer, the exact methods they plan to use, and an agreement with an accredited museum for the curation of the artifacts collected.

Part of the permit process includes a consultation with Native Americans to ensure that the archaeological research will not disturb any remains the relevant descendants deem sacred. In the case of Lizard Man Village, the Forest Service conducted the necessary liaison with the Hopi tribe. Lizard Man Village was not seen as of particular cultural interest to the tribe, so permission to excavate was granted. In 1983 when we began to excavate, our permit allowed us to excavate human burials. At the time of this writing, this is no longer possible, so we now avoid areas of a site where burials are likely to be found. Obviously, even when there is no intent to discover a burial, any digging may accidentally do so. In general, the current policy in areas ancestral to the Hopi is that, when possible, burials should be avoided, and if uncovered they should be left in place and re-covered. Particularly in the case of construction projects, this is not always possible. In such cases, the bodies are removed and suitably reburied. The 1990 Native American Graves Protection and Repatriation Act (NAGPRA) requires that all federal agencies and federally-funded institutions inventory their skeletal remains and Native American artifacts and share these inventories with Native American groups to determine which are sacred items, funerary goods, or other items of profound cultural significance. They then consult with relevant Native American groups about which items should be returned or reburied. Ultimately, the burials that we excavated at Lizard Man Village may be reburied; however, that depends on the wishes of the Hopi.

It is the belief of most archaeologists, myself included, that in our studies of the past we are, in fact, respectful of the dead. I feel that by attempting to understand the ancestors, both my own and others, I honor them. It is my hope that archaeological information about distant ancestors is important and interesting enough that Native Americans will support and participate in archaeological work here in the United States, just as I support and am interested in research on my European ancestors both abroad and in this country. The alternative is loss of the human heritage as destruction of archaeological sites by looters and development continues to increase.

All cultural remains obtained from federal lands must be curated by certified facilities that qualify under government standards for both storage and public accessibility. Conservators are responsible for assuring that a minimum of damage occurs to artifacts as they are stored and displayed. Techniques for artifact storage and restoration are constantly improving. For example, epoxy glues, which were previously used to reconstruct broken pottery vessels but which have been found to yellow and become brittle with age, have been replaced with newer polymer glues. Acid-free paper or polymers that do not cause damage to materials with which they come in contact have become the norm for storage containers and tags. Computers also have revolutionized collection inventories.

When possible, it is preferable to centralize the collections from a particular area, so we chose the Museum of Northern Arizona, which already houses Sinagua materials for the Lizard Man Village collections. The curation of artifacts is extremely expensive for museums. It requires hours of personnel time—up to an hour per artifact for initial cataloging and storage, appropriate storage materials, and space. Like the Museum of Northern Arizona, many museums rely heavily on private donations and are severely underfunded and overcrowded. Contract firms, excavating or collecting as part of a major construction project, put curation costs directly in their budget and reimburse the museum for the time it takes personnel to process artifacts and for the long-term costs of maintenance and space use. As a small, low-budget academic project, we were unable to do this. Instead the museum agreed to allow us to provide personnel to catalogue the artifacts and to purchase appropriate storage boxes. As the site is on Forest Service land, the Forest Service will ultimately be responsible for long-term storage costs.

The importance of curating artifacts in a museum where they will not only be well preserved but available to researchers and others interested in the past cannot be underestimated. The past is a finite resource. Furthermore, some of the sites already excavated, such as Wupatki, are relatively unique because of their size or features. Thus, already excavated sites are continually being studied and restudied. New excavation is also necessary, however. We continually find new ways to study and interpret what we find. Accordingly, archaeologists collect more kinds of information and throw away less as time goes on. This means that old museum collections can be used to answer some kinds of questions, but not others. Only by using a combination of newly discovered data and the information accumulated in the past can archaeologists do a competent job of investigating the past.

Describing and Surface Collecting the Site

The first season we used a transit (figure 2.1) to construct a contour map of the site and to lay out a grid of ten- by ten-meter (32.8 feet by 32.8 feet) squares from which we could then collect the artifacts found on the surface. The transit is a piece of surveying equipment that allows the calculation of a direction, distance and relative elevation of any point relative to the location of the transit by sighting through the lens to a scaled rod. With the aid of a transit, very accurate maps of a site can be drawn and collection grids plotted. Today a transit is rather outmoded, although still in use because some projects can not afford more modern equipment.

Right after our last field school at Lizard Man Village I received a National Science Foundation grant to purchase an electronic distance meter and other necessary equipment to allow computer-assisted mapping in future field schools (figure 2.2). The electronic distance meter (EDM) emits a laser that is reflected off of a prism to determine the location of the prism relative to the EDM. This information is then recorded into a hand-held computer along with

Figure 2.1 *Neil Weintraub and Kathy Kamp mapping the surface of Lizard Man Village using a transit.*

Figure 2.2 *Becky Wallace and Tom Berger use an electronic distance meter to map the site of Fortress Hills Pueblo.*

other data about the object being recorded. Each evening back at the dig house the day's data can be transferred to a computer and maps can be generated immediately. This type of computerized recording, which is becoming a standard feature of most excavations, increases both efficiency and accuracy and allows for more rapid data analysis.

Surface maps and collections are a standard part of any excavation strategy because, although they do not directly reflect subsurface remains, surface remains provide a rough idea of the density and temporal variability in use of the different areas of a site. When combined with detailed maps of other surface features, such as rock alignments and depressions, surface collections provide interpretive data themselves and aid in planning the most effective excavation strategy.

As a part of the initial mapping and setup we established a site *datum*, a stable point of reference from which excavation units and rooms could be plotted as they were excavated, and recorded its position by sinking a metal rod deep into the ground. This allowed us to come back each year and accurately plot new information on a continuing map (figure 2.3). Ideally, it will permit the excavators of the future to reconstruct our excavations.

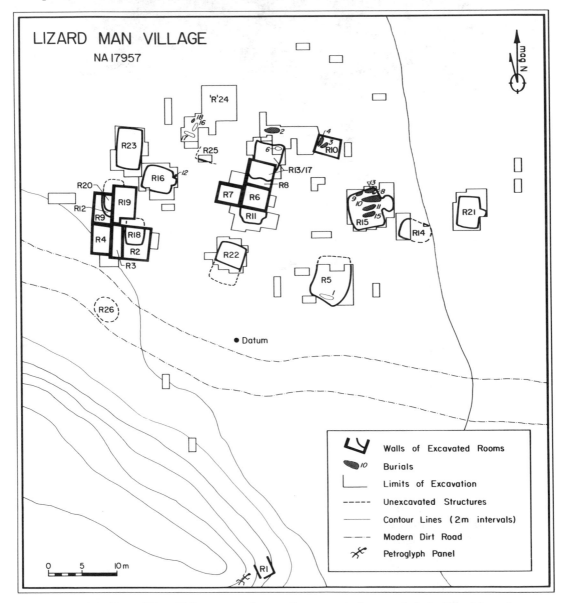

Figure 2.3 *Lizard Man Village site plan with excavated rooms labeled; test trenches are shown but not labeled. The datum is located at thirty meters north and twenty meters west on the site grid system.*

The Basic Excavation Strategy

Designing an excavation strategy is a complex process, requiring the development of systems for recording data and processing artifacts in the field as well for deciding exactly where to dig. The specific techniques used in the field depend on the goals of the research, preservation, and the available equipment and personnel. For example, when Hole, Flannery, and Neeley (1969) went to the Deh Luran Plain in Iran to investigate the development of agriculture, they were most interested in obtaining a comprehensive understanding of subsistence patterns. This necessitated the recovery of large quantities of plant and animal remains but required less knowledge of architectural detail. Thus, not being concerned with exposing entire dwellings, they excavated in small units and used *flotation* (a technique for separating carbonized plant remains from the dirt matrix by utilizing the fact that they float in water) on all of the excavated dirt.

Since we were interested in understanding a small village as a whole community in as much detail as possible, we believed that it was desirable to acquire as much knowledge about structures in the village as possible, and a basic understanding of the use of exterior spaces was also necessary. The strategy for gaining information about architecture was obviously to identify structures and systematically investigate them. Unfortunately, while some of the structures were easy to locate on the basis of surface remains, others were not.

The pueblo rooms (figure 2.4) the Sinagua built in this area are aboveground masonry structures; thus, the presence of quantities of building stones makes them relative easy to identify from surface remains. Sometimes it is even possible to trace the outlines of the ancient stone walls. In contrast, the pithouses (figure 2.5) are single-room semi-subterranean dwellings. Even in antiquity only the upper portions of the walls and the roofs would have been visible. Since they were constructed primarily from perishable materials, such as wood and brush, they are much more difficult to discern today. Occasionally, the pits in which they were constructed were lined with stones that peek above the ground, testifying to the pithouse's presence. Other times plaster or timbers had served to stabilize the pit walls, or the masonry slabs had been removed in antiquity to serve as construction materials for later dwellings, leaving only a slight pit depression as a clue to the existence of the room. Several times, because of a slight depression in the ground, we felt there was possibly a pithouse at a given locale but found only exterior surface; other times we thought we would be investigating an exterior plaza area but discovered pithouses instead. This nicely illustrates the potential inaccuracy of data collected by relying strictly on surface indications.

One of our largest structures, Room 15 (figure 2.3), was discovered in an area that we thought would be simply an exterior activity surface. The third season Amy Henderson, an archaeologist and the scientific illustrator who does all our final illustrations and illustrated this book, had come to the site to work for a week. She and our laboratory supervisor, Sara Bruins, a student veteran of the previous season, were to excavate a test trench in an area

Figure 2.4 *Reconstruction of a pueblo room block from Lizard Man Village. This is Room Block 2 as seen from the vantage point of the basalt ridge to the south of the village. Room 2/3, discussed in detail in chapter 3, is the lower room in the foreground. Room 19 has not yet been constructed in this view. The village of Fortress Hills Pueblo can be seen on the hill in the distance. The San Francisco Peaks are at the far left.*

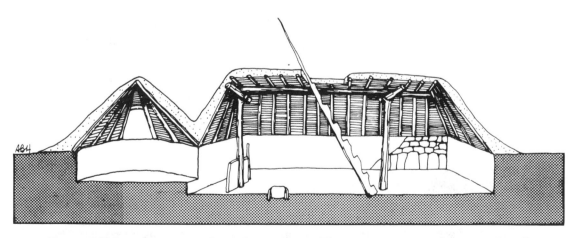

Figure 2.5 *Reconstruction of a pithouse room. This reconstruction shows an Angell-style alcove pithouse similar to Room 15. Note the door in the entry alcove. The cutaway on the back wall shows the masonry beneath the plastered surface of the wall.*

of *midden* not yet examined. Theoretically, this would be a short project, completed within the week. Instead the two discovered a lovely plastered floor and a fragment of slab-lined wall. We assumed (wrongly) that the room would be the equivalent of a shallow, slab-lined pithouse that we had excavated in the previous season. Two of the student excavators, Kirsten Pogue and Karen Brockman, were then assigned to a similar slab-lined pithouse, but one with a very poorly preserved floor, walls that had primarily been disassembled in antiquity, and little in the way of artifacts. My co-director husband, John, and I thought that we would do them a favor by transferring them to this similar but much better preserved room. In retrospect, we realized that we had about tripled their workload, which some would argue was no favor at all! To make the story short, the shallow "room" we had found was just the entryway to a much larger and deeper room, which contained several burials. Our decision to continue excavating that room, not even visible from the surface, added over thirty-five thousand sherds and hundreds of artifacts to our grand total. Incidentally, this excavation made it necessary for us to work many longer-than-normal excavation days, wash sherds until dark, then do paperwork sometimes as late as midnight, only to start again the next morning at 6 A.M.

Difficulties in locating structures had a distinct effect on our exploration of exterior areas. We had decided to use a one- by two-meter test trench as the basic excavation unit for nonarchitectural areas, primarily because it is a convenient size for an excavation team of two, allowing them to work comfortably, keep busy, and finish the unit within a couple of days to a week, depending on the depth of deposition in the unit.

Since it was obvious from the outset that it would be impossible to excavate 100 percent of the exterior areas, we needed to devise some type of sampling scheme. Several options are available. Many projects currently select some type of random sampling design. A random sample is advantageous because it allows the use of techniques for statistical inference. A simple random sample divides a site into units, such as two- by two-meter squares, and assures each unit an equal probability of being selected for excavation. Stratified random samples divide the sampling universe into sections based on some type of criteria and take a random sample of units from each of the sections. For example, a Puebloan site might be divided into room-block areas, central plaza areas, and peripheral regions. Equal percentages of each section could be sampled, or the percentages might vary from section to section. Numerous other sampling strategies are available (for a readable discussion of sampling options consult Redman, 1974).

An alternative sampling strategy is the use of a judgment sample. In the end, because of our desire to locate and excavate as high a percentage of structures as possible, we utilized a judgment sample. This means that we excavated particular types of locations in order to maximize the probability of obtaining certain types of remains. We were interested in excavating all of the rooms; therefore we tried to excavate all areas that had surface features suggesting the possibility of structures. In addition, we sampled other open areas, hoping to discover any rooms not visible from surface indications. There are advantages and disadvantages to this course of action. On the one hand, it allowed us to position units to minimize the probability that a structure could lie between units and also to investigate any areas that showed possible surface indications of architecture, such as depressions or stone slabs protruding from the surface. On the other hand, unless a strict random sample is done, statistical tests are suspect, since sampling procedures may have introduced systematic biases.

For four six-week summer excavation seasons, John and I led field schools of nine to eleven students in the excavation of Lizard Man Village. During this time period, we dug a total of twenty rooms and forty-one test trenches (figure 2.3). We feel confident that most of the structures on the site were discovered, although several were only partially excavated and one was left completely untouched because of its location in the center of the road. Exterior areas were less completely explored. About one-tenth of the exterior surface area was excavated. While this doesn't sound like much, on many sites, particularly large ones, less than 5 percent is often the best that can be done with available resources. Although some exterior features such as hearths and storage bins were encountered, prehistoric ground surfaces, which were 10 to 30 cm below the modern surface, were hard to identify because of extensive rodent disturbance and the relatively soft, sandy soil. In the course of sampling exterior areas and room interiors, we also encountered fifteen complete burials and scattered human bone indicating an additional thirty-seven individuals. This is neither a complete nor possibly a representative sample, since most of the burials came from room interiors where they had been placed after abandonment of the room.

Recovering What Remains

Once an archaeological site has been excavated, much of the information it once contained has been destroyed. As objects are removed from the ground, their exact positions, unless carefully recorded, are lost forever. Ideally, the archaeologist would like to be able to completely reconstruct the site on paper or computer from field notes. Obviously, this is an unrealizable ideal. Nevertheless, given the constraints of time and current technology, it is incumbent upon archaeologists to record as much detail as possible. Our students occasionally lament the fact that the paperwork associated with an excavation seems endless, but detailed records are necessary not only to aid our memories but so that other archaeologists can analyze our data with new techniques or with different questions in mind, perhaps many years in the future.

To standardize recording and insure that important observations are not neglected, we utilize a series of forms to supplement a daily work journal kept by each excavation team. There are separate forms for each excavation *level*, for every kind of sample taken, for features such as hearths or pits, for room floors, for walls, for roof fall, for burials, for profiles, and simply for recording the list of artifacts discovered. The forms are organized to demand redundancy in recording. Although this may at first seem inefficient, it has occasionally saved the day, when excavators found that they had neglected to record an important observation on one form but had noted it elsewhere. In addition to notes and drawings, the site is comprehensively photographed during excavation (figure 2.6).

Most excavation is done with trowels, carefully removing the dirt to reveal artifacts and features, although in fragile contexts such as on floors brushes are used. Among the dubious joys of excavation are the all-penetrating clouds of dust raised as dirt from excavations is sifted through screens. Screening 100 percent of the dirt is routine in most modern excavations (figure 2.7). Even the most careful archaeologist working with a trowel and brush may well miss small artifacts, and the sifting process provides an extra assurance of the most complete recovery possible. At Lizard Man Village we used quarter-inch mesh screens mounted on towering wooden tripods for all the excavated dirt, and we put fill from burials or other contexts where we felt there might be very small artifacts through an additional one-eighth-inch sieve.

Figure 2.6 *John Whittaker braves the "photo tower" to get a better picture of a room. Richard Wallace and Steve Hington provide support.*

As we dug, we separated all the excavated contexts into natural *stratigraphic levels* based on visible changes in soil color, composition, or consistency. This variability in soils signals different depositional events and is thus important for later interpretation of the site. When *natural levels* were more than 10 cm thick, we divided them into *arbitrary* 10-cm sublevels to increase the excavators' vertical control. The test trenches automatically provided small, controlled horizontal exposures. To increase horizontal control, larger room units were divided into quadrants when the locations of all four walls could be estimated from surface indications, and into a series of test trenches when the exact room configuration could not be determined (figure 2.8). When *features* such as pits or hearths were encountered, the dirt from them was excavated separately and the location of the feature recorded.

Figure 2.7 *Dana Robson screens the excavated dirt.*

The goal of subdividing excavations so minutely is to maintain tight control on the exact location, or *provenience*, of artifacts. The most general provenience consists of a vertical level and sublevel, a horizontal unit and subunit, and, when applicable, a feature association. Very common items such as unmodified animal bones, broken pottery sherds, and the small, stone *flakes* that are the debris from chipped stone tool manufacture were separated only by this general provenience and artifact type. Other artifacts such as shell ornaments, bone tools, projectile points, and grinding stones, were given individual identifiers called field numbers. When possible their exact find spots, called *point proveniences*, were mapped, but many small objects were discovered simply in the screens, in which case a more general provenience was recorded.

Maps were drawn of each level and sublevel. Within excavation units, the position of an artifact or feature relative to the excavation unit was mapped using a tape and compass to measure from an excavation unit datum point whose location with respect to the main site datum had been recorded. Both horizontal and vertical measurements are necessary. We obtained vertical measurements by stringing a horizontal line, using a line level, then locating the point to be measured with a vertical string and *plumb bob* (figure 2.9). Unfortunately, this technique often seems to require at least three hands (our students have found that bare feet and prehensile toes help some). Furthermore, on windy days tapes can be incredibly hard to manage; frustration increases while accuracy declines. To some extent, this situation has been helped by the use of electronic equipment such as the electronic distance meter (EDM) described earlier. Nevertheless, while an EDM can provide quick and accurate positions for features and artifacts and, for us, has partially

Figure 2.8 *Kathy Kamp, Rex Osae, June Krell, and Lindy Lopes draw the strati-graphic profile of Room 4. Note that the room is excavated in quadrants to provide both north-south and east-west profiles.*

superceded the use of a tape and compass for this purpose, it does not pro-duce detailed drawings of things like features or room walls or floors. This means that the traditional drawing techniques are still an essential part of most excavations.

The validity of the levels identified during excavation can be checked by examining the patterns revealed in the side walls of the excavation units, called *profiles*. If an examination of the profiles suggests that the investigator was too compulsive about dividing the soils, levels can easily be combined in later analyses. Obviously, separating levels once they have been excavated is more difficult, but the use of the arbitrary 10-cm subdivisions is some help in this regard. Subdividing larger units such as rooms produces numerous profiles which can be cross-checked against the excavated stratigraphic levels as well as assuring some horizontal controls in the separation of artifacts. The record of profiles is often published in the form of idealized stratigraphic drawings (figure 2.10), which summarize the evidence to present an inter-pretation of the depositional history. The actual cut shown in figure 2.10 never existed at any one time in the excavation of the site but is a composite of drawings from several rooms and a number of stages of excavation. This profile cuts Rooms 2/3, and 4 roughly from east to west. The exact position

Figure 2.9   *Barb Cardell and Kevin Rhodes map a point provenience using a tape, compass, and plumb bob system.*

of the cut (shown in figure 3.2 in the next chapter) was chosen to maximize the number of features that could be depicted.

In addition to collecting artifacts and recording information about architectural features such as hearths, postholes, and pits, we also collected numerous samples. Some of the samples were sent in for immediate analysis, and some were curated for the future simply because we did not have the money necessary to pay for analysis. Some were kept in the expectation that interesting analyses that are either very experimental now or have not yet even been conceived of will be possible in the future. The fill from hearths, storage pits, garbage dumps with visible carbonized matter, and a selection of other representative proveniences were collected for flotation, a technique for recov-

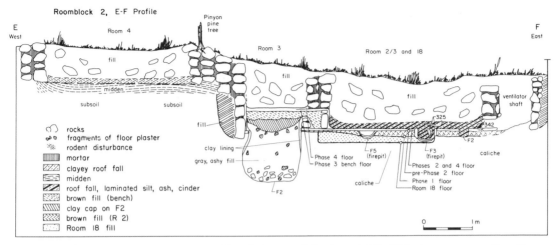

Figure 2.10 *Stratigraphic profile of Rooms 2/3, 4 and 18. This is a composite of several profile drawings and corresponds to a section cutting the rooms as shown by the line in figure 3.2. This profile was chosen to include the largest number of features.*

ering preserved plant remains that is described in more detail in chapter 7. Other samples of dirt were collected as pollen samples. Still others were collected as sediment samples, a record of the soil type of a particular provenience. Floor clay, wall plaster, and volcanic cinders were collected in the hope of analyzing their constituents or matching them to geological sources. Acid washes are taken from metates and the interior of whole vessels in hopes of obtaining information about what plants were ground, cooked, or stored from the pollen they left behind. Carbonized material is collected for possible carbon 14 dating, wood for dendrochronology (described in chapter 4) and burnt clay for archeomagnetic dating (also described in chapter 4).

Completing the Excavations

Kent Flannery (1982) has written, in a rather humorous article famous to archaeologists, that archaeology is "the most fun you can have with your pants on." However, it is also often hot (or sometimes cold), buggy, tiring, and dirty. You get used to eating sandwiches with brown fingerprints on them because there is no water available for washing before lunch. You find you are able to rise at 5:30 A.M., work on the site until 3 P.M. or so, and come home to artifact washing, paperwork, cooking and camp chores. A student once remarked, with some surprise in his voice, that "Field school was no vacation."

Sometimes the site stubbornly refuses to yield its information; at other times the pace is exhilaratingly fast, with numerous and interesting discoveries. Finally, and usually for me far too soon, the excavation season is over. It is somehow an archaeological truism that no matter how carefully you plan things there is always far more that needs to be done than the time allows. Not surprisingly, the most exciting discoveries always come near the end when excavations are deepest. Often they also seem to occur at the most inconvenient possible time, such as right before afternoon summer rains pelt the site or on the last day of the season. Nevertheless, at some point digging must stop.

At a few excavations, where sites are being reconstructed as tourist attractions, the excavated architecture is stabilized and left exposed. Most excavations lack the funds for stabilization and the necessary subsequent maintenance and supervision of the ruins, so excavations are backfilled. Although it is sad to see the hard work of an excavation season disappearing under dirt and rocks, replacing the excavated soil probably ultimately provides the best protection for the ruins.

Chapter 3

FROM POTSHERDS TO PEOPLE
Interpreting the Past

For traditional Hopi the world that humans inhabit today is the fourth in a series of worlds, each successively abandoned because of overcrowding or strife (Eggan 1994). When the third world became too corrupt, the good people decided to escape to the world above by climbing a reed and exiting through a hole in the sky, called a *sipapu*. The good people left first and closed off the reed so that the evil men and women who were trying to follow could not. Soon, however, a child of the *kikmongwi*, a religious and secular leader, died, making it apparent that at least one witch had succeeded in entering the fourth world and bringing along sickness and death. Since no one confessed to sorcery, the kikmongwi threw up a cornmeal ball to divine the identity of the culprit. At first, the people wanted to throw the witch back into the third world, but he (or she, depending on the version of the story) pleaded to be allowed to stay in the upper world. When the kikmongwi showed the people that, despite having died, the child still lived and was happy in the world below, visible through the kiva's sipapu, they decided not to return the witch to the lower world. So, almost immediately, the fourth world too was populated by evil as well as good.

At this point, the fourth world was still cold and dark, but, with the aid of the Flute Priest, Spider Woman crafted a sun and moon. The people were then ready to disperse. They split into groups—ultimately to be known as clans—living, working, worshiping, and occupying a sequence of villages. During their travels, various clans met and dwelt together in symbiotic relationships. Some of this history is remembered as part of a rich oral tradition recording the journeys of clans and the establishment of villages. In addition, the many ruins scattered over the Southwest and studied by archaeologists shed light on the migrations.

Archaeological Interpretations

The archaeologists' interpretations of Pueblo history, as we will see, differ in many specifics from the Hopi explanations but essentially are an attempt to trace the movements of people that the Hopi stories record, to provide explanations for these migrations, and to understand changing lifestyles. The goals, then, are not really mutually exclusive. It is principally the methods of inquiry and interpretation that differ.

While for Puebloan groups their oral history is the fundamental source for reconstructing the past, for the archaeologist the major clues are ruins and artifacts. As archaeology has developed as a discipline, it has developed more systematic and more scientific ways of interpreting the archaeological remains. In the 1960s and 1970s a major goal of many archaeologists was to discover laws of human behavior or at least identify systematic relationships between behaviors and material culture that could be used to reliably interpret archaeological remains. This search continues today, although in a somewhat less idealistic vein. Both controlled experiments and ethnographic research conducted by ethnoarchaeologists help devise more reliable ways of reconstructing the past from the material evidence. While, unfortunately, few simple and invariable relationships between behavior and patterns of material culture have been discovered, it is clear that the systematic study of such relationships is central to the development of archaeological interpretation.

The Relationship Between Behavior and Material Remains

First, it must be acknowledged that in ongoing societies material objects divulge information about culture. Some conclusions can be reached in a fairly straightforward manner. For example, piles of wood shavings and sawdust allow the easy conclusion that woodworking of some sort has occurred in the vicinity. The presence of carpentry tools would further strengthen this conclusion.

Other types of issues may be harder to assess from material evidence alone, even in ongoing societies. Thus, the age or gender of the carpenter, for example, is not obvious from the debris of woodworking. If we believe that we can make an intelligent guess about the gender of the carpenter, it is only because carpentry currently has a fairly strong, although by no means invariable, correlation with a specific gender in our culture. Obviously, this type of interpretation is only an informed guess, and you might well feel somewhat uncomfortable with it. Inference like this becomes even more difficult when we do not already know the basic cultural patterns. There is no guarantee that men were the primary carpenters in the society we are studying. An idea of the likelihood of men doing most of the carpentry can be assessed by cross-cultural comparisons. In the sample of 164 societies for which Murdock and Provost (1973) were able to obtain information on woodworking activities, 159 allocated woodworking tasks exclusively to males, three predominantly to males, one predominantly to females, and one had equal participation. This suggests that on statistical grounds we are still fairly safe in postulating a male carpenter. Nevertheless, ideally the archaeologist would like to be able to discover social patterns that existed in the past but may be rare or extinct today, and inferences simply on the basis of statistical comparisons to modern societies will not allow this.

Some societal characteristics are also harder to discover than others. Postmarital residence patterns, descent, political systems, gender roles, and religious beliefs are reflected in material culture in subtle ways and are therefore hard to discern. For example, in Christian symbolism the fish signifies Christ because the Greek letters in the word "fish" are the same as the first letters in the phrase, "Jesus Christ God's Son Savior." Occasionally the fish also symbolizes baptism because both fish and baptism are associated with water. While an analysis of Christian art would certainly reveal that the fish was one of the important symbols, it would take considerably more astuteness and imagination to discern the exact meaning. The problem is magnified in the case of less common symbols such as the fly, which signifies evil, or the goat, which, because of the Biblical passage about separating the sheep from the goats, denotes the damned.

A short moment's reflection will show that dress, diet, residential architecture, and many other aspects of material culture all yield information about personal and group identity. Nevertheless, analysis techniques for interpreting the evidence are not inherently obvious and often depend on considerable prior cultural knowledge. Ultimately, however, the accuracy of archaeological conclusions rests on the ability to make appropriate generalizations about how specific patterns in material culture reflect human behavior. Archaeologists have spent considerable effort attempting to understand patterns of material remains in extant cultures and to formulate generalizations about the regularities that will help archaeologists to interpret the past.

Site Formation Processes—
Artifact Distributions

Unfortunately, even in the rare sites like Pompeii which reflect special types of catastrophes and an unusual level of preservation, archaeologists do not find artifacts exactly as they were in the ongoing cultural system. As objects are abandoned or discarded to eventually become part of an archaeological site, the process of interpretation becomes more and more complex.

Schiffer (1976, 1987) and others have studied the processes of site formation in some depth, using both experiments and ethnographic studies. Much of what remains on archaeological sites might best be termed garbage. There are two major ways of treating garbage. Some trash is merely left in the location of use. Thus, the candy wrapper is thrown to the ground or the waste flakes from making a stone tool are left in place rather than being cleaned up. This type of garbage, called *primary refuse* by archaeologists, gives information about the location of activities at a site. Thus, used condoms, beer cans, and an abandoned campfire on a beach provide clues to a number of social activities that took place at that specific site.

The second means of dealing with trash is to gather and redeposit it. Garbage dealt with in this way is called *secondary refuse*. Modern garbage dumps are obvious examples of secondary refuse, but secondary refuse may at times be scattered instead of deposited in segregated areas. Floor sweepings tossed into the yard are an example of secondary refuse disposed of outside of a formal garbage disposal area. Much of the refuse found both in modern contexts and at archaeological sites is secondary refuse. Objects found in this type of context provide information about activities that occurred in a broader area. Thus, beer cans found in the town dump obviously do not mean that people actually sat on the garbage to drink their beer (although we can't rule out the notion that this occasionally occurs) but do demonstrate evidence of beer consumption in the area served by the landfill.

Sometimes artifacts are simply abandoned *in situ*. This *de facto refuse* can occur when a group leaves objects at a site, either because they plan to return later or because they are unable or unwilling to remove the items when they depart. Usually the bulk of de facto refuse is relatively cheap or very heavy. Pompeii is a classic and extreme example: a community whose inhabitants were killed or driven away by a sudden disaster. There most of the artifacts simply lie in place. A less extreme example occurs when a house burns down and objects are left on the floor and not later scavenged. In the southwestern United States the most complete archaeological assemblages have been obtained on the floors of rooms destroyed by fire. Of course not all burned rooms have been abandoned because of a catastrophic fire. Some rooms burn long after they have already been deserted. Other times, as in some areas of the prehistoric Southwest, dwellings are ritually burned, perhaps because their owner has died, perhaps because unfortunate events have occurred in the dwelling, or for other reasons. In this case, the objects remaining in the room may be a subset of the original furnishings or may even have been introduced especially for the ceremony.

Unfortunately for the archaeologist (although not for the prehistoric inhabitants), there are no burnt rooms at Lizard Man Village and almost all of the artifacts are secondary trash. A few exceptions occur on house floors or roofs and appear to be items simply abandoned when the group left, examples of de facto refuse. In most cases these are large, heavy ground stone tools such as the manos and metates used to grind corn, or heavily used and broken artifacts, still perhaps useful but not really worth the effort of moving. The fact that most artifacts are not in their locations of use means that some types of analyses are not meaningful. Comparing the frequencies of ceramic forms left *in situ* on the floor of a room might reveal room function, but doing the same analysis of secondary trash in the room fill only tells what types of refuse were thrown into the room after it was abandoned, suggesting nothing about actual room use.

Even when architecture is abandoned or artifacts are discarded, their history does not end. Humans and other animals dig pits, shuffle through the dirt, collect and scavenge, and in many other ways alter the distribution of artifacts. At Lizard Man Village on several occasions we found pottery rim sherds that we were able to put together from rooms on opposite sides of the site. Either adjacent portions of the same broken vessel were initially discarded in very disparate locales or later disturbances moved the artifacts dozens of meters. Not only the position of objects but their very incidence can be altered post-depositionally. If an area is fairly heavily populated, scavenging is likely to ensure that few useable and portable artifacts are left on a site.

The Differential Preservation of Artifacts

Nature also takes its toll on archaeological remains. Time alters the exact position of the remains at the site. Luckily, much of this change follows physical laws and is thus predictable. For instance, artifacts tend to be washed downslope rather than uphill and smaller, lighter objects are more likely to be transported farther. In addition, only a portion of the material record survives. In most climates, organic remains decay; structures collapse; soils are deposited; vegetation grows. The rates of transformation depend on local climate and soil conditions. Organic remains decay less rapidly in very dry climates, where they become desiccated; in wet, submerged conditions which lack the requisite bacteria and oxygen for decay; or where extreme cold preserves through freezing. Bone preserves well in basic soils, while pollens do better in the acid conditions which destroy bone.

We know from materials found in dry caves that the Sinagua wove blankets, baskets, and sandals and made digging sticks, bows, arrows, and wooden weaving implements. In most Sinagua sites these organic artifacts decayed long ago. Pottery, chipped and ground stone, shell, minerals, and bone are the most frequently preserved types of artifacts, since they do not decay readily. For organic remains, burning is sometimes the best protection from decomposition. Carbonized materials cannot be metabolized by bacteria and so remain preserved. Most of our knowledge of prehistoric plant consumption has been gained through the analysis of carbonized plant remains. Occasionally, buried primarily organic artifacts that have not been burned survive, even in the Flagstaff soils, which are moist for part of the year. Notable are wooden or basketry artifacts such as those found with the "magician" burial, which were somewhat protected from decomposition by heavy coats of mineral paints or arid conditions.

At Lizard Man Village one of the burials included an armband made of juniper bark, painted with calcite, hematite, azurite, and limonite in a geometric design (figure 3.1). Bracelets like this one and jewelry of other organic materials such as seeds once may have been fairly common among the Sinagua. If so, most have decayed by now.

The discovery of the bracelet at Lizard Man Village caused considerable excitement, both because such finds are rare and because we were initially unsure about how to remove the armband from the ground without damaging it. The armband was found late in the afternoon after most of the excavation team had already left. It was our policy to complete burial excavations in a single day, if possible, to minimize the damage to bones that may occur if they dry, then are moistened by dews, then dry out again. Despite the fact that the normal field day was over, we had remained to complete this one task.

Only John, the two student excavators, Sara Bruins and Gweneth Johnson, and I remained. Gwen discovered the armband with the memorable words, "There's something blue!" John carefully uncovered the top face of the band using a photo lens-cleaning brush of the type with a small air bulb and a fine brush. Now we could see the design, but we had no idea how to remove

a

resin
element

0   25 mm

☐ White   ▨ Red   ■ Black

▦ Yellow   ▨ Blue   ⬚ Design Unknown

b

Figure 3.1 *Armband from Lizard Man Village: (a) The armband in situ as excavated,
(b) A drawing of the armband showing the design.*

the artifact. It was positioned just below the elbow, which meant that part of it was under the bone. Furthermore, it was extremely fragile and currently being supported by the earth matrix.

John decided to sleep on the site near the burial so that it would not be disturbed by animals overnight. We drew and photographed everything, then covered it with a tarp. I went into town to get John a bit of supper, soap and a jerry can of water so that he could wash, and a sleeping bag. Most important, however, I started to make phone calls to see what kind of advice I could get about removing the armband.

I was ultimately sent to Elaine Hughes, a conservator then working for the Museum of Northern Arizona. The next day work was pretty much suspended, as we all watched her pedestal the arm, encase it in a plaster cast, and remove the whole as a unit. We took the cast to the lab at the Museum of Northern Arizona and excavated the now-exposed back of the armband under a microscope. Still we were in a quandary; no one knew how to remove the soil supporting the interior of the armband without damaging its structure.

Luckily, an old boss of ours, Keith Anderson, then at the National Park Service's Western Archaeological and Conservation Center in Tucson, came to visit the site. We knew that the conservator there, Brigid Sullivan, was excellent at this type of task and hoped to convince Keith to allow her to work on the armband. He assured us that the archaeological rumor mill had already alerted her to the discovery and she was dying to see what she could do. She carefully excavated the armband and placed it in its own case on a stiff supporting band. Techniques in the conservation of artifacts are constantly improving. This is an area of active, technical research and, thanks to conservators, many artifacts such as the bracelet that in the past would have been damaged extensively or even totally lost during recovery are now preserved.

An Example of Formation Processes at Lizard Man Village

To illustrate the operation of *formation processes*, let us think about what happens as a deep subterranean room is constructed, used, abandoned, and eventually decays, using as an example one such room at Lizard Man Village. In chapter 4 we will use this same subterranean room to show how a sequence of events can be reconstructed using archaeological evidence.

Construction of Room 2/3, an Elden Phase (A.D. 1150–1250) habitation room (figures 2.3 [location on site plan], 2.10 [profile], and 3.2), first required digging a large pit. This would have been considerable work for the Sinagua, as their digging tools would have been primarily wooden digging sticks and baskets. On some of the pit walls at Lizard Man Village it is still possible to see the marks produced by these digging sticks. The pit for this room would have been about five meters by six meters (16.5 feet by 20 feet), a lot of dirt to move, even with metal shovels and buckets. Construction of the pit cut through an earlier pithouse, which we designated Room 18 (rooms are simply numbered as they are identified), shown by a dotted line on figure 3.2, phase 1 (See also figure 3.3, phase 1). Next the pit would have been lined with masonry and the gap between the masonry and pit walls filled in with smaller rock rubble and dirt. Above the pit the masonry walls were free-standing and the room was built about a meter (3 feet) above the ground before the roof was added. A flat roof would have been constructed of large wooden beams crossed by smaller ones, brush, and finally clay. Entry was by ladder through an opening in the roof. Ventilation was provided by con-structing a masonry-lined shaft to the east of the room that drew air to the level of the floor. This allowed air circulation and helped reduce smoke from the fire, as cooler air came down the shaft and warm, smoky air rose up and was drawn out the entryway. Floors would have been made of clay, walls plas-tered, and other desired features such as hearths and storage pits con-structed.

Historically, among the Hopi the men constructed the room walls and the women were in charge of plastering them. The resulting dwelling belonged to the women. Unfortunately, no means for determining gender roles in either construction or ownership of prehistoric architecture has yet been developed. At one time it was hoped that fingerprints in wall plaster would provide a vital clue to the sex of the plasterer. Unfortunately, it is not possible to reliably dis-tinguish male and female fingerprints. Perhaps, in the future, some creative archaeologist will figure out a method.

While we have never tried replicating pithouse construction, others have. Glennie (cited in Varien 1984) took 467 person hours, about 58 eight-hour days, to construct a pithouse 5 meters (about 16.5 feet) in diameter. While this provides only the roughest estimation of construction times, it does dem-onstrate the considerable time and effort that went into the initial construc-tion of Room 2. When the room was complete it would have had the floor plan depicted in figure 3.2, phase 1.

The story of a dwelling is never finished when its initial construction is done, however. Many dwellings have very complicated life histories, with many remodelings. This should not come as a surprise to any of us. Any building with a long life span is likely to have been altered in response to the changing needs that a household experiences as children are born, grow, marry, and leave the house or bring spouses and their own children into the household, as the social or economic position of the household changes, as styles change, or simply because time and use have caused degradation in the original structure and a need for refurbishing.

Room 2/3 at Lizard Man Village, our illustrative case, was initially a sin-gle large room. The pit was dug down to the calcified layer of subsoil called caliche in the Southwest, which was leveled and smoothed off to form the ini-tial floor surface. A round firepit was dug near the center of the room (phase 1, figures 3.2 and 3.3). Subsequently a new clay-plastered floor was put in and the positions of several pits in the floor changed, but the original fireplace continued in use (figure 3.2, phase pre-2). Later the fireplace was covered by a second plastered floor, and a new, slab-lined central hearth was con-structed. At about the same time, a large, deep storage pit with a stone rim was dug through the floor in the southeast corner of the room (phase 2, fig-

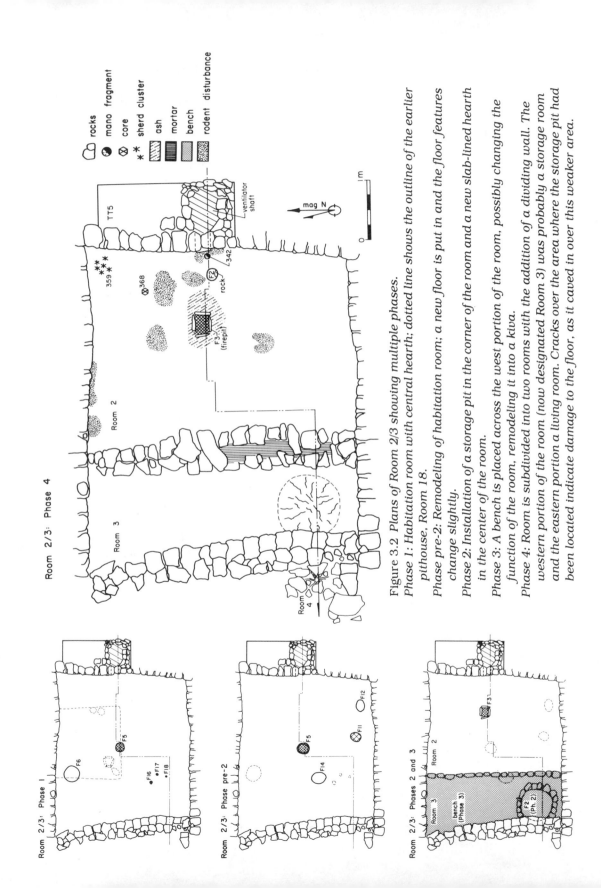

Room 2/3: Phase 4

Room 2/3: Phase 1

Room 2/3: Phase pre-2

Room 2/3: Phases 2 and 3

Figure 3.2 Plans of Room 2/3 showing multiple phases.

Phase 1: Habitation room with central hearth; dotted line shows the outline of the earlier pithouse, Room 18.

Phase pre-2: Remodeling of habitation room; a new floor is put in and the floor features change slightly.

Phase 2: Installation of a storage pit in the corner of the room and a new slab-lined hearth in the center of the room.

Phase 3: A bench is placed across the west portion of the room, possibly changing the function of the room, remodeling it into a kiva.

Phase 4: Room is subdivided into two rooms with the addition of a dividing wall. The western portion of the room (now designated Room 3) was probably a storage room and the eastern portion a living room. Cracks over the area where the storage pit had been located indicate damage to the floor, as it caved in over this weaker area.

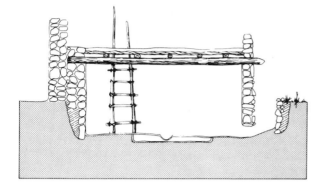

Phase 1: Room 2, a habitation room with a ventilator shaft to the east, is constructed over the remains of the earlier pithouse, Room 18.

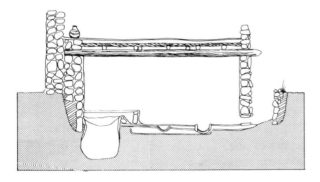

Phase 2: Room 2 is remodeled with a new floor, slab-lined firepit, and deep storage pit.

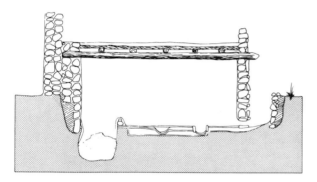

Phase 3: The storage pit is plastered over and covered by a low bench across the western end of the room. The room is now seen as a kiva.

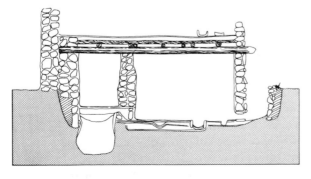

Phase 4: The room is now subdivided into two rooms: Room 3, a storage room, and Room 2, a habitation room.

Figure 3.3 *Diagram showing the major construction phases of Room 2/3:*

ures 3.2 and 3.3). Until this point analogies with historic puebloan homes suggest that the room is likely to have been living quarters for a family.

Later, the residents filled in the storage pit with ashy debris, plastered over the top of the storage pit and built a low bench over the entire west end of the room (phase 3, figures 3.2 and 3.3). The garbage in the pit fill included a piece of burnt wood which dendrochronology tells us died sometime after A.D. 1197. This means that the pit was filled in and covered by the bench no earlier than A.D. 1197. Ethnographic analogy suggests the possibility that the construction of the bench indicates a change in room function from a residence to a ceremonial room (a kiva), an interpretation discussed in more detail later.

Eventually, the inhabitants remodeled again. This time they built a wall along the bench top to subdivide the room into a large room (Room 2) with a central hearth and a smaller room (Room 3), which contained no features, on the surface that had been the bench top (phase 4, figures 3.2 and 3.3). The remodeling may have signaled the return of the dwelling to primarily a living structure, with the small room serving as a storage room. This interpretation may be strengthened by the fact that probably at about the same time (or at least fairly late in the life of the room block) a second kiva-like structure with a bench, Room 19, was built adjacent to Room 2/3 (see site plan, figure 2.3).

Even after Room 2/3 was abandoned, its history did not end. When they left, the inhabitants removed almost all of their possessions, leaving only a couple of heavy metates on the roof and perhaps a few no longer useable items such as a mano fragment and a *chert* core. Alternatively, many of the smaller items may have been thrown into the room after it was abandoned. Worldwide, abandoned structures are commonly used as garbage dumps. There does not seem to have been much trash deposition in Room 2/3, however. Perhaps this is because the room was abandoned toward the end of the site's occupation.

After abandonment a layer of dust, dirt, and cinders accumulated on the now unswept floors. This layer was particularly thick near the ventilator shaft, where dirt could blow in from the outside. The room, no longer maintained, began to fall apart. Plaster started to peel off of the walls and the roof began to decay and leak, leaving thin lenses of water-laid mud across the room. Finally the roof began to fall in. As the roof weakened, the two large metates fell through it, broke on the hearth stones and remained resting on the layers of mud from the roof and blown-in cinders, awaiting the archaeologist to discern from these clues that they had originally been on the roof rather than on the floor. Perhaps the abandoned village was visited by adults from nearby villages, who scavenged for usable items, or by children who played at the site, making stacks of pottery or inventing games with discarded animal bones. Eventually the masonry walls of the room began to fall down as the mortar washed out and the frosts pried the stones apart. Generally, the first stones tend to tumble to the base of the wall, but, as the pile grows, others roll or bounce to the center of the room. As earth and stones accumulate, the cross-section of the fallen wall debris begins to look like a smile (figure 2.10). As time passed at Lizard Man Village, the walls decayed; wind and rain brought in dust, dirt, and artifacts such as sherds from the surrounding trash. Finally, the walls became stabilized, as dirt mixed with garbage and wall stones reached and eventually surpassed standing wall height and the central depression filled. When we first identified Room 2/3 the surface indications consisted merely of artifacts (primarily sherds), a few scattered wall stones in the vicinity, and a slight depression (figure 3.4). The pile of rocks we excavated looked nothing like the home abandoned by a Sinagua family, but a knowledge of formation processes allows us to reconstruct its history and envision it as it once was (figure 2.4).

Figure 3.4 *Photograph of Room 2/3 area before excavation.*

Interpreting the Artifacts

Once excavations are complete, only a small fraction of the interpretive job is done. Numerous hours must now be spent in the lab and at computers, analyzing artifacts and provenience information. Archaeologists can use excavation data to search for answers to an infinite number of questions about the lifeways of the past. The exact issues investigated vary somewhat from project to project. Basic to any investigation, however, is knowledge about what each artifact was used for, who made it, and when it was made. Here I will discuss some of the analytic methods used to decide function and cultural affiliation. Additional comments on artifact analyses and specific examples are scattered throughout the other chapters. Because it is such a large and complex topic, I have devoted an entire chapter to dating techniques.

Typologies

Archaeologists usually start analysis by organizing artifacts using some kind of a typology or classification system. This activity is a necessary part of both human thought and human communication. There is not a single correct typology for any group of objects. Just as in our own culture ceramics may be classified by material of manufacture (ironstone, melamine, china), by manufacturer (Spode, Wedgewood), by date of manufacture, by status (good china, everyday china), by form or morphology (plate, cup), by function (dinner plate, cereal/salad/soup bowl), or a myriad of other ways, it is likely that the prehistoric cultures archaeologists study had a similar diversity of typological schemes. Archaeologists devise typologies to solve particular research problems such as dating, determining cultural affiliation, or discussing the activities that the artifacts imply.

The construction and use of typologies depends on the categorization of an artifact's *attributes*, or properties. In ceramic analysis, for example, typologies are often based on variability in paste (the clay part of the ceramic), *temper* (nonplastic inclusions), manufacturing techniques, decoration, and form. The inhabitants of a region tend to produce specific, recognizable types of pottery that usually change through time. Thus, during the occupation of Lizard Man Village the Sinagua were manufacturing primarily plain reddish-brown ceramics, while the Kayenta produced a variety of types including painted wares with black designs on a white background. Both of these ceramic styles changed through time, making it possible to identify a general time and locale of manufacture by applying an appropriate typology.

Determining Function

Some typologies are specifically designed to address issues of function. Clues to artifact function are provided by ethnographic analogies, experiments, usewear analysis, chemical residues remaining on the object, material science studies of its physical properties, and the archaeological context. An example or two will show how these types of evidence are used to devise and support claims about the function of prehistoric artifacts.

The chipped stone points commonly found on sites in North America and elsewhere provide a simple example. Archaeologists may initially suggest that a particular type of point was normally mounted on arrows, because there are good ethnographic examples of that type of use for similar points. The hypothesis is strengthened by experiments showing that it is indeed feasible to construct a usable arrow with such a point. It is also possible to show that the point was not suitable for arrow use. This is certainly true of some of the larger point types. The assertion is further strengthened by the discovery of blood residues on some points, breakage patterns on the tips of points that would most likely be due to impact with another object, or the discovery of points actually embedded in bone. (Of course, the discovery of a completely preserved arrow would be the clincher, but that is hard to count on!)

Among the most enigmatic artifacts at Sinagua sites are roughly finished cylinders of vesicular basalt (figure 3.5). Our students nicknamed them "petrified turds," but archaeologists usually designate them by the more staid morphological descriptor, "basalt cylinder." Possible functions for the cylinders, suggested on the basis of both ethnographic analogy and logic, include weights, tools for removing the kernels from dried corn, tokens for relay races, plaster smoothers, abraders for working wood or sandstone, toys, phallic symbols, and tools for thinning ceramic vessels. An examination of the cylinders under a simple 10-power hand lens shows discernable wear on many of the basalt cylinders.

Intrigued by this odd artifact, I designed an experiment to evaluate some of these alternative hypotheses. First I replicated several cylinders, then used one to shell corn, one to work wood, one to polish a ceramic disk, and one to thin an unfired ceramic bowl. Each activity was performed for six hours by whomever I could con into it, and the resulting wear on each basalt cylinder was examined under a stereo-microscope at a range of magnifications from ten times to one hundred times. Figure 3.6a shows an example of the usewear found on an archaeological specimen of a basalt cylinder. Figure 36b is an unused, freshly-manufactured cylinder. Figures 3.7a through 3.7d show the types of usewear produced by the four types of experimental use. A close comparison of the photographs shows that the experiments allow several hypotheses to be eliminated. The cylinders were clearly not used to shell corn, work wood, or polish clay surfaces. The wear on the cylinders was, however, very similar to that produced by scraping a ceramic vessel. Furthermore, despite having already been washed, about one-fourth of the cylinders had clay imbedded in vesicles. This may be another kind of use residue, the result of working clay. Based on this usewear study, I have tentatively suggested but not definitely proven that those mysterious basalt cylinders may, in fact, be part of the equipment for pottery manufacture.

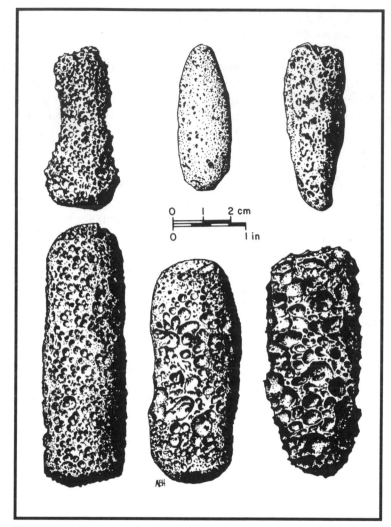

Figure 3.5 Basalt cylinders.

Artifact Styles

Function may require that artifacts have certain attributes and make others highly desirable, but in addition to purely functional features, all objects have a stylistic dimension. While in theory style is separate from function, in practice the two may be very difficult to distinguish. For example, the style of a dress may also affect functional qualities such as warmth, durability, or ease of movement. Similarly, the exact form of a ceramic vessel or the use of a clay *slip* to alter the pot's color may be a stylistic choice but may also have functional ramifications.

Generally an object's style is interpreted as having primarily symbolic

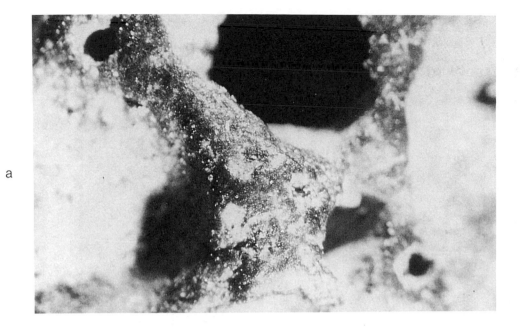

a

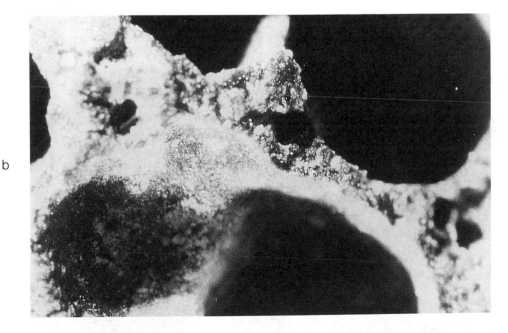

b

Figure 3.6 *(a) Photograph showing usewear on an archaeological specimen viewed under 40X magnification. Note the polishing and rounding of the vesicle wall top and sides. Worn vesicle cross sections tend to be rounded. (b) Photograph showing unused basalt cylinder replica under 40X magnification. Note the irregular topography of the top of the vesicle wall and the sharp, unworn vesicle edges.*

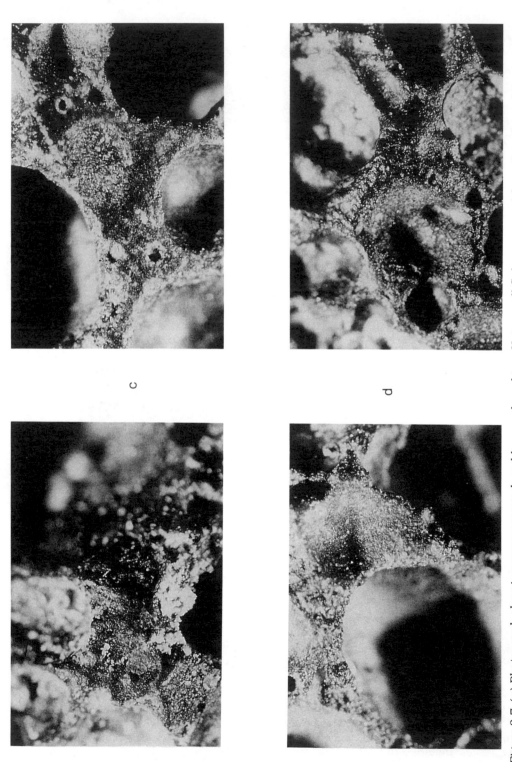

Figure 3.7 (a) Photograph showing usewear produced by wood working. Note small flakes removed from the edges of the vesicles and smoothing on vesicle tops. Vesicle cross sections tend to be peaked. (b) Photograph showing usewear produced by removing kernels from dried corn. Note crushing of vesicle edges and removal of some small flakes. Cross sections of vesicle walls tend to be peaked. (c) Photograph showing usewear produced by simulated floor polishing. Note flattened vesicle wall tops. (d) Usewear produced by smoothing and polishing a clay vessel. Note the polished and rounded vesicles. Cross sections tend to be rounded.

and communicative functions. The choice of a dinnerware to serve guests may well communicate information about the status of both host and guest, as well as define the nature of the occasion. Weddings and picnics, dinner for the boss and dinner for a casual family friend all have their own rules of etiquette that are expressed partly in material objects. The use of a particular object itself may communicate information. A wedding ring, regardless of its style, says that the wearer is married. In other cases, the nuances of style are crucial. Thus, a necklace in the form of a cross suggests that the wearer is Christian, while a hand of Fatima usually indicates a Muslim.

As in the example above, personal and group identities are not infrequently signaled by style. We are all aware that dress may vary with national identity. In archaeology, too, regional variability in artifact styles is often interpreted as meaning cultural identity. As mentioned previously, the prehistoric Puebloan populations of the Colorado Plateau are distinguished from the Sinagua primarily on the basis of differences in their pottery styles. Obviously, pots are not people, so cultural affiliations determined in this manner may be inaccurate. We know that today some groups consider themselves ethnically and politically different from others without manifesting significant visible cultural differences, while others show such differences but see themselves as ethnically the same. Nevertheless, in many areas variability in material objects does correspond to ethnic diversity, and some objects may intentionally be used to signal group identity. Thus, to assume that variability in artifact styles roughly corresponds to overall cultural and ethnic variability is not entirely without justification and, at the moment, is the best method the archaeologist has for delineating cultural units.

As we know from watching clothing, cars, and numerous items in our own culture, styles also change through time. This fact can be used to help date archaeological proveniences and will be discussed in more detail in the next chapter.

Examining Patterns and Context

A knowledge of *context*, the relationship of artifacts to one another and in space, is vital to the successful interpretation of archaeological sites. At the simplest level, four unworked stones are just rocks, but placed in a circular configuration with ash in the center they have an entirely new meaning. Now they are part of a hearth. A projectile point at an animal kill site is a hunting tool, embedded in a human skeleton it is recognizable as a weapon of war, when found with manufacturing debris it documents the efforts of an artisan, and in a burial it represents an offering with symbolic meaning. Once removed from its original context, the artifact loses some of its potential for revealing information about the past.

To look at a slightly more complex example of the way that archaeologists put together information about artifacts and context to arrive at an interpretation, let us examine Room 2/3 again. First, note that this room is not isolated but belongs to a suite of rooms, Room Block 2 (figure 2.3). The room block includes two adjacent surface rooms (4 and 9). Room 4 had a very poorly preserved, unplastered floor and lacked any type of hearth or firepit. Room 9 had a slab-lined hearth and a large storage pit in one corner. Room 2, which we described earlier, was constructed immediately to the east of Rooms 4 and 9 and was later remodeled with the addition of Room 3. Room 19, another large semisubterranean room with a bench, was added in the latter part of the room block's occupation, possibly around the time that Room 2/3 was subdivided.

As early as the late 1800s Mindeleff ([1891] 1981) made detailed descriptions of Hopi architecture. These subsequently have been supplemented by many ethnographic reports. In 1968 Hill systematically reviewed the archaeological implications of the ethnographic information on room function, developed a series of statements relating room characteristics to functions, and applied them to Broken K Pueblo near Snowflake, Arizona. He proposed three room types: living rooms (large rooms with firepits, mealing bins, and ventilators), storage rooms (small rooms with no firepits and few features), and special rooms (analogous to kivas, used for ceremonial events and as as mens' houses). Since then, other room-use typologies have been devised, but Hill's scheme or variants of it remain the core of much of the current analysis of room function in the Southwest.

Following Hill's assertion that hearths tend to be associated with habitation rooms and benches with kivas, we have tentatively identified Room 9 as a habitation room, Room 19 as a kiva, and Room 4 as a storage room. As described earlier, Room 2/3 is seen as having a series of functions: built as a habitation room, remodeled into a kiva, and finally subdivided into an eastern habitation room and western storage unit (probably when a new kiva, Room 19, was constructed). The interpretation of room function at Lizard Man Village had to be made using only information about architecture and the context of room features such as hearths. Artifacts in good, interpretable contexts on room floors would have added to the confidence of our interpretations but simply weren't available, since the rooms had all been cleaned out as they were abandoned.

The context of these rooms as a unit, in relation to one another and to the site as a whole, is important in our interpretations. That these rooms are spatially distinct from the other room block suggests the possibility that they constitute a separate social unit. Functionally, this also makes sense. At any one time, there would have been one or two habitation rooms (Rooms 9 and 2), one or two storage rooms (Room 4 and later Room 3), and, after an initial phase which lacked any visible ceremonial room, a kiva (Room 2 and later Room 19). If this interpretation of the room block is correct, the room block probably housed one or two households that shared communal ceremonial facilities.

Given this interpretation, we can go one step further and attempt to determine the number of people who might have inhabited the room block. The two major methods for determining population size are: (1) to make a calculation based on the size of the area inhabited and (2) to figure out the number of households, then multiply by household size. Let us examine the rationale behind these two approaches and apply them to the room block we have been discussing.

In a classic study, Raoul Naroll (1962) looked at the relationship between household size and average floor area of the dwelling for a sample of eighteen societies worldwide. He concluded that a rough estimate of ten square meters (about 108 square feet) per person of floor area could be used to calculate the average household size. Thus a dwelling size of forty square meters (430 square feet) would suggest four members in a household. There are numerous criticisms of Naroll's model. For instance, it is not clear what should be included in the dwelling area. Should storage areas be counted? What about communally-used living space? We know, for example, from the metates that once rested on the roof of Room 2/3 that roofs were a work area for the Sinagua, effectively an extension of the household space. Should roofs be logically incorporated in the calculation of living space? It has been suggested that in some areas exterior spaces are so important that they should be included. Furthermore, Naroll's model does not take into account the enormous variability in house size in some cultures that relates to variables such as economic status rather than household size. Another problem with Naroll's figure is technical rather than theoretical. Brown (1987) replicated Naroll's original study and asserted that some of the cases had been incorrectly coded. He proposed an alternative figure of six square meters (64.5 square feet) per person. Unfortunately, this figure suffers from the same theoretical problems as Naroll's.

Despite the unreliability of such estimates, it is interesting to apply them to the data from a site and compare them with the population estimates obtained using other kinds of information. Room Block 2 measures a total of about sixty-three square meters (678 square feet), including Rooms 2/3, 4, 9, and 19. Assuming that all the rooms were occupied simultaneously, this would imply a population of approximately six people, if the ten-square-meters-per-person figure is used, and ten people with the six-square-meters-per-person estimate.

An alternative method of calculating population size is to multiply the postulated number of households by an estimate of household size. Based on analogies with modern pueblos, a figure of 6.1 persons per household has been used for prehistoric pueblos. This would lead to an estimate of twelve persons for the two households occupying the room block, which is not too disparate from the ten persons calculated based on six square meters per person. Cross-culturally, nuclear families tend to have an average of five to six members. This would give a range of ten to twelve people as the most likely estimated population for the room block. Neither of these techniques is infallible, but together they do give us a general notion of how large a group may have occupied the dwelling unit we just explored.

Advantages and Disadvantages
of Archaeological Data

Clearly, archaeological data is limited in its scope and provisional in its interpretations. We will never be able to interview the ancient Sinagua, to share
their personal joys and triumphs, to explore their concerns, to understand
their hopes and fears. Neither will we be able to view a ceremony, record the
sacred songs, describe the kinship system, or document the political machi-
nations that may have occurred as some villages were abandoned and others
established.

Nevertheless, the archaeological data has advantages as well as limi-
tations. First, the archaeological record may be less biased than written documents or contemporary interviews. All documents are consciously drafted
by an author or authors, for a particular audience, and with a specific agenda.
Thus, it goes without saying that all documents have inherent biases in both
what they present and how they present it. The same is clearly true of personal interviews and oral histories. A portion of the material record may be
viewed as an explicit attempt at communication in a very analogous manner.
Clothing, architecture, and art all have a distinct communicative element that
is manipulated by humans. Other parts of the archaeological record may be
termed nonreactive. They are the unconscious by-products of human activities and are not consciously manipulated in response to the opinions of other
individuals. A study by Bill Rathje (1978) of the University of Arizona illustrates this nicely. He asked people from one area in Tucson about their
household's alcohol consumption, then examined the area's garbage for alcohol containers. Perhaps it is not surprising that most individuals admitted to
far less alcohol consumption than the average indicated by the analysis of the
garbage.

Second, archaeology provides a picture with incredible time depth. Ever
since humans have inhabited the earth, wherever they have lived, they have
left behind a material record of their presence. Ethnographic studies are limited by the field season of the ethnographer and the life spans of the members
of the culture. History is limited to the places and times with written documents. Archaeology explores the most remote human past and thus is ideally suited to the study of broad themes in culture change, such as the
relationship between humans and their environment, the evolution of economic and political stratification, or the role of warfare.

Chapter 4

CHARRED BEAMS AND MAGNETIC PARTICLES
Dating the Site

One of the initial steps in an archaeological analysis is to obtain dates for both the overall occupation of a site and for the sequence of events that occurred at it. Dating establishes the relative contemporaneity of events in a region and at individual sites, and permits the investigation of change through time.

Relative Dating Techniques

The determination of a chronological sequence that is not tied to specific dates or date ranges is called *relative dating*. Relative dating merely establishes the order of events, specifying which happened first and which happened more recently. The analysis of a site's stratigraphy and of changes in the styles of artifacts through time can produce relative dating information.

At some sites the dating information has allowed the reconstruction of fairly definitive sequences of room construction, use, and abandonment. Obviously this is the ideal, as it allows the researcher to determine which structures are contemporaneous, and thus to reconstruct the configuration of the village and chart changes through time on both a local and a regional level. Unfortunately, many sites are not easily dated. The attempt to provide secure dates for Lizard Man Village provided frustration and headaches, while costing not insignificant funds in dating attempts that have been only partially successful. The following sections describe three methods of relative dating that were used during the excavation of Lizard Man Village.

Stratigraphy

The examination of *stratigraphy*, the vertical sequence of layers, reveals information about the unfolding of events. The analysis of stratigraphy is one of the most common means of relative dating. The *law of superposition* states that a level that directly overlays another will be the more recent of the two. This is a fairly obvious principle, easily illustrated by constructing a stack of blocks. The first one laid down is on the bottom and subsequent additions can be "dated" by their position in the sequence. Absolute depth is, however, not a simple indication of relative age. Sometimes deposition is very rapid and other times it is slow. Sloped surfaces or the digging and refilling of pits often yield situations where more recent strata are physically lower than older layers.

The profile from Room 2/3 discussed earlier (figure 2.10) provides a convenient real-life example of stratigraphic analysis. Often, diagrams such as this one take considerable study before they can be completely understood. In essence, the profile provides a record of all the events I described in the section on formation processes, and it is a knowledge of these processes that allows us to accurately interpret the stratigraphy. Figure 4.1 provides a simplified diagram showing how the stratigraphy shown in the profile was produced. The earliest human modification to the area below Room 2/3 was the excavation of a deep pit. As I discussed in chapter 3, this pit formed the basis of a deep pithouse, Room 18. While the pithouse had a hearth in the floor (figure 3.2), it is not shown in the figure 2.10 profile because the cross-section chosen for this profile does not cut across the section of the floor containing this feature. After its abandonment, the pithouse designated Room 18 was at least partially filled in with dirt and debris. This fill is shown on the profile by a stippled area. Presumably the pit edges and possibly the fill once continued up to the surface, as shown in figure 4.1. The occupants of Lizard Man Village disturbed the area, however, when they decided to build Room 2/3. They dug down to and a bit below the hard caliche subsoil, then leveled off the surface to construct a floor. The sequence of floors and fill is fairly simple to follow. The area around the pit and bench is worth noting. You can see that a thick plaster floor was constructed across the entire room. The deep storage pit was then dug into it, presumably used for awhile, then filled in and capped over so that the bench could be made. If you were just relying on absolute depth to judge relative age, you would jump to the conclusion that the material in the deep pit was the earliest in the Room 2/3 area. An examination of the stratigraphic layers, however, clearly shows that the clay lining of the pit superimposes the phase 2 floor and is, hence, later than it. Further perusal of the profile should be consistent with the sequence of Room 2/3 events described in chapter 3.

The interpretation of the metates on the roof also provides an example of the way stratigraphy yields information about a sequence of events. Figure 4.2 is a photograph showing a close-up of the stratigraphy underneath the metates. The metates do not rest directly on the floor; instead, they rest on layers of light ash and darker roofing material. This suggests that when the room was abandoned the metates were sitting on the roof, rather than on the room floor. When we excavated Room 2, we found that over much of the room a layer of cinders mixed with dust lay directly on the floor. This layer does not extend across the entire floor of the room but is concentrated in the vicinity of the ventilator shaft. Since the ground surface outside the room contains many cinders, the logical explanation is that after the room was abandoned, when it was not longer being maintained, cinders blew into the room through the ventilator shaft and perhaps through the roof opening as well. The cinder layer is so thin on the portion of the floor where the metates fell that it is not visible in the photograph, but it was apparent during excavation. Immediately above the cinders is a light-colored ash lens, debris from the room's hearth. This lens only exists on portions of the floor in the immediate vicinity of the hearth. The roof collapsed onto this layer of dust, ash, and cinder; and because the metates were resting on the roof, they came down as well. Stratigraphically, they are located within the layer of

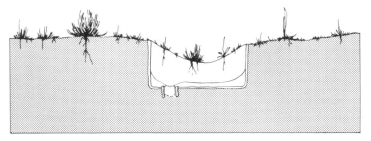

Room 18 is dug, occupied, and abandoned, then begins to fill with dirt and debris.

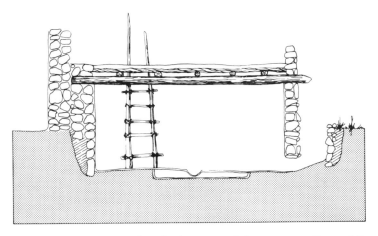

Room 2 is constructed in the location of the previous Room 18.

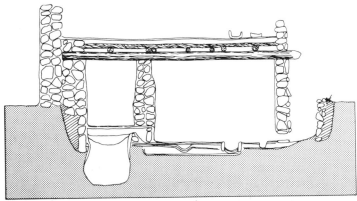

A stratigraphy builds in Room 2 as a result of sequential re-modeling. Eventually the room is abandoned.

Figure 4.1 *Simplified schematic showing how the stratigraphy in Room 2/3 was produced. Compare this diagram to the room profile shown in figure 2.10.*

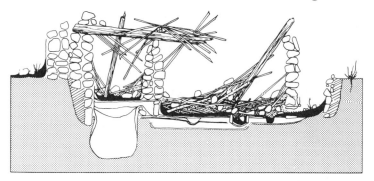

After abandonment cinders, dirt and trash accumulate on the floor. The metates on the roof fall through as the roof weakens with time. Eventually the whole roof caves in.

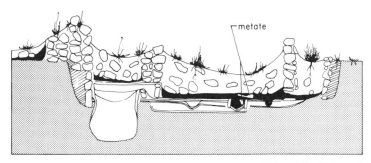

Gradually the walls crumble and the room fills with dirt and debris.

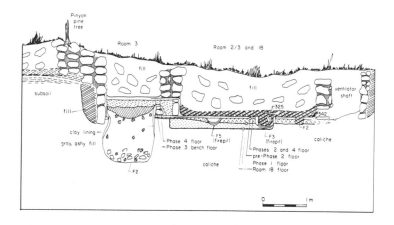

The archaeologist excavates the room and constructs a profile drawing showing the stratigraphy produced during the room's history.

Figure 4.2 *Close-up of stratigraphic position of metate fragments showing the stratigraphy. Immediately above the floor is a thin layer of cinders. Above that are layers of ash and roofing materials upon which the metates lie.*

roofing materials rather than on top of it. They probably fell through the roof as it began to weaken and decay but before the entire roof collapsed.

As each level of the room is exposed, it is possible to see, to a certain extent, what the room would have looked like in that phase of its occupation. The most recent phases are revealed first and the earliest last. For example, figure 4.3a shows the Room 2/3 floor with a bench, plastered floor, and central slab-lined hearth. The ventilator, which is also associated with this level, is in the wall at the front of the picture, so it is not visible. During actual occupation of the room, the walls would have been plastered. Traces of plaster still remain at the base of the walls but elsewhere have been washed off by exposure to the elements. Figure 4.3b shows earlier phases of the room's history. This is what the room looked like when excavation was complete. The early Room 18 is visible as a rectangular depression in the lower right of the photograph. The slab-lined hearth of Room 18 is still intact; however, portions of the two later fire features (the clay-lined firepit in almost the exact center of the room and the slab-lined fire pit of the final phases located on the center line of the room, immediately in front of it) have been partially removed in the excavation of Room 18. The large storage pit is in the back left. These two photographs can be compared to the floor plans shown in figure 3.2. By putting together information about floor plans such as these and stratigraphic profiles, it is possible to reconstruct a reasonably accurate picture of the history of a room or an entire site.

Figure 4.3   *Above, photograph of Room 2/3 showing the benched phase. Below, Barb Cardell stands in the Room 2/3 after the final excavations. Room 18 is visible in the frontright.*

Seriation

As we all know from our observations of fashion or cars in our own society, styles tend to change through time. The study of changes in artifact styles can produce a *seriation*, a sequence, usually gradual, of stylistic changes through time. Once a seriation is constructed, there is no *a priori* way to tell which styles are earliest. The starting point and direction of a series of changes can only be determined by looking at the stratigraphic distribution of the styles or other chronological evidence. Absolute date ranges for artifact types can only be obtained when secure dates are systematically associated with a particular artifact style.

When datable artifacts are deposited within a stratigraphic level, they can be used to date the level. Unless the stratigraphy is disturbed, an artifact type must be at least as old as the oldest levels in which it is found. Thus, a pottery vessel style found in a level that dates to about A.D. 600 must be at least that old. The reverse is not true, however, since old items can be reused, kept as heirlooms, or even found and kept. We can find seventeenth-century silver in use today. Perhaps even an antique teaspoon is occasionally lost. That does not mean that the level in which it is found (along with paper clips and 1996 pennies) dates to the 1800s. We know that this hypothetical level must date to the 1800s or later because of the spoon. The pennies, however, let us know that it is 1996 or later and give the clue that the silver was an antique at the time it was lost. Levels with similar artifact assemblages should be roughly contemporary. This allows us to posit, for instance, that a plaza surface in one part of the site was in use at roughly the same time as similar trash was being deposited in another area behind a house.

Ceramics: An Example of Seriation and Stratigraphy at Work

Archaeologists have already seriated both Sinagua architecture and the pottery types found on Sinagua sites and have correlated these styles with absolute dates, primarily those obtained from dendrochronology (discussed in a later section). Over the years archaeologists have devised a large number of Southwestern pottery types, identifiable by differences in attributes such as color, temper, techniques of manufacture, shape, and painted designs. *Types* tend to be made by a particular cultural group for a limited time and are thus useful for dating sites. Types are further clumped into wares. A *ware* is a group of pottery types which are technologically similar. Thus, painted wares can be contrasted with plain wares or wares can be categorized on the basis of color into white, red, and brown wares. Specific named wares such as Tusayan White Ware or Tsegi Orange Ware are expected to indicate particular cultural traditions in pottery making within a single area.

For instance, in the Sinagua region the local brown wares are called Alameda Brown Ware, and, if anyone refers to an Alameda Brown Ware type such as Angell Brown, it is immediately understood that it was manufactured in the Sinagua region. These undecorated ceramics are fired in an oxidizing atmosphere, yielding a red or reddish brown color, and are made using a paddle-and-anvil technique (see chapter 8 for more details of manufacture). Although rough date ranges are known for local Alameda Brown Wares, various trade wares are even more useful for dating Sinagua sites. Undecorated Sinagua pottery changed slowly over time, but the designs on painted trade wares changed more rapidly and, therefore, give more precise dates. Tusayan White Wares and Tsegi Orange Wares from the Kayenta region and Little Colorado White Wares from the Winslow region are particularly useful, since their date ranges are well understood and their designs are distinctive.

Figure 4.4 shows changes in ceramic decorations for the Kayenta area, a region that exchanged a considerable number of ceramic vessels with the Sinagua. The designs change through time from the large blocky shapes of the Black Mesa style to the finer geometics of Flagstaff and Tusayan. Gradually the relative proportions of black paint to white background slip change. At first the white areas are large. When stripes appear, the black stripes are separated by large areas of white. Later black areas predominate, and the white areas between are so fine that the design almost appears to be white against a black background. These ceramics generally have been assigned date ranges by examining instances when they occur directly on floors in rooms for which absolute dates are available.

Sites are normally dated by examining the entire assemblage of pottery types found, the proportions of each type, and their known date ranges. Table 4.1 shows some of the ceramic types found in the Sinagua area, with associated date ranges. A short perusal of the table shows that dating with ceramics is not very precise, since many of the pottery types have fairly large time spans.

Furthermore, if one thinks back to the site formation processes discussed in chapter 3, it becomes clear that the manufacturing date of a few sherds found in a specific context is unlikely to securely date that context. The caveats are many. Some ceramic vessels may have very long use-lives, being kept as heirlooms for generations. Even after a vessel has been broken, sherds may remain in use for a long time, recycled as jar lids or scrapers, inserted into the spaces between wall stones as chinking, and so forth. Trash is likely to have mostly contemporary sherds, plus a few older ones mixed in from the scatter of trash that covered the whole surface of the site. Patterns in the data are the key. Numerous sherds with overlapping date ranges provide an indication of the time period for a deposit. Archaeologists have divided the chronology of the Sinagua into a sequence of dated time periods (table 4.2). Table 4.3 shows the ceramic types indicative of each of the major Sinagua time periods.

Figure 4.4 *Changes in ceramic style decoration in the Kayenta area: Above left, the earliest designs, Black Mesa, followed by Sosi and Flagstaff. Tusayan, lower right, is the most recent style in the sequence.*

Table 4.1 **Date Ranges of Major Ceramic Types Found at Lizard Man Village**

Ceramic Type	Date Ranges (A.D.)
Rio de Flag Brown	775–1065, perhaps to 1175
Angell Brown	1075–1150 or 1200, most abundant 1075–1125
Sunset Red/Brown	1065–1200, perhaps to 1300
Youngs Brown	1075–1150 or 1250, most abundant 1090–1130
Coconino Red-on-buff	1080–1100
Black Mesa Black-on-white	875–1150, most abundant 1000–1130
Sosi Black-on-white	1075–1200
Dogoszhi Black-on-white	1075–1200
Flagstaff Black-on-white	1085–1270, most abundant 1100–1200
Kayenta Black-on-white	1260–1300, most abundant 1260–1285
Tusayan Black-on-white	1125–1300, most abundant 1250–1300
Holbrook Black-on-white	1075–1300
Padre Black-on-white	1085–1200, based on similarity to Dogoszhi
Walnut Black-on-white	Between 1065 and 1100–1250 or 1150–1225
Tusayan Corrugated	Best between 1000–1280
Moenkopi Corrugated	1125–1285 or 1300
Deadmans Grey	775–1200, most abundant 850–1150
Medicine Black-on-red	1075–1125, not well dated
Tusayan Black-on-red	1065–1200, most abundant 1050–1150

Date ranges based on Breternitz, 1966 and Downum, personal communication.

Table 4.2 **Dating Scheme for the Northern Sinagua**

Pre-Eruptive
Cinder Park Phase, A.D. 600–700
Sunset Phase, A.D. 700–900
Rio de Flag Phase, A.D. 900–about 1064

Post-Eruptive
Angell-Winona Phase, A.D. 1064–1100
Padre Phase, A.D. 1100–1150
Elden Phase, A.D. 1150–1250
Turkey Hill Phase, A.D. 1250–1300
Clear Creek Phase, A.D. 1300–1400

Table 4.3 **Ceramic Dating Criteria for Rio de Flag through Turkey Hill Phases**

	Ceramic Types	
Phase	**Dominant**	**Present**
Rio de Flag	Black Mesa Black-on-white Coconino Gray Medicine Gray Tusayan Corrugated Rio de Flag Brown Deadmans Black-on-red Deadmans Gray	Angell Brown Winona Brown (rare–late) Medicine Black-on-red (late)
Angell-Winona	Black Mesa Black-on-white Holbrook A Black-on-white Angell Brown Rio de Flag Brown Winona Brown Sunset Brown Tusayan Corrugated	Coconino Red-on-buff Winona Red-on-buff Winona Corrugated Youngs Brown Medicine Black-on-red Citadel Polychrome
Padre	Sosi Black-on-white Holbrook B Black-on-white Winona Brown Sunset Brown Tusayan Corrugated	Flagstaff Black-on-white Walnut Black-on-white Coconino Red-on-buff Winona Red-on-buff Winona Corrugated Moenkopi Corrugated Youngs Brown Turkey Hill Red Medicine Black-on-red Citadel Polychrome
Elden	Flagstaff Black-on-white Walnut Black-on-white Sosi Black-on-white Dogoszhi Black-on-white Tusayan Corrugated Moenkopi Corrugated Winona Brown, Sunset Brown Sunset Red Tusayan Black-on-red	Wupatki (Tusayan) Black-on-white Angell Brown Youngs Brown Turkey Hill Red Citadel Polychrome Tusayan Polychrome
Turkey Hill	Wupatki (Tusayan) Black-on-white Flagstaff Black-on-white Walnut Black-on-white Leupp Black-on-white Tusayan Corrugated Moenkopi Corrugated Sunset Red	Polacca Black-on-white Kiet Siel Gray Winona Brown Turkey Hill Red Tusayan Black-on-red Citadel Polychrome Tusayan Polychrome

Kiet Siel Polychrome
Kayenta Polychrome
Kintiel Black-on-orange
Kintiel Polychrome

From Wilson 1969, modified by Peter Pilles for use in the Coconino National Forest.

The classification of whole pots and broken pottery sherds is the initial step in dating a site by ceramic criteria. The Coconino National Forest archaeologists who initially discovered Lizard Man Village dated it to the Angell-Winona to Padre Phases on the basis of the types of the pottery sherds seen on the surface. During our excavations we collected over a quarter of a million pottery sherds. Fear of incipient insanity prohibited the classification of the entire collection, so we analyzed only a little over 100,000 sherds, all the sherds from on or near room floors plus a large stratigraphic column from each room.

Sunset and Angell Brown, both locally-made Sinagua types dominate the collection and comprise, respectively, 42 percent and 41 percent of the sherds. Youngs Brown, another Sinagua type, accounts for an additional 3 percent. Rio de Flag Brown, the major pre-eruptive local type, is fairly scarce (about .5 percent), suggesting that no one lived at Lizard Man Village before the eruption of Sunset Crater. No trade wares were extremely common but significant numbers of Deadmans Gray, Tusayan Corrugated, Moenkopi Corrugated, Black Mesa Black-on-white, Sosi Black-on-white, Flagstaff Black-on-white, and Holbrook A Black-on-white were identified. A perusal of table 4.3 shows that these are primarily ceramic types listed as characteristic of the Angell-Winona through Elden Phases. The beginning of the occupation span is suggested by the virtual absence of Rio de Flag Brown, which precludes much pre-eruptive occupation. The ending date for the occupation is suggested by the paucity of ceramic types typical of the Turkey Hill Phase. In particular the very late black-on-white types like Kayenta and Tusayan Black-on-white are extremely rare. Thus, the ceramic types at Lizard Man Village suggest an occupation roughly from the Angell-Winona through Elden Phases, about A.D. 1065 through 1250.

In addition to dating the site as a whole, sherds can be used to help date specific contexts. The one caveat here is that there must be a sufficient number of sherds in the depositional context to provide a reliable pattern. The section below describes dating on the basis of changes in architectural styles, and how a seriation of architectural styles, stratigraphic sequences, and ceramic dates can be combined to provide more secure dating of the architecture.

The Architecture at Lizard Man Village

The architecture at Lizard Man Village includes both rectangular masonry blocks of contiguous rooms, similar to those found in modern pueblos, and isolated wholly or partially subterranean pithouses. A variety of types of evidence from Lizard Man Village and elsewhere shows that the pithouses predate the pueblo room blocks. Based on construction materials, shape, and depth, there are four types of pithouses at Lizard Man Village. The following list is a seriation of the architecture from the earliest styles to the latest.

1. Four pithouses (Rooms 11, 12/20, 16, and 18; see figure 2.3 for location on site plan and figure 4.5 for excavation photo) had plastered walls. None of the walls would have been full height, and presumably the rooms would have been covered by a pole-and-brush superstructure. Most of these rooms were disturbed by later pueblo room construction, a phenomenon easily explained, if they had long been abandoned and were mainly filled in with dirt and debris by the time the pueblo room blocks were constructed.

Figure 4.5 *Sara Croft and Jon Till excavate the floor of Room 11, an example of the earliest pithouse type, the plastered-wall pithouse.*

2. Masonry-lined pithouses with an alcove entry to the east (figures 4.6 and 4.7) are characteristic of the Angell Phase (A.D. 1064–1100). Both of the Lizard Man Village Angell pithouses (Rooms 15 and 21) were big. Pairs of large postholes along a central axis and several other postholes along the periphery of the room supported an earth and timber superstructure (figure 2.5). The relatively early date of this style is verified by the presence of numerous intrusive burials in Room 15. Several of the burials are positioned along room walls showing that, while the pithouse had already been abandoned, the room outlines were still visible at the time of the interments.

Figure 4.6 *Photograph of Room 15, an example of the classic Angell pithouse.*

3. The third type of pithouse (Rooms 5, 10, and 14; figure 4.8), like the Angell pithouse, is slab-lined. It is shallower, however, and lacks an alcove entry. Room 10, the only completely excavated example of this pithouse type at Lizard Man Village, has several large postholes, which would have supported a pole-and-brush dwelling. Like the Angell pithouses, two of the shallow slab-lined pithouses (Rooms 5 and 10) have intrusive burials that date to the Elden Phase, based on the ceramic types included in the offerings. This suggests that the pithouses had been abandoned long enough before the burials for soil to build up and provide an area in which to dig.
4. Isolated, deep, rectangular, masonry-lined pithouses were dated to the Padre Phase (A.D. 1100–1150) by McGregor. Three of these at Lizard Man Village (Rooms 13/17, 22, and 23; figure 4.9) appear intermediate in style between the shallow pithouses and the subterranean rooms that are a part of pueblo room blocks and are discussed with the pueblo architecture below. Pairs of large central postholes supported a roof. Two of the rooms (Rooms 13/17 and 22) appear to have been subdivided by a central wall.

Room 15

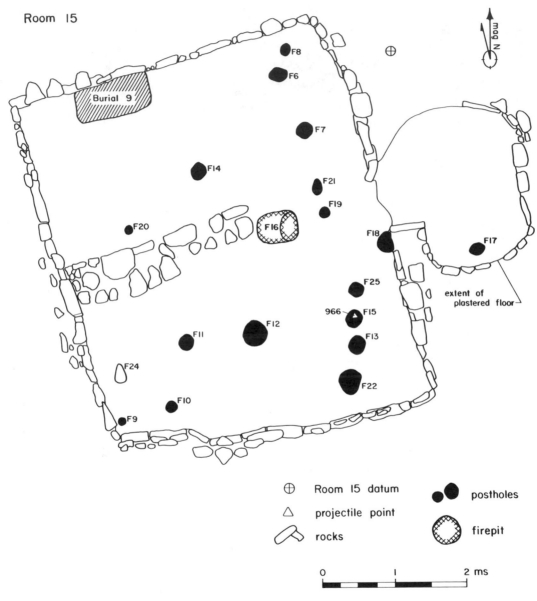

Figure 4.7 *Floor plan of Room 15.*

As pithouses dwindled in popularity, here and throughout the Southwest in general, they were superseded by groups of contiguous masonry rooms. While there is considerable debate among archaeologists about the reasons for the switch in habitation form, it is generally agreed that pithouses are more effective for retaining a stable temperature because of the extra insulation from the surrounding earth. Thick insulating walls on above-ground structures can minimize this advantage, however. Furthermore, the above-

Figure 4.8 *Lisa Piedescalzi and Jackie Jendras in Room 10, a shallow, slab-lined pithouse.*

ground portion of pithouses may have been less well built and thermally-effective than pueblo walls.

Pueblo rooms, on the other hand, are seen as more responsive to demographic changes, because construction costs for new rooms can easily be decreased by adding rooms that share walls with the existing dwelling. Pueblo rooms are also easier to subdivide, providing more opportunities for separating people and activities. It should be noted, however, that rectangular pithouses are just as easy to partition as pueblo rooms. The shape, rather than the overall architectural style, is really the critical variable. In the Sinagua area Padre Phase pithouses (A.D. 1100–1150) are, in fact, rectangular, so this argument seems to have less relevance.

The relative construction costs of pithouses and pueblos are in dispute. The consensus seems to be that pithouses require more effort, but some archaeologists have also argued that the need for larger pieces of wood to make pueblo roofs implies that the investment is larger for pueblo rooms. The exact relative costs of the two construction techniques probably depends on locally available resources. Basically, however, both types of rooms require high energy expenditures; neither fits well with the model of a quickly built or readily mobile residence. Another issue for consideration may be relative maintenance costs. Pueblo rooms tend to have a longer uselife because they are less susceptible to infestation by insects.

Figure 4.9 *Dana Robson and Amy Naughton in Room 23, a deep, rectangular masonry pithouse.*

A worldwide sample of eighty-four ethnographic cases examined by Gilman (1987) shows that most recent pithouse dwellers live in fairly small pithouse villages during the cold season, when they primarily utilize stored food. The rest of the year their existence is more mobile, and they occupy less permanent structures. Pueblo dwellers tend to reside in somewhat larger units and have a bit less mobility. Gilman argues that with increasing dependence on agriculture, particularly in a rather uncertain environment, prehistoric Southwesterners found it necessary to store foods for long periods and to increase food-processing time. According to her, both of these activities require increased spatial differentiation, which is easier to do in rectangular structures. Although, as noted above, this part of her argument does not seem particularly relevant to the Sinagua area with its rectangular pithouses, she further argues that food stored in underground pits is more susceptible to vermin and to dampness due to water seepage than that stored above ground. Thus, when there is a need to store food for periods in excess of a year, as there may have been once prehistoric Southwesterners started to rely heavily on agricultural products, above-ground storage facilities are desirable. It is probably no coincidence that the earliest above-ground rooms in the Southwest are storage rooms rather than habitation rooms.

Lizard Man Village boasts two room blocks (figures 2.3 and 4.10). One has a semi-subterranean room (Room 6) and two above-ground rooms (Rooms 7 and 8). The other (already described in chapter 3) has two semi-subterranean rooms (Rooms 2/3 and 19) and two above-ground rooms

Figure 4.10 *Neil Weintraub, Hilary Thompson, and Sandra Raimondo sit in Room 6, a semi-subterranean living room of Room Block 1. Room 7, an above-ground storage room, can be seen behind it.*

(Rooms 4 and 9). As discussed previously, the room blocks appear to include both living and storage rooms and can be interpreted as the residence for one or two households. Only Room Block 2 appears to have any specialized ceremonial spaces, which may suggest that the residents of the two room blocks shared a single kiva.

Since the trade wares characteristic of the Angell-Winona Phase are different from those found in the Elden Phase, it should be possible to seriate the rooms at the site based on the ceramics found on or near room floors. Unfortunately, in this case, the number of trade wares is too small to allow reliable statistical comparisons. There are, however, plenty of the locally made types. Sunset Red/Brown and Angell Brown are roughly contemporary, although Sunset may have become popular later and lasted a bit longer than Angell. Table 4.3 shows both Angell and Sunset as dominant types during the Angell-Winona Phase (A.D. 1064–1100). In the later Padre (A.D. 1100–1150) and Elden (A.D. 1150–1250) Phases Angell is still present, but Sunset becomes more dominant. Rooms occupied earlier should have a higher ratio of Angell to Sunset sherds than those occupied later. In other words, rooms that have a higher proportion of the later Sunset sherds and thus a lower ratio of Angell to Sunset should date later than those rooms with relatively more Angell sherds, and, thus a high Angell to Sunset ratio. Thus, a ratio of 1:0.7 (Angell:Sunset) should suggest an earlier room than a ratio of 1:1.5). Sherd ratios from lower stratigraphic levels should date a room more accurately than those from upper levels, since upper levels are more likely to contain trash from well after the abandonment of the room. As it turns out, the ratio of Angell to Sunset sherds nicely separates pueblo rooms from the earlier pit-houses. Pueblo rooms from both room blocks tend to have more Sunset sherds than Angell sherds (table 4.4). The exceptions to this (Room 6, upper fill and Room 4, lower fill) are close to a 1:1 ratio. The lower levels of pit-houses, on the other hand, tend to have more Angell sherds than Sunset sherds. This is not always true of the upper levels of the pithouses, however, as might be expected if mixing with later levels were occurring. One would predict that more contamination with later sherd types would occur near the late room-block areas than more distant from them. An examination of table 4.4 shows that this expectation is also upheld. Ideally, it would be possible to use the ratio technique to corroborate the seriation of the pithouse types. Unfortunately, there are no patterned differences in ratios between pithouse types. This could suggest contemporaneousness of the structures or simply that the technique is only sensitive enough to detect rather large time differences.

Absolute Dating Techniques

Techniques which allow the archaeologist to assign a specific calendric date or range of dates to an event are called *absolute dating* methods. New research is constantly increasing the number of absolute dating techniques available to the archaeologists. I will discuss only a few of the more common and reliable techniques here. Each technique can be used to date specific types of materials and has a date range for which its use is most appropriate. Dates, however, must be interpreted with care. It is the archaeological context and an understanding of the formation processes discussed in chapter 3 that give the date cultural meaning.

Carbon-14 Dating

Carbon-14, which can be used to date organic remains, only tells us when an organism died. It does not directly reveal when the cultural event of interest took place. A very old piece of antler can be collected and used to form a tool. Carbon-14 dating will tell us when the animal lost the antler, not when the tool was manufactured.

Carbon-14 dating, developed by Willard Libby in the 1940s, is one of several *radiometric dating* techniques. Carbon exists as three different *isotopes*, ^{12}C, ^{13}C, and ^{14}C. The ratio of the isotopes is stable in the atmosphere over short time periods. Since all living things incorporate carbon via their

Table 4.4 **Angell:Sunset Ratios by Level, Room and Area of Site**

Room Block 1 Rooms	Upper Fill Levels	Lower Fill Levels
Room 6	1:0.96	1:1.27
Room 7	1:1.38	---
Room 8	1:1.57	1:1.36
Room Block 2 Rooms		
Room 2	1:1.49	1:2.65
Room 3	1:1.39	1:1.10
Room 4	1:1.79	1:0.82
Room 9	1:1.22	1:1.56
Room 12	1:1.25	1:1.65
Centrally-Located Pithouses		
Room 13/17	1:1.22	1:0.86
Room 11	1:1.04	1:0.53
Room 12/20	---	1:0.56
Room 22	1:0.84	1:0.35
Room 23	1:2.6	1:0.3
Room 16	1:1.07	1:0.74
Peripherally-Located Pithouses		
Room 5	1:0.32	1:0.23
Room 15	1:1.41	1:1.0
Room 21	1:0.33	1:0.26
Room 10	1:0.87	1:0.91
Room 14	1:0.53	1:0.39

metabolic processes, the percentages of the isotopes in organic matter reflect atmospheric ratios. When an organism dies, its carbon intake ceases. Although the other two carbon isotopes are stable, the ^{14}C disintegrates into ^{14}N at a set proportional rate called a half-life. The half-life for ^{14}C is now generally accepted at 5,730 years, which means that in 5,730 years one-half of the ^{14}C in the original organic material will have reverted to ^{14}N; after 11,460 years or two half-lives only one-fourth of the ^{14}C will remain. The length of this half-life allows the calculation of dates between 100 and 70,000 years ago. Carbon-14 dates are usually given as dates before the present (B.P.), which is arbitrarily defined as 1950. Because the proportion of ^{14}C in the atmosphere has varied over time due to fluctuations in solar radiation, changing B.P. dates into calendar years is not straightforward. The calibration table that has been devised, primarily by calculating the ^{14}C dates of precisely dated wood samples, shows a wiggly, slightly curved relationship between ^{14}C counts and calendric date.

Because of inherent inaccuracy due to such factors as counting errors, ^{14}C dates are always given with a standard deviation. There is approximately a 67 percent probability that the real date will lie somewhere within a range of the quoted date plus or minus one standard deviation, and a 95 percent probability that it will lie within two standard deviations. Thus, a date of 800 B.P. with a standard deviation of 50 would mean that there is a 67 percent probability that the true date falls between 850 B.P. and 750 B.P. and a 95 percent probability that it lies between 900 B.P. and 700 B.P. The size of the standard deviation varies but is rarely less than 50 or 100 years. Thus, for areas where more precise dating methods are available it may normally not be worth the expense to process ^{14}C samples. At Lizard Man Village, for example, while we had many samples of organic material, primarily pieces of charcoal, which could be dated using the ^{14}C dating technique, we have not had any of them processed. The ^{14}C dates would be expected to have ranges of error no better than the date estimates from pottery analysis. Therefore, we decided to spend our always limited financial resources on techniques that would be capable of providing more precise date ranges. The three absolute methods we used are tree-ring dating, archaeomagnetism, and chronological correlations with dated artifact types from other sites. We did, of course, collect samples for ^{14}C dating in case, at some time in the future, we wanted to conduct further analyses. These samples must be collected and stored with care so as not to contaminate them with the modern carbons found in organic matter such as paper.

Dendrochronology

The most precise dating technique available, tree-ring dating, or *dendrochronology*, is capable of assigning an exact year date to the time of death of a piece of wood. The method (figure 4.11) is based on the fact that trees grow two rings per year, a large, thin-walled ring in the spring and a denser, darker ring in the fall. In many tree species, the width of the rings varies from year to year, reflecting differences in temperature and precipitation. Thus, a span of several years will produce a distinctive tree-ring pattern. As every child knows, it is possible to count the rings in a tree stump to estimate the age of the tree. A. E. Douglass, who developed the method of tree-ring dating while doing research on the relationship between sunspot cycles and climatic variability, utilized this information combined with the knowledge of yearly variation in ring width to establish tree-ring patterns for the four-corners area of the Southwest. He started with living trees and worked his way back into prehistory by matching ring patterns in these trees with patterns in roof beams from historic buildings and abandoned pueblos. Once a master chronology has been established for an area, it is possible to collect wood samples with at least twenty rings and date them by matching the ring patterns with the master sequence. Since climatic variability is a fairly local phenomenon, regional sequences must be developed for each area. The Southwest is one of the best-studied areas for dendrochronology. The technique was invented

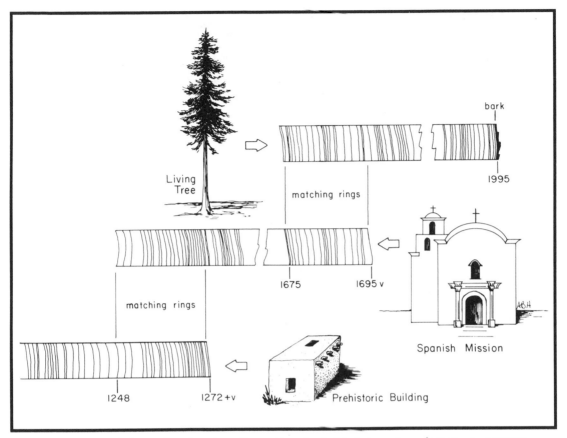

Figure 4.11 *Schematic showing the rationale behind tree-ring dating. A master chronology is built by starting with living trees and matching ring patterns of successive specimens, working backwards. Unknown samples can then be dated by matching a sequence of ring patterns to the master chronology. The v after a date indicates that the bark and some outside rings are missing.*

there, wood preservation is generally good, and there are several tree species—most notably Douglass fir, yellow pine, and pinyon—which are sensitive enough to climatic variability to provide excellent temporal indicators.

In standing architecture such as some of the Southwestern cliff dwellings, tree-ring samples are collected by drilling small cores from existing timbers. In sites such as Lizard Man Village only carbonized wood is generally preserved. Most charcoal samples are very fragile, so they are stabilized by imbuing them with a mixture of paraffin and kerosene, then tied with string and hung or set out to dry (figure 4.12). When the kerosene has evaporated, the samples are wrapped in cotton and sent to a specialized lab such as the Laboratory of Tree-ring Research at the University of Arizona for analysis.

Dendrochronology, like many of the archaeological dating techniques, does not directly date an archaeological event. It provides information about when the tree from which the sample was obtained died. When the outer ring

Figure 4.12 *John Whittaker and Melinda Lopes collecting carbonized wood from Lizard Man Village.*

of the tree (which can be identified by the presence of beetle galleries or traces of bark) is present, an exact date of death, usually referred to as the cutting date, can be calculated. Often samples do not include the exterior ring. This is indicated by a "v" for a few missing rings or "vv" for many missing rings. When rings are missing, the last datable ring provides an estimate that is from a few to many years too early. Even when the outer ring is present, tree-ring dates are not always easy to interpret. The context of the sample tells the investigator whether the date should reflect the construction of a roof or other architectural feature, the last burning of a hearth, or the deposition of some hearth materials into garbage deposits. Cultural factors affect interpretations too. Wood can be reused or cut and stockpiled for later use; dead wood can be collected and used, especially in hearths; some wood can be from repairs rather than from initial construction. To an extent, these problems of interpretation can be minimized by using multiple samples and looking for patterns in the tree-ring dates.

Some sites yield numerous dendrochronological samples. From the viewpoint of the archaeologist, burned rooms with carbonized roof beams are ideal. The pattern of dates from the beams can be used to date the construction of individual rooms. If several rooms can be precisely dated, the sequence of construction may reveal interesting social phenomena. For example, Dean (1970) was able to compare the development of two Tsegi Phase cliff dwellings, Kiet Siel and Betatakin, located in northern Arizona in what is now Navajo National Monument (and both open to the public). Kiet Siel started as isolated clusters of five to six rooms, each around a courtyard and presumably representing some type of family unit. Later these were joined by similar units, probably immigrants. In a final phase, growth was by the addition of single rooms and is interpreted as due to natural reproductive increases. Betatakin, in contrast, started in A.D. 1267 as a few families occupied clusters of rooms. The original occupants were joined by a large influx of immigrants using stockpiled wood. This is shown by the pattern of dates from roof beams. Most of the roof beams date from A.D. 1269 and 1272, but there are a few beams cut between A.D. 1275 and 1278 mixed in among them. Dean argues that Betatakin was settled in a planned move by a community from elsewhere that prepared for the move by cutting wood for several years before the actual new construction.

Alas, Lizard Man Village has no nicely burned roofs. Nevertheless, we optimistically collected any carbonized wood that might come anywhere close to having enough rings to allow dating. We sent a total of 129 specimens to the Laboratory of Tree-Ring Research at the University of Arizona for analysis. Only eight of the samples provided dates, and of these only one (from a storage pit found in a test trench) is a cutting date (table 4.5). Some samples are so small that it was not possible to establish a ring pattern; others are juniper, which does not date well in the Flagstaff area. The few dates we obtained were interesting. Most of the dates fall within the accepted date ranges for the Angell-Winona to Elden Phases (A.D. 1064–1250), although one (from the fill of the pit-house, Room 11) is a bit later than expected. A.D. 1250 is usually considered the

Table 4.5 **Tree-Ring Dates from Lizard Man Village**

Excavation Unit	Context	Dates (A.D.)
Room 2	pit associated with early floor	1049–1118 v
Room 2	storage pit under later bench	1102p–1197 vv
Room 4	midden fill under room?	1015–1094 +vv
Room 4	midden fill under room?	967–1062 ++vv
Room 8	fill	1195fp–1247 +v
Room 11	fill	1205–1261 vv
TT16	large exterior storage pit	1141–1219 r
TT22	storage (?) pit	1091 fp–1200 vv

Key:
vv = Cannot tell how far last ring is from true outside.
v = No true outside, but subjective judgment that last ring is close to cutting date.
+ = One or more rings may be missing near the end of ring series.
++ = A ring count is necessary beyond a certain point because cross-dating ceases.
r = Outer ring is continuous around surviving circumference, cutting date.
p = Pith ring present.
fp = Curvature of inside ring indicates that it is far from pith.

end of the Elden Phase, yet this date indicates use sometime after A.D. 1269. This may suggest some post-Elden Phase occupation, a notion that is supported by the presence of a few late pottery sherds. Current descriptions of the Flagstaff area propose that small villages such as Lizard Man Village are generally abandoned by the end of the Elden Phase. At any rate, the phases used by archaeologists are artificial constructs, designed to help us better understand the past. The archaeological equivalents of the Baby Boomers or the X-Generation, they have fuzzy beginnings and endpoints which probably reflect gradual rather than abrupt changes of lifestyle.

The sad fact of the tree-ring data from Lizard Man Village is that, while it confirmed the time range known from architectural types and sherds, it provided little new information. The tree-ring dates do make sense, however. The earliest dates are from midden deposited prior to the construction of Room Block 2. Both are missing many rings, so we don't know exactly how late they are. The next date comes from an early pit in Room 2 and the third from fill in the storage pit under the bench. Again, we do not have exact dates for these, but the general sequence does make sense, as does their general time frame.

Archaeomagnetic Dating

Archaeomagnetic dates, which can be obtained from well-burnt hearths or any other stable, well-baked clay feature, provided another hope for dating constructions at Lizard Man Village. *Archaeomagnetic dating* is based on the fact that the direction and intensity of the earth's magnetic field have varied over time. Clay contains small iron particles, such as magnetite and hematite, which are attracted to magnetic north and align with it. When the clay is baked, the particles' orientations are fixed until the clay is reheated. Thus, the magnetite and hematite act as a compass record of the moment when the clay feature was last burned. To obtain a date estimate, the direction and intensity of orientation of the particles are measured with a magnetometer and compared with a master chart of the known magnetic pole positions through time (figure 4.13). These master curves (which are regionally specific) are available for the Southwest, where they have been constructed using hearths that are also associated with good ^{14}C or tree-ring dates. However, the curves are still being refined. Two curves, each based on a slightly different set of empirical observations, compete for acceptance in the Sinagua area and are constantly being revised. We worked with Jeff Eighmy of the Archaeometric Laboratory of the Department of Anthropology at the University of Colorado, so it was his curve that was used to interpret the Lizard Man Village samples.

The collection of archaeomagnetic samples is a long, tedious process, often made even less pleasant in the Southwest by the hot climate of the area. John, who takes our samples, always groans a bit when we find a nicely preserved, well-baked hearth because he knows it means he will have to spend much of a day in the heat, sitting still, getting cramped and well-baked him-

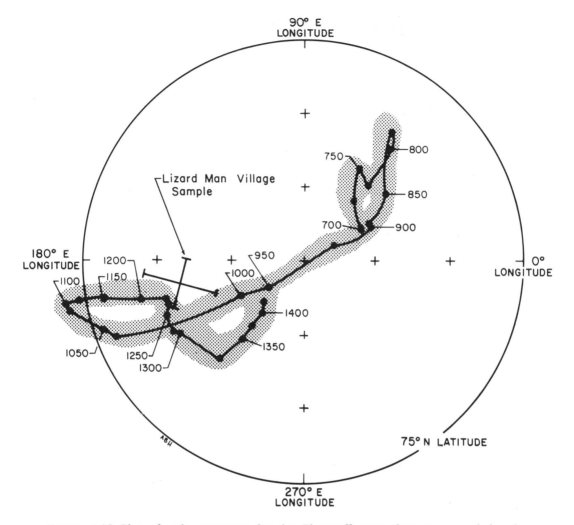

Figure 4.13 *Plot of pole positions for the Flagstaff area that was used for the archaeomagnetic dating, showing one of the samples from the fire feature in Room 16 plotted as the large X. The estimated date for this sample is A.D. 1005 to 1020 or A.D. 1175 to 1250. Two possible dates are proposed because the sample plots are in an area where the curve intersects itself.*

self. The clay samples needed for archaeomagnetic dating must preserve the original orientation of the clay. A small cube of hearth clay is isolated without moving it, and a metal mold is placed around it (figure 4.14). The mold is then filled with plaster of paris, fixing the position of the clay sample. The orientation of the cube to the present true north is meticulously recorded so that the analyzing lab can determine the exact orientation of the magnetite and hematite particles in the sample.

Figure 4.14 *John Whittaker collects an archaeomagnetic sample.*

The first season at Lizard Man Village no one had the necessary expertise for collecting archaeomagnetic samples, so although we found several hearths, including one with particularly nice burnt clay, all were covered in the backfill without being sampled. The second season a friend of ours, Richard Ciolek-Torrello, taught John how to take samples and we re-excavated that hearth. We thereafter took archaeomagnetic samples like mad, hoping that, in part, this technique would help us compensate for the paucity of good tree-ring dates.

In the end we were frustrated in this attempt as well. Part of the problem was that the magnetic properties of the volcanic rocks on the site caused too much interference. We had noticed this problem earlier when trying to use compasses to do mapping. As an excavator took a compass from standing height to a position near the ground in the vicinity of masonry structures, the position of the compass needle would change discernibly. While this was convenient for mapping, for archaeomagnetic samples it was disastrous. Jeff Eighmy examined eight samples for us (table 4.6). None of the samples from slab-lined hearths could be dated at all. Even the dates from clay-lined fire-pits appeared to have problems. Several samples simply fell into a portion of the curve where there is overlap, and two different dates are possible interpretations. Other dates simply did not make much sense, given our knowledge of the archaeology.

Putting It All Together

Ideally multiple tree-ring dates from each of the rooms at Lizard Man Village would have allowed us to figure out the sequence of room construction. Archaeomagnetic dates from a series of hearths each associated with floor surfaces would have revealed the date the hearth was last used. The date of the last fire might then have been used as a rough index of abandonment of

Table 4.6 **Archaeomagnetic Dates from Lizard Man Village**

Excavation Unit	Context	Dates (A.D.)	Comments
Room 5	Feature 2, firepit	1005–1020 or 1190–1250	Later date range preferable as site lacks pre-eruptive pottery, but is probably too late
Room 6	Feature 3, slab-lined hearth	undatable	no date
Room 9	Feature 2, slab-lined hearth	undatable	no date
Room 16	Feature 1, fired basin	1005–1020 or 1190–1250	later date preferable as site lacks pre-eruptive pottery; basin is post-room abandonment
Room 17	Feature 10, firepit	940–1000	Date suspect because site lacks pre-eruptive pottery
Room 19	Feature 2, firepit	1015–1065 or 1150–1315	Latter dates preferable as site lacks pre-eruptive pottery
Room 21	Feature 2, firepit	1010–1125 or 1125–1300	Correct date probably somewhere in the middle
Room 22	Feature 5, firepit	off curve	no date

the living rooms, or at least a change in use to a room function no longer requiring a hearth. Rooms lacking hearths could theoretically be dated by artifact floor assemblages. All together this information would allow us to establish a definitive sequence of use for architectural structures, tell us whether any of the pithouse types were contemporary, let us know whether the room blocks were constructed at the same time or sequentially, and provide better information for estimating population size.

Ideal worlds rarely exist. Lizard Man Village was no exception. Despite our efforts, instead of having numerous unambiguous absolute dates, we have a few slightly ambiguous ones. These do provide valuable information, however. First, we know the basic time span during which Lizard Man Village was occupied (about A.D. 1070–1275). This allows us to talk about the village as part of a general pattern at a particular time, in the context of other sites that would have been its contemporaries. Even without absolute dates it is possible to place sites in a chronological framework. The site that we excavated immediately after Lizard Man Village is a smaller nearby site called Fortress

Hills Pueblo. Based simply on the pottery types that are found there, the room block at Fortress Hills Pueblo appears to have been occupied a bit later than those at Lizard Man Village. Sunset Red/Brown sherds dominate Angell Brown even more at Fortress Hills Pueblo than in the Lizard Man Village room blocks, and late trade wares such as Tusayan Black-on-white and Kayenta Black-on-white are much more common.

While it was not possible to provide an exact sequence of room construction and occupation dates at Lizard Man Village, it was possible to tell that the pithouses were occupied prior to the pueblo room blocks by comparing the ratios of local ceramic types. It is also possible to show some sequences of events by using the law of superposition and examining stratigraphic relationships across the site. For example, since the pits dug to construct Rooms 6 and 19 cut through the fill of Rooms 11 and 20, we know that plastered wall pithouses had been abandoned long enough before the room blocks were constructed that the pits had already substantially filled in. The burials found in rooms such as 5 and 15 were dug long enough after the rooms had been abandoned to have allowed the fill through which the pits were dug to accumulate but recently enough so that the wall outlines were still fairly clear. Bodies were often placed right along walls, and the burial pits are oriented parallel to them.

Thus, we know that Lizard Man Village was occupied for about two hundred years. At no time, however, was the village very large. We can chart the approximate size of the village by noting the number of dwellings of each type. While we can not prove that houses of the same style were occupied at exactly the same time, this is a reasonable hypothesis, especially since they tend to cluster in particular areas of the site. The earliest pithouses, those with plastered walls, were in the western portion of the village. The next, Angell pithouses with alcove entries, were in the eastern portion, followed by shallow slab-lined pithouses in the central and eastern parts of the village, and by deep-masonry, Padre-style pithouses in the western sector. Finally, the two room blocks were constructed. Each pithouse type is represented by two to four dwellings, never a very large number. Likewise the room blocks are small, one with three rooms and the other with a maximum of five.

No matter which one of the previously-discussed techniques for estimating population we use, the population of Lizard Man Village remains extremely low. If we assume some two to four family units, the estimate is never more than twenty or twenty-five residents. Using floor area as an estimator results in an even smaller population, but this estimate is very tentative because several of the early pithouses are partly obliterated by later construction, meaning that we can only approximate their total floor areas.

Chapter 5

PERSONALIZING THE PAST

Hopi Edmund Nequatewa (1993) tells about the time when as a boy he got angry at his young aunt because she accidentally released a dove he had shot and wounded but not killed. Furious, he threatened to shoot her. Then, as she was running away, he actually did. She went home to his parents and grandfather with the arrow still embedded in her hair to prove the misdeed. Edmund was lucky because, consistent with Hopi reluctance to punish children too severely, he had only to suffer a serious talk about shooting and safety. In his autobiography, another Hopi, Don Talayesva (1942), depicts himself as quite a hellion as a child and later as a bit of a womanizer. Like most lives, his had periods of happiness and others of despair. Despite his successes in ceremonial matters and his status as Sun Chief, Don Talayesva suffered sadness and some loss of prestige because none of his children lived past infancy. There is no reason for us to think that the Sinagua had life stories that were any less individual or dramatic. Each of the Sinagua of Lizard Man Village would have had his or her own personality and history. Some Sinagua had a sense of humor, some were flirtatious, some prudent, some cross and some mild. Some lived long and some died young. Some were lucky and others seemed to find misfortune wherever they went. Unfortunately, neither Puebloan history and legend nor archaeological interpretation incorporate individual personalities and the vitality they lend to actual, living societies.

Most archaeological reports are about constructs rather than people. The discussion centers around settlement patterns, typical architecture, subsistence strategies, and trade networks rather than people. This focus does not imply that archaeologists are not interested in the individuals that populated their sites; it simply means that the archaeological database yields very little direct information about the details of individuals' lives. The use of admittedly fictitious stories is a vehicle for personalizing prehistory, for reminding us that the past is more than systems, trends, and theories. Ideally, however, this type of archaeological depiction differs from popular fiction about prehistoric time periods in several ways.

The archaeological drama is not simply a random tale. It is engineered to illustrate specific themes in the prehistory of a particular area and time period. As with a novel, the characters are fictional, although they may be inspired by actual burials or artifacts. The basic description of the setting and the culture must be consistent with known evidence. This means that, just as with any archaeological description, some of the background details will be securely documented, while others are more speculative. Obviously, the exact words, feelings, thoughts, and dreams of the inhabitants of long-abandoned villages can only be surmised; however, attempting to do so not only emphasizes the humanity of the past but leads the archaeologist to ask new questions and resolve details. In this section I present my attempt to fictionalize the lives of the residents of Lizard Man Village. The story's consistency with the archaeological evidence can be tested with a careful reading of the subsequent chapters, and I challenge the reader to think about which aspects of the story are well documented and which are speculative as they read the remainder of the book.

One of the things that becomes immediately obvious when attempting to construct a story about the past based on archaeological information is the large number of gaps in one's knowledge, not just about individuals but about culture as well. A good story demands details. If food is an element in the tale, it is not enough to say that the Sinagua ate corn; they must have prepared it in specific ways and had favorite and less-favorite recipes. Analogously, for a tale to work, the characters must be portrayed with familial relationships, work roles, and belief systems.

The very act of formulating a story demands that the archaeologist think about issues that are usually ignored in most theoretical models, because they are seen either as less important or simply as too difficult to discern. Similar challenges confront the museum curator fabricating a reconstruction or artists like Amy Henderson, who drew the illustrations included in this book. It is no accident that some of the first (and few) archaeologists to include short tales of the past in their presentations were explicitly interested in engendering the past. Try to write a story, no matter how short, without attributing gender roles! Similarly, age is generally neglected by archaeologists. Where are all the children who romped in the distant past? It is certainly possible to discuss abstract models of societies solely in terms of concepts such as exchange systems or settlement patterns, but once people enter the picture it is impossible to envision them without age or gender.

Generating stories about the past also allows the archaeologist to talk about and think about the past in ways not allowed by the rigors of strict scientific method. We are encouraged to think about the meaning of past events. How did infant mortality affect people? How did they perceive the changes occurring in their own culture? One of the most memorable papers that I have heard at a professional archaeological meeting was also one of the most dangerous for its presenter (archaeologists are not encouraged to think in terms of stories!). After a traditional exposition of changes in settlement patterns (read by her graduate student co-author), Ruth Tringham presented a short story depicting a young woman's reaction to the isolation imposed by the new scattered farmsteads. Obviously this part of the paper was strictly imaginary, yet it provoked me to ponder the past in provocative new ways.

Once these types of issues and their importance are brought to the fore, they will probably not recede. They challenge the archaeologist to go beyond the speculation inherent in stories and to search for more solid answers. Thus, stories raise issues, generate hypotheses about the past, and in the end lead to new, different, and better research.

In addition, stories personalize the past. They remind us that ultimately we excavate to understand people and their lifeways. Together with more traditional scientific approaches, such stories can help us to visualize the past and to build a respect for and common humanity with those who inhabit it.

The Birth: A Story from Lizard Man Village

A crisp breeze made her face tingle as she sat in the dark atop the basalt ridge behind the village, stroking her belly, thinking of the past and dreaming of the future for the child that stirred within her. Above, the sky was clear, sparkling with a million stars. Periodically she could feel small spasms, twinges of pain, a signal that the birth was not too far away, but she remained serene, composed, aware that she probably still had hours to wait. The air smelled slightly of fires from the village, and occasional sounds—laughter, a children's quarrel, a dog barking—reminded her that she was not wholly alone and that the warmth and security of family lay close at hand.

At twenty-one she already had one child, a son, a charming, boisterous boy of four, always ready to laugh yet sometimes, like his father, showing a serious side. She almost laughed out loud to think of the way he occasionally imitated his father in demeanor and speech, mimicking his parent's favorite phrases even to the exact tone and way of holding his head and body. Sometimes Elder Brother chided her and her mother for spoiling the boy. That was really not fair. After all, his father *was* teaching him how to farm and hunt. Their young son helped carry water to the small seedlings, so that they might survive even when rains were not forthcoming. Regularly, he went to the fields near the village with the older boys to help chase crows and other predators from the crops. He hunted with the tiny bow and arrow his father had made him, catching butterflies and even the occasional lizard. Maybe it was sometimes fun, too, but what did that hurt? Hard work, responsibilities, and sorrow would come soon enough into his life. Why not let him enjoy these few years of childhood? Suddenly she had an overwhelming urge to hold the boy tight, to assure both him and herself that all was well in the world. The hunger was so fierce that it scared her. Somehow, her son was too perfect, too wonderful. What if something were to happen to him?

Rationally, she knew that he was safe; after all he was with her own brother and his wife's family. Elder Brother had married a woman from Walnut Canyon and gone to live with her there and farm her family's fields. Still, while less than an easy day's walk away, the canyon seemed an entirely different world. The more abundant water and slightly higher elevation made the vegetation more lush. Ponderosa pines dotted the canyon tops, dwarfing the pinyons and junipers of Lizard Man Village. Standing water in the canyon floor assured the ability to water crops even in relative droughts. She knew her son would sneak away with the other boys to play in the shade of the canyon bottom near the water during the heat of the day, and she envied him slightly.

Once when she was a girl, she had visited Mother's Brother far away in a village on the other side of the Little Colorado River. Usually he came to Lizard Man Village to visit, but this time her whole family had gone to his new home, to see a multitude of cousins and to attend the marriage of one of his daughters. The family had come laden with gifts—pinyon nuts, shell jewelry, obsidian arrowheads, and some of Grandmother's favorite corn cakes. They had initially felt some trepidation, since the people that Mother's Brother had married into and now lived with spoke a different language and had somewhat different customs. But they had returned confident in the knowledge that their relative had become part of a good family on whose help they could rely in hard times. They had also brought home gifts from Mother's Brother's family. She still had a lovely white bowl painted in intricate black designs. A second bowl, just as lovely and even larger, had cracked when her son had accidentally dropped it. She had tried to mend it, but in vain. Now all that remained were a couple of spindle whorls she had made with the broken pieces. Every time she spun they reminded her of her journey and of her childhood.

Her twenty-some years had been good, although not always easy. She thought of her own childhood, remembering the warmth of a skin coverlet on a cold morning, Grandmother's rabbit stew and cornmeal dumplings, the stories of Grandmother, Mother and Mother's Sister, who had told her of the olden days when they were children—of her relatives, her ancestors, and of the gods. Her favorite story was about the little horned toads that she had often caught and played with as a child: One day when Coyote was walking past Horny Toad's farm, he asked Horny Toad to show him around. So Horny Toad showed him the farm, and when Coyote was just about ready to leave he bent his head down and, "Gulp," he ate Horny Toad! Horny Toad began to climb up Coyote's stomach. First he gave a little tug on the liver, and yelled, "I am pulling on your liver, Coyote." Next he gave a little sharper scratch on Coyote's heart, and yelled, "I am scratching on your heart, Coyote." Then, he grabbed the esophagus and began to squeeze. Suddenly Coyote fell over dead. Horny Toad crawled out of his mouth and lived happily ever after.*

She whispered a prayer to the gods for her children's welfare, the one child already a part of the world and the other yet to be born. Older Sister had had such problems with her children. Several boys had died in infancy. Then finally she had borne a daughter, a bright and pliant child who charmed everyone with her sparkling eyes and constant teasing. The year the girl had been born was a year of relative plenty, followed by two harder years when the harvest did not do well and food stores ran out. Only a knowledge of wild foods to be used primarily in hard times, some good and others rather nasty tasting, saved the group from starvation. Nevertheless, Sister's Daughter had thrived, small for her age, perhaps, but intelligent and happy nonetheless. Alas, when she was only three and playing in the ruins of an abandoned village nearby, she had fallen through the roof of a decaying pueblo room and broken her leg. The village was seldom visited, at least not by adults, so Sister's Daughter might have lain there, alone and crying, not to be found until it was

*This is a story based on Hopi and Navajo tales of Coyote and Horny Toad, as told to me by my daughter, April.

too late. Fortuitously, an older child had been there to carry her home. Nevertheless, her leg had healed badly, and forever after the child walked with a severe limp. Unable to play as robustly as her age mates, Sister's Daughter stayed near home, becoming even more her mother's darling. Her mother, one of the better potters of the tribe, taught her how to make pots. Initially, she made only tiny doll dishes and small animals and figurines. At the mere age of five, however, she precociously began to make small, adult-sized bowls. Her tiny hands carefully shaped the base, smoothed the coils, and burnished the exterior. Sister's Daughter looked forward to the day when she would be able to use a paddle and anvil like her mother to make a large, thin, even bowl or a gracefully curving jar. Her mother radiated a quiet pride, sure that her offspring would someday be a renowned craftswoman.

Perhaps someone was jealous; perhaps there was witchcraft at work. Whatever the reason, ever since she had broken her leg, the girl's health had remained fragile. Illness alternated with health until one day, at the age of only six, Sister's Daughter breathed her last. Family and friends had done all they could. They had used all their own knowledge of herbal remedies. They had called a woman from New Caves whose curing abilities were well known. They had had a healing ceremony. Nothing had helped.

They laid the small body in a grave where the walls of the pithouse in which Grandmother had been born could still be discerned. There she could join her other relatives for a happier life, without illness or hunger. To help her on her journey and to show their love, her relatives dressed her in her best clothes, with a necklace of shell beads and a carved frog shell necklace around her neck, and placed pottery, food and two of her favorite shells in her grave, then covered it with wooden slabs and earth.

At first it had seemed that Sister and Sister's Husband would never cease to mourn. Now, the child had been replaced with another, but at times, especially during the season of the pinyon harvest, at ceremonies, or at other times especially pleasing to children, Sister would become quiet and thoughtful. While they never discussed it, intuitively she knew that in some way the loss of this child had imbued her sister with a dull ache that would never leave. She stroked her belly carefully again and prayed that, for this child, all would be well, that there would be no shallow grave, and that someday she would be the awaiting the birth of a grandchild instead of her own child.

Perhaps she should find her husband to tell him that her time was soon to come. It would be comforting to feel his strong arms around her. But he would be in the kiva, passing time with the other men, and might not appreciate her intrusion. If he were to react wrongly to her summons, the entire moment would be destroyed. Yet, she toyed with the idea; he was, after all, generally a gentle and loving husband, and she knew he looked forward to the child.

It was difficult for him, living apart from his birth family, particularly his mother and his younger sister, about whom he worried. His sister's husband had a reputation as a womanizer, spending many of the hours when he was supposed to be in the fields or out hunting in pleasant dalliance instead, becoming angry when his faults were noted. It was rumored that sometimes Sister-in-law's Husband beat her. Probably they would divorce soon, but until then she knew her husband worried. He was, after all, the head of the household, responsible for his sister's welfare. At least Sister-in-law had women kin at home to defend her. As long as her mother and sisters were around, things could never be too bad.

Then, if Sister-in-law did divorce her husband, there would be the question of who would farm her fields. Either she would remarry immediately or Husband would be responsible for caring for his sister's fields as well as his own. The family needed a minimum number of males to provide for its needs. She understood the problem and she sympathized with his sister. Many marriages were short-lived, especially until children came. In a system where a man's primary responsibility was to his sisters and their children, loyalties were often divided.

Her own first marriage at the age of fifteen had been very brief, but she was confident that this one would be different. Both she and First Husband had been very young, and he had been restless, always flirting with other women, preferring visits to other villages and gambling to working the fields. Her husband now was different. Although his body did not rouse in her the passions of her earlier alliance, he was older, dependable, and very kind. He did his duty, to her, to his own family, and to the community. In the end, she thought, this was the best type of husband to have.

She got slowly to her feet. Now it was surely time. In the back of her mind, while she had been thinking and enjoying the breeze, the stars, and the smell of wood smoke, she also had been listening to her body. The contractions had grown hard and sharp. She walked carefully down the basalt ridge to the familiar plaza of the village, and down the ladder into her mother's house, hopeful for the child, its future, and all the happiness that life could bring.

It was early dawn. Still she struggled. A woman who understood such matters had been summoned to help her sister and mother, since this child was reluctant in the coming. She pushed and pushed. Finally she saw her child, a son. She had thought she might feel disappointment if the child were a boy again. After all, a girl would stay with the family, carry on the lineage, and be both companion and friend. The moment she saw the child, however, she was more than satisfied. Pride surged within her. Surely this was the best thing she had ever done, and this child was the most beautiful infant she had ever seen. She closed her eyes and said a brief prayer, attempting to allay her sudden fears that this one moment had used up all her store of good fortune and that she would never be lucky enough to see her children grown.

Chapter 6

THE PEOPLE OF LIZARD MAN VILLAGE

As discussed in chapter 4, the site that today is called Lizard Man Village represents the remains of a sequence of villages, each occupied by a relatively small number of individuals. The main scientific goals of archaeology are to reconstruct the past, and ultimately to better understand the way cultures work and how and why they change through time. In addition to these theoretical goals, however, most archaeologists are also fascinated with the past for its own sake and yearn to gain insight into the lives of the individuals who populated it. We would like to understand how they lived and what they thought, to obtain a sense of humanity not only across space, but through time as well.

The Analysis of Burials

Burials provide us with the means for getting as close as we can to actually meeting the occupants of Lizard Man Village. With an entire skeleton we can determine the age of the individual, the sex of adults, general body build, health and nutrition, and, to a certain extent, physical appearance. The treatment of the body and the goods buried with it give glimpses into the funerary ritual accorded the deceased and possible insights into his or her status in the community.

In addition to skeletal remains contained in formal burials, loose fragments of human bone are scattered throughout the site. This dispersion has occurred because over the years digging has exposed some of the buried remains. Some of the digging occurred as part of the normal activities of the village when pits were dug to store foods, bury garbage, and obtain building materials. Animals also contributed to part of the process. A dog may have buried a coveted bone, accidentally disturbing the dead, or a rodent may have dug its burrow right through a burial pit. Some of the disturbance, however, was due to pot hunting at the site. As mentioned earlier, digging for artifacts is illegal on government property, and grave robbing is illegal wherever it occurs. Despite this, because Native American pottery, historic bottles, and other artifacts are saleable, the destruction of archaeological sites continues. Burials are particularly vulnerable, since they sometimes contain whole pots and other valuables. At Lizard Man Village the south half of Room 15 had been greatly disturbed by looters. Large portions of several bodies were missing, and there were many isolated bones. Because pot hunters are not interested in recovering information—merely artifacts—burials tend to be disrupted rather than carefully excavated. The bones, particularly skulls, are occasionally sold, but more often skeletal fragments are ignored and simply strewn on the ground.

In addition to being very disrespectful of the dead, the disruption of burials and other archaeological remains by looters causes an incredible loss of information. When grave goods are dissociated from their original recipients, it is no longer possible to reconstruct either social identity or mortuary ceremony or to explore the way that these varied with age, gender, health, or other personal characteristics. Nevertheless, isolated bones can still provide clues to the lives of the prehistoric Sinagua. Age can be determined for many of the individuals represented by isolated bones or very incomplete bone clusters and sometimes pathologies can be detected.

Methods of Osteological Analysis

As the body first develops into adulthood and then begins to age, both the bones and teeth are continually changing. During childhood, biological changes occur relatively rapidly and are quite predictable, so age can be determined with relative accuracy, usually within a few months or years. After reaching age twenty-five or so, when alterations to the skeleton are primarily degenerative, there is considerable variability between individuals; therefore, age estimates are given in much larger ranges.

Tooth eruption rates are well documented and children's ages can be estimated by looking at the number of deciduous and, later, permanent teeth that are present (figure 6.1). Thus, we decided that a child buried in Room 15 (described below as Burial 9) was five to six years old because it had a complete set of deciduous teeth, permanent teeth developing, and a first molar in the process of erupting. Even after the last adult teeth appear, change continues as tooth surfaces are worn. Tooth wear can be used as a very rough index of age, although the rate of wear will obviously vary, depending on diet. Teeth exposed to coarse diets and food with a high grit content will wear much faster than those exposed primarily to softer, cleaner foods. Use of the teeth as tools will also produce distinctive wear patterns and may accelerate wear.

Bones also provide important clues. As the body matures, the cartilage at *epiphyses* of long bones and other primary centers of ossification, such as the junctures, or *sutures*, in the bones of the skull, is replaced by bone and growth ceases. The time ranges for the fusion vary considerably among both individuals and groups, but general ranges are known, and the amount of fusion can be used to estimate the age of the individual at death. Even after maturity some ossification continues, and the age of mature adults can be estimated based on the amount of fusion of cranial sutures and changes in the morphology of the *pubic symphysis* in the pelvis, as well as the tooth wear mentioned earlier.

The age of the woman interred in Burial 2, who is described in more detail below, was determined using information about both bones and dentition. She had all of her permanent teeth with the exception of the third molar, which suggests an age of between fifteen and twenty-one (figure 6.1).

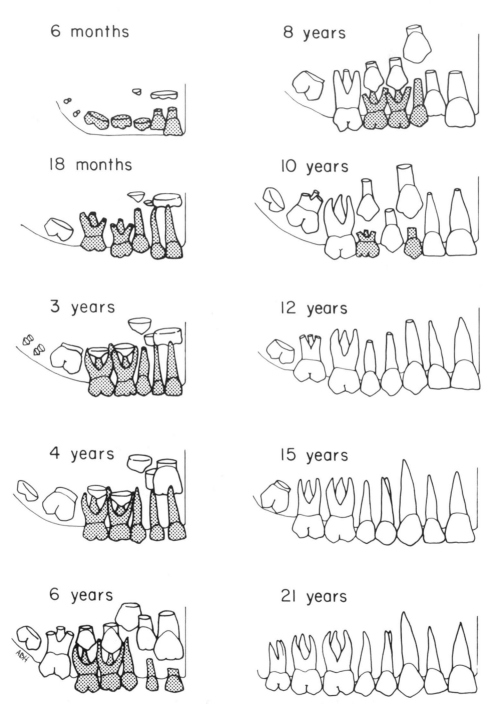

6 months

18 months

3 years

4 years

6 years

8 years

10 years

12 years

15 years

21 years

Figure 6.1 *Tooth eruption sequence used to age pre-adult individuals. The stippled teeth are deciduous.*

Figure 6.2 shows the bones that were to determine the age of her skeleton. Several bones that generally fuse by age nineteen or twenty are unfused, suggesting an age under twenty. On the other hand most bones that fuse in the fourteen- to eighteen-year range are fused, and several that fuse around age eighteen are almost but not quite fused. This seems to suggest an age in the upper teens, perhaps eighteen or nineteen.

Because of its adaptive relevance for childbearing, the best bone for determining sex is the pelvis (figure 6.3). The wider sciatic notch and larger sub-pubic angle of women provide a larger birth canal—a distinct evolutionary advantage, given the relatively large head size of human babies. Cranial morphology also provides a clue to sex, but since there is overlap in the range of variability between males and females, it should be used with some caution. In general, males tend to be more robust, with larger jaws, brow ridges, and muscle markings than females. All of these differences become pronounced only at puberty, however, making it difficult to determine the sex of preadolescent skeletons.

Burial Descriptions

At Lizard Man Village, fifteen burials were excavated. Descriptions of a few of these will give some idea of the type of variability in both the health of individuals and the way their bodies were treated after death.

The first burial we discovered (figure 6.4) was in a shallow, slab-lined pithouse. The body was lying on its back with its head to the east along the south wall of the pithouse. The shallow burial pit cut through the pithouse floor, but no attempt had been made to repair the floor. This means the body, that of a woman of about thirty years of age, was buried after the pithouse had been abandoned and filled but while the configuration of the room was still apparent, allowing her body to be perfectly aligned with the wall. Because the body was very close to the current ground surface, it was in poor condition. A large root had pierced the skull; there was evidence of considerable rodent gnawing on many of the bones; and many of the smaller bones, such as the hand bones, were missing. The woman's height, estimated from her long bones, was about 5'1" (157.5 cm). The back of her skull was flattened (figure 6.5), suggesting that she had been carried on a hard cradleboard as an infant. Because the jaw had been disturbed by a root, many of the teeth were missing. Those recovered did not suggest particularly good dental hygiene. Three cavities were observed in the seven teeth that were recovered. In addition a third molar had been lost before death, probably because of an abscessed gum, and all the teeth were quite worn. She did not have arthritis or any other disease that affects the bones, however, and no cause of death could be discerned. No artifacts appear to have been placed in the grave. Although half of a broken argillite ring and two *Olivella* shell beads were found in the burial pit fill, it also contained other trash, so their inclusion was probably accidental.

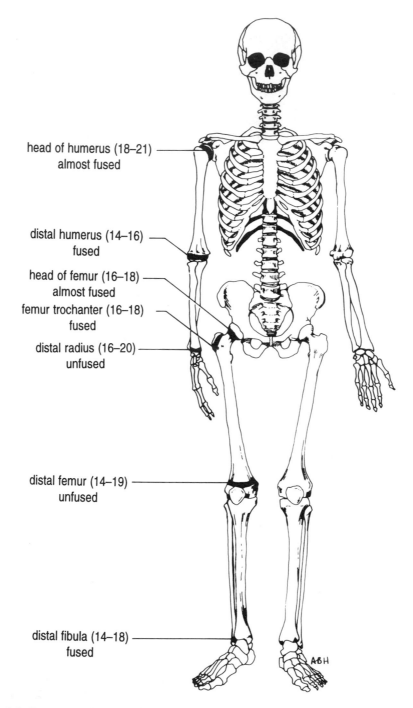

head of humerus (18–21)
almost fused

distal humerus (14–16)
fused

head of femur (16–18)
almost fused

femur trochanter (16–18)
fused

distal radius (16–20)
unfused

distal femur (14–19)
unfused

distal fibula (14–18)
fused

Figure 6.2 *Diagram showing the bones used to age Burial 2. Ages shown are fusion times for the epiphyses indicated. The individual's age appears to be about eighteen or nineteen.*

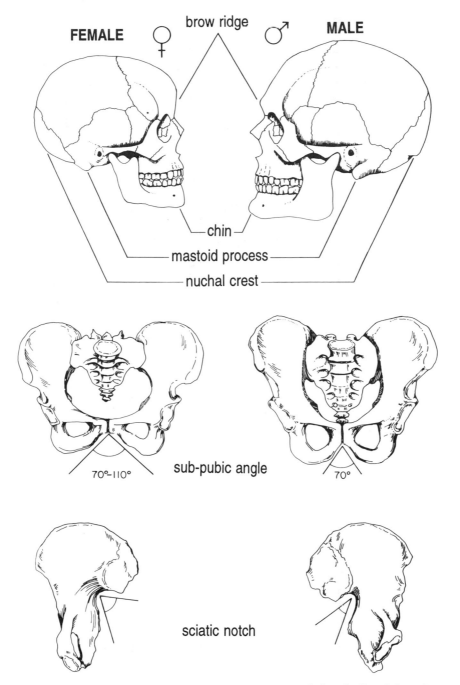

Figure 6.3 *Skeletal clues to determining sex. In general the skulls of females are more gracile than those of males. Brow ridges, mastoid processes and nuchal crests are smaller, and chins tend to be more pointed. On the pelvis the sub-pubic angle and sciatic notch are both larger in the female; the pelvis is configured to produce a larger birth canal.*

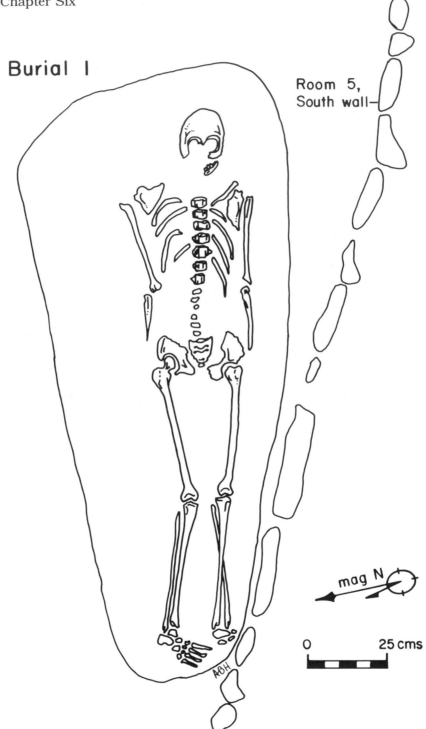

Burial 1

Room 5,
South wall—

mag N

0   25 cms

Figure 6.4 *Burial 1, a woman placed extended in a pit dug along the wall of an abandoned pithouse.*

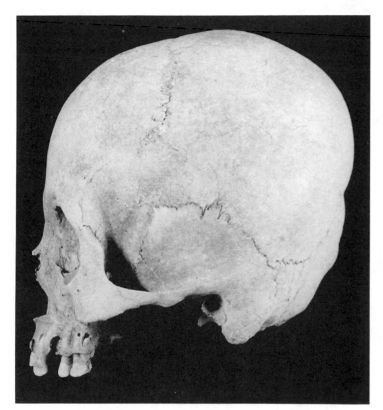

Figure 6.5 *Photograph show-ing the skull of an individual who had been placed on a cradle board as an infant.*

Burial 2 (figure 6.6), that of the young woman discussed earlier in the section on aging skeletal re-mains, was almost not discovered. One of our excavation teams, Sara Bruins and Gweneth John-son, was excavating a test trench in a mid-den area. They were already almost a meter (three feet) deep, bored with the enterprise, and with only a maze of rodent holes at the bottom of the pit. Eager to start excavating the room that had been allotted to them, they asked to omit cleaning out the holes. Thoroughness demanded that the rodent holes be cleaned out to ensure that they really were rodent holes, and to gauge the amount of rodent disturbance, so we persevered in our demands, and they excavated. In one of the "rodent holes" was a human foot.

The second burial, a deeper and more complex grave containing numerous offerings, was quite a contrast to the first. The pit was dug about a meter (3 feet) deep, cutting through trash midden and into the subsoil. As in the case of Burial 1, the woman had been laid on her back with her head to the east. Red staining on the back of the pelvic bones suggests that hematite was sprinkled into the grave before the body was laid to rest. Fabric impressions in the soil along the back of one of the arms show that the body had been wrapped in some type of cloth. The woman was adorned with the juniper-bark armband described ear-lier and a shell bracelet. We do not know what else she wore for her burial. Nine ceramic vessels, three of them imports from the Puebloan groups to the north and the rest local types, and a human figurine of unfired clay were placed with the body. The grave was then covered with slabs of conifer wood.

The woman herself appeared to be in good health. She had no arthritis and her teeth were strong and even, with no abscesses or cavities and little wear or buildup of calculus deposits. No cause of death could be determined; how-

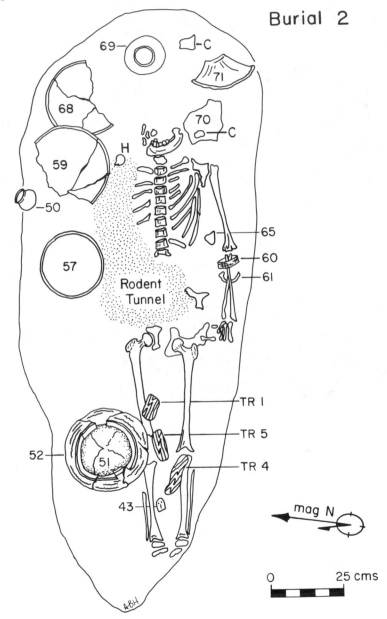

Burial 2

Figure 6.6 *Burial 2, a young woman buried in a deep pit at the edge of the village. Artifacts are identified by their field numbers: 43, human figurine of unfired clay; 50, small Sunset jar; 51 (inverted into 52) deep bowl of late Flagstaff Black-on-white with damaged rim, mend holes, and handle broken off; 52, large Moenkopi Corrugated jar containing three pots; 57, medium bowl of Sunset Brown; 59, large Sunset Brown bowl; 60, painted fiber armband; 61, shell bracelet; 68, large Sunset Brown bowl; 69, medium Sunset Brown jar; 70, large Sunset bowl; 71, large sherd of Alameda Brown Ware. TR (tree-ring) numbers are pieces of wood. C=Cranial fragment. H=Humerus head.*

ever, she was of childbearing age, always a time of physical stress for women. The relative abundance of grave goods and the elaborate treatment of the burial might suggest one of a number of things, including high status, numerous relatives, a well-loved individual, or a cause of death requiring special ceremonies and specific goods to guarantee a successful journey in the afterworld.

Perhaps the burial that made many of us feel saddest is that of the five- or six-year-old child (figure 6.7) that I referred to in the previous discussion on using dentition to determine age. The bones tell the clear story of a very sickly child, but the large quantity of grave goods interred with the body attests to the fact that he or she was probably very important to someone.

The health of this child, which is too young to sex, was probably always precarious. Anemia is indicated by pitting in the left eye socket. The scientific name for this condition is *cribra orbitalia*. Thin horizontal lines of opaque enamel referred to as *hypoplasias* appear on several teeth. These hypoplasias are caused by interruptions in normal tooth growth due to systemic stresses such as disease or malnutrition. A radiograph of the femur showed Harris lines, a similar phenomenon in bone growth. Again, the lines appear if bone growth has been retarded, usually due to illness or lack of food. The child was short for the age indicated by tooth eruption patterns. The shaft ends of long bones were flared (figure 6.8), which may be an indication of either scurvy or rickets. Scurvy is caused by vitamin C deficiency, while rickets is a result of vitamin D deficiency. The child's dental health was also poor. Already it had five cavities and an unhealed abscess. In addition, the child had been crippled by a broken leg that had not healed properly and was, hence, shorter and probably considerably weaker than its mate. Probably a year or more before the child's death, the right femur had been broken (figure 6.8). It had not been set straight and a large, bony callus had formed around the break point. Although considerable healing had occurred, the bone was still undergoing some remodeling. The lower leg bones of the broken leg were very bowed. Perhaps the bone softened during a period of confinement after the accident, then was stressed by the child walking on it before it had regained its strength. Several other long bones also have areas of very porous surface bone, indications of a systemic infection at the time the bone was being laid.

This crippled child had more offerings than any other burial we excavated at Lizard Man Village. The child, wearing a necklace of almost two hundred *Olivella* shell beads accented by a large shell pendent carved into the shape of a frog, was placed in a deep pit which was then covered with split juniper. Two *Pecten* shells drilled to hang as pendents were found at the knees and pelvis; it is possible that these were worn as jewelry also. Ten pots, all of the locally-made Sunset Brown type, were placed in the grave. One of the small bowls contained a powdery white material, probably kaolin, through which three fingers had been dragged. Possibly the powder was used as a body paint during the funeral ceremony. Several of the pots are somewhat unusual in form. Two imitate large bivalve shells such as *Laevicardium*. One of these is very well-made and highly polished, while the other is visibly

Burial 9

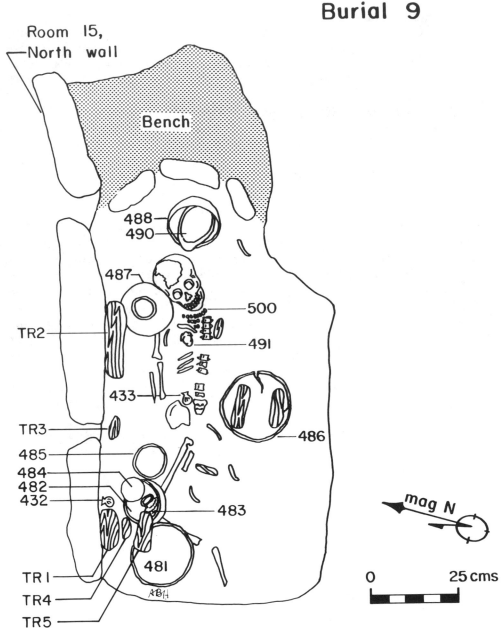

Figure 6.7 *Burial 9, a child buried along the wall of Room 15. Artifacts are identified by their field numbers: 432 and 433, Pecten shells; 481, medium Sunset Brown bowl; 482, small Sunset Brown bowl; 483 and 484, small Sunset jars nested inside 482; 485 small Sunset Brown bowl, white organic crust with finger striations inside; 486 medium Sunset Brown bowl; 487, medium Sunset Brown jar; 488, small Sunset Brown bowl; 489 and 490, shell-shaped Sunset Brown bowls, inside 488; 491, shell frog pendant; 500 165 Olivella shell beads, in mass with detectable rows. TR (tree-ring) numbers and similarly shaded pieces are wood.*

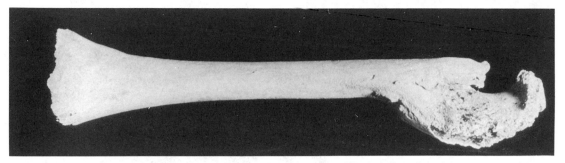

Figure 6.8 *Right femur showing healed fracture and flared distal end.*

cruder. Two small jars, one corrugated and the other with a long neck not characteristic of Sinagua jar styles, also seem a little less expertly made. Perhaps these are the work of the child or one of its siblings.

Just describing individual burials provides a partial picture of a few of the individuals who once lived at Lizard Man Village. The objects with which they are buried gives insight into funerary ritual, and their health and bone structure tells something about the lives they led. Additional information about the village population can be derived looking at patterns in the entire group of burials excavated, rather than concentrating on the details of individuals.

Demography

In order to understand the dynamics of population structure, it is useful to construct a life table—or in this case a mortuary table. To do this, it is necessary to work with burials that are all roughly contemporary. The ceramic types used as burial offerings all date fairly late. Flagstaff Black-on-white and Walnut Black-on-white are fairly common imported wares, and several of these have designs that look very late for their types; some of the latest pottery at the site came from burials (figure 6.9; compare with figure 4.4). As mentioned earlier, several of the burials are also intrusive into earlier pithouses. These two pieces of evidence suggest that all the burials represent a late population at the site or even some individuals interred in an ancestral residence. Therefore, we are treating all the burials from Lizard Man Village as if they represent a single population dating to the puebloan occupation. We do not know where the occupants of the pithouses buried their dead.

While the number of burials excavated at Lizard Man Village is too small to allow the construction of formal life tables, it is possible to see some trends. Table 6.1 lists both the burials and fragmentary remains by age and, when possible, sex. Most obvious, is the youth of many of the deceased. Thirty-seven of the fifty-two individuals (71 percent) were under the age of eighteen when they died. Thirty-two of these were under age twelve. About 30 percent of the remains represent children a year old or less. All of the adults in the sample for whom ages could be determined also died young. Only a single individual is over age forty. The lack of any very old individual is probably

Figure 6.9 *Black-on-white trade wares found in and used to date burials. Note the failry high percentage of black to white on these, dating them as relatively late.*

Table 6.1 **Age Structure of Burial Population at Lizard Man Village***

N	Fetal	0–1	1–6	6–12	12–18	18–30	30–40	>40	Adult
1	A	6	9	16 m	3 m	2 f	1 f	4 m	G
2	E	8	C	B	J	11 m	10 f		Q
3	O	12	H	N	K	13 m			S
4	CC	18	P	BB	15 m				T
5	GG	F	DD	LL	17 m				X
6	JJ	L	EE	MM					Z
7	M	HH	NN	D f					AA
8		R	II						FF
9		Y							OO
10		KK							

*Numbers are for complete burials, letters for isolated bones. Sex of burials is indicated by "m" or "f." Isolated adult bones could not be accurately aged and are all in the "adult" column.

a sampling problem, due to the small number of adult burials for which an age could be determined. However, both the high infant mortality and the relatively young ages of adults at death reflect the harsh realities of life at Lizard Man Village and are consistent with demographic profiles from other Southwestern sites with larger burial populations.

Stature

Physical anthropologists have devised formulae for calculating height using long bone length. Only four of the adult skeletons had long bones preserved well enough for good stature estimates. The females stood approximately 157 cm (5' 2") and 147 cm (4' 10") and the males were 161 cm (5' 3 1/2") and 160 cm (5' 3"). All of the adults were fairly short in comparison to other Southwestern Native American populations, but not outstandingly so. For example, males at Mesa Verde averaged about 2 cm (1") taller than the Lizard Man Villagers, while Mesa Verde women were about the same average height. At Pueblo Bonito in Chaco Canyon, on the other hand, the men were about 9 cm (3.5") taller and the women about 5 cm (2") taller.

Children were also short in comparison to some other Native American populations. For example, the five- to six-year-old child in Burial 9 was the height of a three-and-a-half to four-and-a-half-year-old child at Indian Knoll (a site in Kentucky dating about 4000 B.C.) or a two-and-a-half to three-and-a-half-year-old child from the proto-historic plains dwellers, the Arikara. Similarly, the eleven- to twelve-year-old in Burial 16 was only as tall as a seven-and-a-half to eight-and-a-half-year-old Arikara youngster.

Despite a generally small size, the ridges on bones where muscles attach tend to be distinct, suggesting a well-developed musculature. Thus, while the Lizard Man Village residents may have been short, perhaps due to health problems, poor diet, or even simply genetics, they were also a strong, tough people accustomed to active lives in a rugged terrain.

Nutrition

In addition to small body size, there are other indications of nutritional stress. Skeletons show a high incidence of *cribra orbitalia* and *porotic hyperostosis*, pitted bone that occurs in anemic individuals. A high incidence of *cribra orbitalia* is common among prehistoric Southwestern children and may be due to a diet that is high in corn, since corn is a poor source of iron and may even inhibit iron absorption. As human milk is also low in iron, this is especially problematic if children are breastfed well beyond the first six months, then weaned onto a diet of corn mush. Diarrheal infections and parasites such as intestinal worms may also be implicated. Researchers have found numerous eggs of pinworm, tapeworm, and whipworm in fecal matter from Elden Pueblo, which is contemporary to the Elden Phase (A.D. 1150–1250) at Lizard Man Village. Midden and latrine areas in and near the village doubtless harbored numerous diseases transmitted through human waste products. Teeth also confirm a high level of stress related to disease or nutrition. Almost 100 percent of the individuals from Lizard Man Village had one or more hypoplastic lines on their teeth. As mentioned earlier, this is an indication of periodic stress during the developmental period, probably nutritional but possibly also disease-related.

The Lizard Man Village residents had many dental problems. Teeth were recovered for ten individuals over four years in age. Seven of these had cavities, and six had current abscesses, loss of teeth prior to death, or both abscesses and missing teeth. Several individuals must have been in almost constant pain. One man, aged forty to fifty, had seven cavities, five active abscesses, and had already lost one tooth. Another had six cavities. A woman who was somewhere in her twenties had eight cavities, five abscesses, and had already lost five teeth. Another had two cavities, two abscesses, and had lost seven teeth. Even children were not immune. The five- to six-year-old in Burial 9 had five cavities, one abscess, and already had lost one tooth. Probably the high incidence of tooth decay is due, in part, to a high-carbohydrate diet. Populations relying heavily on corn or other starches frequently have tooth problems. One of the changes that can often be observed, if a group shifts from hunting and gathering to agriculture, is a worsening of dental health.

Health

The major health problems were anemia and arthritis. The anemia, discussed above, was probably primarily due to diet. Arthritis (figure 6.10) was almost ubiquitous among the adults. The two of these, together with the frequent dental problems, may have caused some level of chronic ill health among most of the adult population. A consistent toothache, particularly when accompanied by the infection of an abscess, can be quite debilitating. Arthritis is the same way. We may not view it as normally life threatening, but it certainly leads to reduced effectiveness in many tasks.

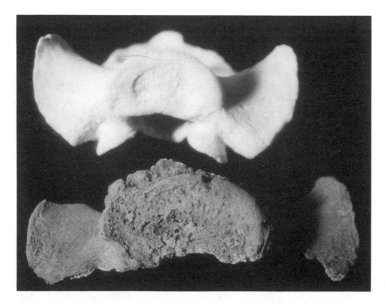

Figure 6.10 *Above, a healthy sacrum; below, sacrum showing the effects of arthritis. Arthritic sacrum shows excess bone deposits.*

The Sinagua lifestyle probably necessitated heavy physical exercise, and the effects are sometimes seen on skeletons. In addition to arthritis, one male, probably between forty and fifty years old, had evidence of *spondy-*

lolisthesis, slippage of the last vertebra of the lower back (the fifth lumbar vertebra), probably caused by strenuous exercise and heavy lifting. In the fourth lumbar vertebra there is also a possible *spondylolysis*, a failure of the neural arch to join with the rest of the vertebrae. While this is possibly congenital, a more likely cause is repeated stress fractures. A similar problem was seen in another male whose estimated age is twenty-five to thirty. His fifth lumbar vertebra shows a complete bilateral spondylolysis and there is also evidence of old injuries at the joint between the pelvis and the spine and at the attachment of one rib to the vertebrae.

In addition to back problems, there were several other injuries. One child of about twelve years of age—perhaps a male, based on the pelvis (but at this young age sex is very hard to determine)—had a fractured rib that was healing at the time of his death. Injuries to the back are particularly common. Burial 10, a woman between thirty and thirty-five years of age, showed evidence of a minor injury to her back. A healed infection or injury to the rib articulation of one vertebra could be seen, and the body of the eleventh thoracic vertebra had suffered a compression fracture and showed some arthritic lipping.

Clues to Personal Status

The rituals surrounding an individual at death may well reveal personal characteristics, social roles, and status. Archaeologists often assume that an analysis of the variability in grave goods and burial treatments will provide information about social organization. This aspect of burial analysis will be discussed in more detail in chapter 10 when we explore various reconstructions of social organization. Burials also tell us something about religious beliefs. For example, the fact that goods are placed as offerings suggests belief in an afterlife of some sort and the need for specific types of items in the afterlife or on the passage to it. The Lizard Man Village burials and other Sinagua burials show several distinct patterns. By the Elden Phase graves tend to be clustered in cemetery areas. Bodies are normally placed in the grave lying on their backs with the body extended and the head to the east. Infants and children are frequently buried with small or miniature ceramic vessels as offerings. We know that rituals surrounding death and burial would have been imbued with meaning and symbolism. Unfortunately, to date the entire corpus of Sinagua burials has not been well studied. This means that, while we are aware of some of the obvious patterns we do not yet know about the more subtle ones, and future study is required before it will be possible to reconstruct and understand the Sinagua treatment of their dead.

Clothing and Jewelry

Part of reconstructing a picture of the inhabitants of Lizard Man Village requires knowing what people wore. Most of the clothing of the Sinagua no longer exists. With the rare exceptions of occasional sandals and pieces of cloth preserved in dry caves or wooden objects like the fiber armband which was protected to an extent by mineral paint, perishables have long vanished. Even relatively imperishable items like shell and stone jewelry often had perishable components and so are no longer completely intact.

We do know that cotton fabrics were probably both abundant and diverse. A greater variety of weaving techniques was used in the prehistoric Pueblos than are found in the Pueblos today (Kent 1983:4). Particularly striking is a lacy, openwork shirt found at Tonto, near the Southern Sinagua region. Fabrics were decorated in a variety of ways. An almost complete cotton blanket painted with elaborate geometric designs was found at Hidden House, also in the Southern Sinagua area (figure 6.11). From two Southern Sinagua sites in the Verde Valley and from Tonto National Monument come examples of the use of embroidery (Kent 1983:38). Thus, Sinagua clothing certainly incorporated a variety of cotton fabrics, some of them quite decorative and elaborate.

Since winter weather is cold and often snowy in the Northern Sinagua

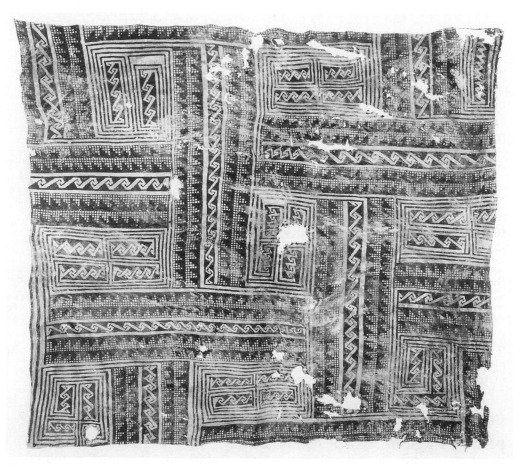

Figure 6.11 *Painted blanket found at Hidden House.*

region, we can be sure the Sinagua had some warm clothing. The Kayenta made rabbit fur blankets by shrinking strips of rabbit fur onto yucca cords and then weaving this yarn onto a weft of yucca fibers (Kent 1983:90). The Sinagua probably had similar fabrics, as well as leather and fur, although no evidence has been preserved. We know from the faunal remains that the Lizard Man Villagers caught plenty of rabbits. Dry cave finds show that feet were protected by sandals, but these might have been augmented by skin shoes during the winter.

The one item of apparel that is fairly abundant at Sinagua sites is jewelry, much of which is more durable than pieces of clothing. Most of the jewelry found on sites is fragmentary, lost beads rather than the complete necklace. Burials, however, do provide complete specimens in a meaningful cultural context, providing information on who wore a particular type of jewelry as well what the complete piece might have looked like.

The Sinagua adorned themselves with necklaces, bracelets, rings, earrings, and probably anklets. Nose plugs (figure 6.12k) worn through a pierced nasal septum are characteristic of Sinagua and were probably worn by males, since they have been found in the vicinity of the nose in several male burials. Lip plugs were also sometimes used. Shell jewelry, imported from the Gulf of California, probably via the Hohokam area, is the most common type of jewelry. Fifty-eight fragments of *Glycymeris* shell bracelets (figure 6.12e) and 388 *Olivella* shell beads (figure 6.12a) as well as a number of different shapes of cut shell beads and pendants (figure 6.12c,d,g,h,j) were found at Lizard Man Village. *Conus* shells were modified into tinklers (figure 6.12i) which could be sewn onto clothing or strung together, presumably to produce a type of rattle. The "magician" was presumably carrying such a cluster of tinklers and had them sewn onto his leggings as well (figure 1.5).

Argillite, a red siltstone originating in the Prescott area, is a fairly common material for jewelry, but turquoise is considerably rarer. The Lizard Man Villagers produced argillite ornaments for themselves (figure 6.12k,p,q) but did not work turquoise, presumably acquiring this primarily as finished ornaments (figure 6.12n,o). Bone hair pins occasionally decorated with incising are sometimes found near the skulls or hands of men, which suggests that they adorned men rather than women.

We know from traces of pigment on bones found in burials that body painting was sometimes done, but we do not know whether its use was primarily ceremonial or if it was a part of everyday attire. At Lizard Man Village the lower jaw of Burial 16, an adolescent, probably a male, was stained green from a copper-based pigment. The fairly large quantities of hematite, a red, iron-based pigment found at Lizard Man Village and in other sites, suggest that this may have been a common paint. Several metates from Lizard Man Village have the type of overall stain that would occur if hematite were ground in them and mixed with water or another liquid (urine, for example) to produce a paint. Other pigments include malachite (green), azurite (blue), jarosite and limonite (yellow), tenorite (black), and kaolin (white).

Feathers were also probably used, at least in ceremonial costumes and

a

b

c

d

e

f

g

n

i

j

k

l

m

n

o

p

q

0   1   2 in

0   5 cm

Figure 6.12 *Common Sinagua jewelry types found at Lizard Man Village: (a) Olivella shell beads, (b) whole shell bead, (c,d) cut shell beads, (e) Glycymeris shell bracelet fragment, (f) frog pendant found in Burial 9, (g,h) cut shell beads/pendants, (i) Conus shell tinkler, (j) cut shell beads/pendant, (k) argillite noseplug, (l) pendant made from bracelet fragment, (m) soapstone bird pendant, (n,o) turquoise pendants, (p) argillite pendant with drill-hole mistake, (q) argillite ring made to imitate shell.*

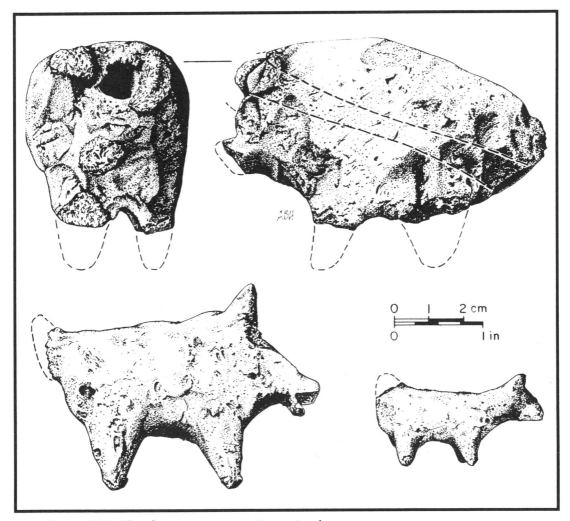

Figure 6.13 *Clay figurines representing animals.*

possibly in personal attire as well. Although it is not always necessary to kill a bird to obtain its feathers, the animal bones found at Lizard Man Village include numerous birds. Of particular interest are small, nonfood species such as meadowlarks that may have been hunted specifically for their feathers.

Other Personal Possessions

Unless an object is found in a burial, it is never archaeologically associated with a single individual. Even items in burials may not have been owned by the person with whom they are interred. Appropriate ceremony for a given age, gender and status may simply have required such an item. Alternatively, some or all of the objects may have been presented to the deceased as part of the mortuary ritual. In some cultures, it is even believed that the dead can transport items to the afterlife for other individuals who have already passed into that realm. Despite these caveats, variability in mortary treatment is generally viewed as a reflection, albeit imperfect, of some aspects of personal status.

In the Sinagua region, containers and items of apparel comprise the majority of burial offerings. Unfortunately for the archaeologist, tools are almost never included in burials, making it impossible to determine possible gender or age differences in the allotment of tasks. In addition to jewelry and clothing, occasionally burials include idiosyncratic items that may well be personal possessions. Some of these yield clues to leisure activities. Beneath the skeleton of one older man were two rectangular bone tokens, probably originally held in a cloth or leather pouch, that may well have been gaming pieces. Other possible gaming pieces, primarily made from shaped and smoothed broken pottery, have been found scattered in fill throughout the site. This should come as no surprise, since Native American groups played a variety of games.

Crudely shaped clay animals (figure 6.13) and miniature vessels found throughout the fill at Sinagua sites may well be children's toys. An adolescent burial at Lizard Man Village included two such figurines. A study of fingerprints on clay figurines that I conducted with two of my students, Jules Graybill and Ian Natowsky, suggests that at least some of the fingerprints are too small to have belonged to adults. It looks as if children at Lizard Man Village made small clay figurines that were later fired, perhaps by an adult potter. The possibility of identifying toys is particularly exciting, since, while we know that children doubtless played and worked at Lizard Man Village and other ancient sites, archaeologists rarely find direct evidence of their presence, and they tend to be woefully overlooked.

Chapter 7

RABBITS
AND CORN
Sinagua Subsistence

According to the Hopi, when Spider Woman first explained their destinies to Man and to Woman, she gave to women the task of keeping the home and storing and preparing the food (Mullett 1987:5), while men were to provide their families with game, weave, and tend the kivas. Certainly, for the Hopi and Zuni these rank as major responsibilities for women and men, although we can not currently demonstrate similar gender roles for the Sinagua.

When Frank Cushing (1920) described Zuni cuisine in the late 1800s, the diet included a wide variety of dishes, some of them quite complex. Corn, the staple, was parched, roasted, boiled, baked, steamed, fried, ground, and made into puddings, dumplings, breads, and mushes. Of particular prominence was a wafer bread (*he'we* in Zuni and *piki* in Hopi) produced by quickly spreading a thin batter over a very hot flat stone, an art that required consummate skill and was passed from mother to daughter. Other widely used indigenous domesticates included beans and squash. Numerous wild plants, such as wild licorice, onion and potato, agave, milkweed, currents, cactus fruits, acorns, pinyon nuts and grass seeds, were collected and provided additional diversity in taste and nutrition.

While there may be similarities between Zuni dishes and those prepared by Sinagua cooks, there are also significant differences. The Spanish introduced peaches, watermelons, and wheat, which were popular domesticates by the 1800s. Likewise, donkeys, chickens, and most notably sheep were brought from the Old World. While donkeys were used more for transport than food, sheep had become a very important subsistence item by the 1800s, although they were supplemented by the traditional game animals and the two native North American domesticated animals, turkeys and dogs. In addition, we know that the wafer bread mentioned above was not being baked until the late 1200s, when the stone griddles required for its manufacture begin to appear at archaeological sites. Thus, an accurate reconstruction of Sinagua diet ultimately rests on the archaeological evidence, although ethnographic parallels can, of course, be illuminating.

Information about prehistoric Sinagua diets comes from several sources. Pollen, preserved vegetal remains, and animal bones provide direct information about the plant and animal species utilized. Agricultural tools, remnants of prehistoric field systems, experimental replications of prehistoric gardens, and modern Pueblo practices enhance our understanding of Sinagua agriculture. The remains of various wild plant species reveal the importance of gathering. Hunting practices can be inferred from hunting equipment, rock art, and the bones of the animals themselves.

Plant Remains

Detailed evidence for dietary practices at Lizard Man Village comes from the analysis of carbonized plant materials. This type of evidence doubtless provides only a partial list of the plant species utilized by the prehistoric Sinagua. Most portions of plants are consumed rather than thrown away. Sometimes the undigested portion of meals can later be recovered, if the archaeologist is lucky enough to discover preserved human fecal remains which can be reconstituted and analyzed. Unfortunately, Lizard Man Village yielded no such treasures.

In most archaeological sites, the plant remains preserved will be those which were carbonized. Because these will be only a small percentage of the total plants used, not all utilized species may be represented. Furthermore, the sample preserved is unlikely to be either random or representative. The way in which a plant is used will strongly affect the probability that it is ultimately carbonized. Frequently, plant parts that are roasted may be burnt in the fire and discarded with the ashes, while those that are boiled or eaten raw are less likely to encounter this fate.

The carbonized remains of plants are collected from archaeological sites using a technique called *flotation*. The basis of this method is quite simple. Excavated dirt is placed in a container of water and agitated briefly. Because the earth is heavy, it sinks to the bottom, while the lighter organic remains float to the top. Sometimes chemicals are added to the water to increase its density, so that somewhat heavier particles will float. Some quite complex machinery is available for flotation and is particularly useful for processing large quantities of dirt, but the basic process can be done with a simple bucket of water and a strainer. After the plant remains are retrieved, they are dried slowly to prevent cracking, sorted, and identified under a microscope. A trained specialist can identify many species on the basis of a variety of often-fragmentary plant parts.

Two paleobotanical specialists have worked on the samples from Lizard Man Village. The best samples from the first three years of excavation were given to Charles Miksicek for analysis. He produced a species list, which includes numerous domesticated species: two races of corn, three types of beans, summer squash, and cotton. Also included on the list were wild plants such as amaranth, pinyon, juniper, wild sunflower, acorn, squaw bush, yucca, and rice grass.

A much more detailed analysis, discussed below, has been attempted by Andrea Hunter, currently at the University of Northern Arizona. Unfortunately, because many of the best samples were in the possession of Miksicek, she had only a few samples to work with: seven flotation samples and five carbon samples from Angell-Padre Phase pithouse contexts (A.D. 1064–1150) and five flotation samples from Elden Phase pueblo contexts (A.D. 1150–1250). These samples, despite their small number, yielded thousands of plant remains and so still allowed for some interesting analysis.

When possible, it is informative to compare the pithouse and pueblo occupations, looking for changes in subsistence strategies. This was done using two indices: relative frequency and presence. Relative frequencies may be calculated as the percentage of a species relative to the total volume of carbon or relative to the total number of a similar type of remains (in other words as a percentage of the total number of seeds, domesticates, rind fragments, and so forth). Presence refers to the percentage of samples containing the species. These comparisons are, however, made tentative by the small sample sizes and by a lack of absolute comparability between the pithouse and pueblo samples, since more of the pithouse samples come from hearths. Despite these caveats, the floral remains yield some fascinating insights into the use of domesticated and wild plants at Lizard Man Village.

Farming Practices

The area the Sinagua farmed around Lizard Man Village is not used for cultivation today. Cultivation is limited both by the paucity of water and by a relatively short growing season. During the occupation of Lizard Man Village, however, the Sinagua, like many Native American groups, grew corn, beans, squash, and a number of other cultigens. This may have been made possible by climatic conditions that were slightly warmer and wetter than today's. As mentioned earlier, plant pollens and the presence of waterfowl and fish bones at sites in the area suggest a slightly more optimal climate for agriculture. By the end of the Lizard Man Village occupation, however, the weather was becoming cooler and drier.

Miksicek has identified at least two races of corn. One is a smaller variety similar to corn cultivated by the modern Pima and Papago tribes of southern Arizona. The second is a larger pueblo flour-type similar to some varieties cultivated by the Hopi today. Sometime between the pithouse (A.D. 1065–1150) and pueblo (A.D. 1150–1250) occupations, the size of the corn kernels and cobs appears to have decreased somewhat. Hunter interprets this as an indication that corn agriculture was decreasingly successful, probably due to the climatic changes referred to earlier. As the climate became drier and cooler, farming would have become more difficult in an already somewhat marginal area.

Both pithouse and pueblo villagers cultivated three types of beans. Two are common varieties of bean (*Phaseolus vulgaris*), one a small navy-type bean and the other a larger kidney-type. The third is a tepary bean (*Phaseolus acutifolius*). Beans have the nutritional advantage of being high in protein and containing an amino acid, lysine, that is absent in corn but necessary in the human diet. The addition of beans greatly improves a diet based on corn. In addition, bean roots harbor nitrogen-fixing bacteria, so they combat soil depletion when planted with other crops or in rotation.

Cucurbitae sp. (squash and pumpkins) and *Lagenaria siceraria* (gourds) were grown in both phases but became more common in the Elden Phase. The only cucurbit species securely identified is *Cucurbitae pepo*, the summer squash species that includes modern zucchini and some pumpkins. The prehistoric squash was probably pumpkin-like, with edible flesh and a fairly hard rind. While the cucurbits are edible, the gourds (*Lagenaria*) are bitter and thus grown for their rinds, which can be used to produce vessels.

Cotton (*Gossypium hirsutim*), while often grown primarily for its fibers, also produces edible seeds. In the early pithouse contexts cotton seeds are rare, but almost half the seeds in flotation samples from later pueblo contexts are from cotton bolls, suggesting a possible increase in use and cultivation of cotton.

Sinagua farming is revealed by tools as well as plant remains. Wooden digging sticks were probably used to plant crops. These were not preserved at Lizard Man Village, since they are of a perishable material, but we know them from historic times and from prehistoric specimens preserved at some dry cave sites in the Southwest. Stone hoes were found at Lizard Man Village, however. These are tabular pieces of basalt flaked to a roughly triangular shape (figure 7.1). The edges of all of the specimens are heavily polished and rounded by abrasion from digging. They were apparently handheld and used to scoop and move the soft cindery soil in gardens. Two complete hoes and four fragmentary ones were discovered in our excavations; however, another archaeologist, Noel Logan, found six complete hoes in a looter's pit at Lizard Man Village several years before we began to work there. He, of course, turned these over to the Museum of Northern Arizona, so that they could later be used for research and become part of the official record for the site.

Hoes are one of the artifact types often associated with one-room structures found scattered throughout the pinyon-juniper. Archaeologists working in the area call these *field houses*. Field houses exhibit lots of individual variability but are generally small—less than 13 m^2 (140 ft^2)—with masonry walls that were less than full height, and would have been topped by a brush superstructure. They tend to lack hearths and have both low artifact diversity and counts. These structures, which may be similar to the field houses used by Zuni and other groups historically (figure 7.2), are very numerous during the Elden Phase, accounting for about one-third of all sites. They are thought to be temporary dwellings located near fields and used during the agricultural season to allow the Sinagua to disperse their agricultural plots, an advantage both where good locations for cultivation are sparse and where localized variability in precipitation may mean the difference between a decent crop and no crop at all.

The perils of agriculture were aptly illustrated to us for two years in a row when we attempted to grow experimental gardens in two areas adjacent to Lizard Man Village. The garden locations were chosen because they seemed likely to have been among those used by the Lizard Man Villagers. One was a south-facing, cinder-covered slope on the opposite side of the ridge that shelters the village. The second was located just to the south of the village in a wash, along which are located several field houses. Both areas had fairly deep soils that should have been useful for trapping moisture.

For seeds we used Hopi short-stapled cotton (*Gossypium hirsutim* var. *punctatum*), Frijol en Seco beans (*Phaseolus vulgaris*), and two Hopi varieties of corn (*Zea mays*), Hopi early sweet corn and Hopi blue corn. Seeds were obtained from Native Seeds/SEARCH, a nonprofit organization dedicated to conserving seeds of traditional crop plants used in the southwestern United States and northwest Mexico, as well as the seeds of their wild relatives.

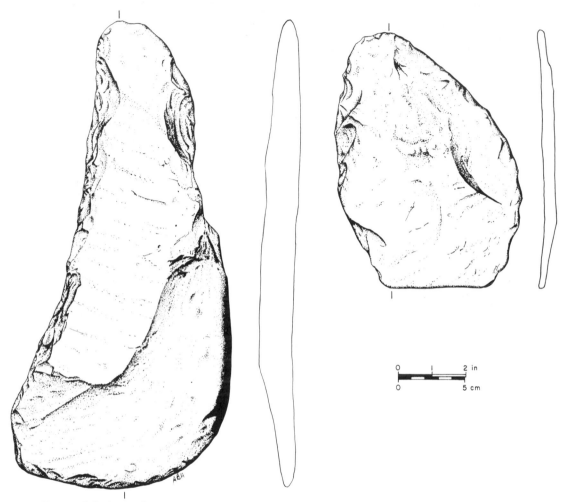

Figure 7.1 *Stone hoes.*

In order to maximize our chances of success, we mimicked Hopi agricultural practices. Hopi do an early planting in mid-April and a later one at the end of May or beginning of June. We planted part of the crop in mid-April and part in mid-May. Bradfield (1971: 5) describes the planting of a Hopi field (figure 7.3).

A Hopi corn field . . . is planted in rows, with some three paces between rows, and three to four paces between the separate "hills" in a row. To plant a "hill," the farmer first pushes the surface layer of sand to one side with his foot; he then goes down on one knee, scrapes a hole about 10 inches deep with his digging stick (commonly, nowadays, a metal tube squeezed at one end to a spud shape), loosens the soil at the bottom for a further

Figure 7.2 *Frank Cushing's drawing of a Zuni farming hut.*

2 to 3 inches with a rotary motion of the stick, and drops the seed—12 to 15 individual kernels—into the hole; finally he pushes back the soil with his hand, first the clay-and-sand loam to fill the hole, then the covering of fine sand on top. This method of planting ensures that the seed itself lies well down into the moist subsoil.

We interspersed the corn, beans, and cotton, planting seeds in clusters some four feet (1.2 meters) apart to maximize the available moisture, put our corn ten inches (25 cm) deep, and even used digging sticks. Instead of a layer of sand on top of the corn our plots had a fine layer of the volcanic ash that blankets the area. We cheated by fencing the plot with four-foot-high wire mesh to help keep out animals, since we did not intend to live in a field house immediately adjacent to the plots.

Neither year produced a crop. Not surprisingly, the limiting factors for us were the same as those frequently discussed for Hopi agriculture: moisture and temperature, complicated by pests. Both the quantity and timing of water was the problem. The first year there was a drought, and the corn died while it still looked like wisps of grass. The second year, although rabbits ate the bean plants, the rains were better and there were a few small ears of corn, but cold weather came too soon for a real harvest.

Part of the problem is that the summer rains generally do not come until early July—too late for maximum effectiveness. Had we watered, our yields would have doubtless been much better. We chose not to, perhaps partly out of laziness, but also because we felt that the paucity of water sources in the region would suggest that the Sinagua were unlikely to have watered their fields very extensively. This may be an unfair assumption, since many Southwestern people carried water to plants as part of their normal agricultural activities.

Another experimental cornfield (Maule 1963), this one planted at Wupatki National Monument thirty years earlier, had similar results. Only the row of plants that were watered produced a crop. It also demonstrated the usefulness of a cinder layer for maintaining soil moisture, thus enhancing the chances of a crop's success. Maule planted four rows of Hopi corn, relying on rainfall for moisture. One row had no cinder cover, one had a one-inch cinder cover, and the other two had two- and three-inch cinder coverings. The seeds from the row covered by one inch of cinder had the best germination and growth rates. This

Figure 7.3 *Hopi cornfield.*

lends credence to the theory that one reason for the fairly intensive occupation of the pinyon-juniper regions near Sunset Crater after its eruption may have been increased agricultural potential due to the advantageous properties of a cinder cover.

    Clearly, the Sinagua were much better farmers than we. Both years we attempted to farm we would probably either have starved or had to use primarily wild foods to get us through the winter. Despite the skeletal evidence that shows the Lizard Man Villagers sometimes knew hungry times, they did manage to occupy the village for about two hundred years. They certainly had established a subsistence strategy that worked at least fairly well.

Historic accounts indicate that farming was not easy for recent Puebloan peoples either. Aridity is the most obvious problem, but rodents, birds and insect pests, sandstorms, and unseasonable frosts can also destroy crops. Don Talayesva, a Hopi born at Oraibi in 1890, describes some of his agricultural problems:

> With plenty of rain and no wind, worms, or rats to destroy our crops, and no weeds to choke them, we would never need to work so hard. But whenever friendly clouds gathered overhead, hostile winds scattered them. The men looked tired and worried and passed each other on the road without comment, each knowing what was in the other's mind—discouragement and a wish for rain. I probably made twenty-five trips to my cornfield to replant, chop weeds, poison rats, set traps for rabbits and spray my crops with a mixture of powdered rabbit intestines, dried roots, dog dung, and water. It took so much strength in herding and field work that I had to cut down on lovemaking from every other night to only once a week. (Talayesva 1942:231)

Scarecrows, such as those recorded at Zuni by Cushing, may have helped discourage some pests. Cushing ([1884]1920:182–83) describes the preparation of a Zuni field (figure 7.4):

> Now comes the time when young Zuni and his elder brother may indulge in fanciful creations which would astound the most talented scarecrow makers of New England. The glossy, large, Southwestern crow or raven is abroad. He sits on every rock, soas through every cloud-shadow, laughs and cackles in every corn arroyo at safe, nevertheless impertinent, distances from the busy planter. He as much as says to his companions, in the language of Zuni crow lore: "Ah! You just wait until those little green

Figure 7.4 *Frank Cushing's drawing of scarecrows in a Zuni cornfield.*

spikes come up! They grow solely for our benefit, that we may have signs whereby to find the good things those long-legged fearful fellows are hiding so deep in the sand. Why that's what our heavy noses are provided for!" Alas, poor birds! Have they forgotten last season? What a shock is in store for them! What disappointment shall soon be attested by the most discordant kaw-croaks of anguish!

The old man is busy setting up cedar poles, at intervals of a few rods, all over the field. Not knowing what these poles were for, you would think an eastern bean-patch or hop-field had been transferred to Zuniland. But if you carefully look, you will see that each pole is furnished at the top with a bunch of its own or some other prickly leaves, so that the crows may not light on it. Moreover, the busy planter is now stringing from one pole to another, cords of split yucca, leaves which, but for their knottiness, would remind you of the telegraph wire of New York City, so thick they are. A sort of network is thus formed all over the field. To make this more imposing, tattered rags, pieces of dog and coyote skins, old shoulder-blades strung two or three together, streamers of moss, in fact streamers of every conceivable thing which has the property of swaying in the wind, are thickly attached to these numerous cords, making them appear much as I fancy a clothes-line would, left by a hurricane.

The necessity of such intensive attention to crops is probably one of the reasons that it was desirable for Sinagua to have temporary quarters located near their fields.

Gathering Wild Plants

Cultivated foods were augmented by gathering a wide variety of wild resources. The unreliability of agriculture in the face of both chronic water shortages and pest infestations doubtless made the existence of alternative food sources critical. A knowledge of plant use was probably passed from generation to generation as it was in the historic Pueblos. Hopi Don Talayesva recalls:

> It was hard to learn what plants we could eat. Some of them were good for food and others for medicine, but still others were good for nothing save to make people sick or crazy. The loco weed would make even a horse crazy. I tried to remember the use of all the plants under my grandfather's instruction. (Talayesva 1942:54)

We know from ethnographic sources that seeds, fruits, leaves, and tubers were all utilized, but seeds preserve best, so plants whose seeds were the focus of interest will be over-represented. Some species, including common purslane (*Portulaca oleracea*), bugseed (*Corispermum hyssopifolium*), pigweed (*Amaranthus spp.*), goosefoot (*Chenopodium spp.*), and sunflower (*Helianthus*), are relatively abundant and frequent in the flotation samples from both the Angell and Elden Phases. All of these had seeds that could be made into bread or mush but had additional possible uses as well. For example, the Hopi boiled sunflower seeds to produce a red dye. They used the flowers for ceremonial decorations and ground them to produce a face powder. Purslane and goosefoot were cooked and eaten as greens.

Amaranth, a weedy plant with numerous small starchy seeds, may have been cultivated rather than gathered wild. On the basis of pollens associated with a system of cinder ridges and mounds some twenty kilometers (twelve miles) east of Sunset Crater, Berlin, Salas, and Geib (1990) suggest that these agricultural features were constructed for the cultivation of *Amaranthus* and or *Chenopodium*. Miksicek thinks that some of the Amaranth seeds recovered from Lizard Man Village resemble cultivated Hopi red-dye amaranth in both size and morphology. Andrea Hunter (1994), however, argues that the quantity of seeds recovered from excavations is well within the potential for easy collection from wild stands and would be very low for a cultivated crop of such prolific seed producers.

According to Hunter, there is also a possibility that the pithouse dwellers of Lizard Man Village cultivated bugseed (*Corispermum hyssopifolium*). Seeds found in feces from Beaucoup Alcove, an Archaic hunter-gatherer site in Utah, prove that bugseed was sometimes eaten. At Lizard Man Village bugseed was found in all but one of the pithouse occupation flotation samples. A total of 3,780 seeds were recovered, representing over 90 percent of the seeds recovered for this time period. Since most of them (3,727 of the 3,780) were from a single hearth, this figure is probably less significant than it seems at first glance. A single mishap, the spill from a vessel in which a batch of seeds was being roasted, could well account for the abundance of seeds from this species. The high frequency and presence of seeds suggests to Hunter that the pithouse residents of the Lizard Man Village may have been cultivating bugseed. If they were, by the Elden Phase pueblo occupation of the village they had ceased to do so. By this time, bugseed only represents about 3 percent of the recovered seeds and is found in only 60 percent of the samples.

Water smartweed (*Polygonium amphibium*), four-wing saltbush (*Atriplex canescens*), peppergrass (*Lepidium spp.*), and dropseed (*Sporo cryptandrus*) are additional sources of seeds. Manzanita (*Arctostaphylos pringlei*), elderberry (*Sambucus spp.*), juniper (*Juniperus monosperma, deppeana, scopulorum,* and *osteosperma*), nightshade (*Solanum*), prickly pear (*Opuntia polyacantha*), and pincushion cactus (*Coryphantha vivipara*) provided fruits and berries.

Nuts, particularly the abundant pinyon nuts (*Pinus edulis*), were an important food source for many historic and prehistoric Native American groups. Today pinyon trees are common around the site, so it is not surprising that they were a significant part of Sinagua diets. While pine nuts were the staple nut whose use appears to have increased through time, Arizona Black Walnut (*Juglens major*) is also found, and there were three fragments of acorn (*Quercus gambeli*) found in pithouse flotation samples.

Figure 7.5 *Two young women grinding corn using manos and metates.*

Processing and Storage of Plant Foods

Artifacts provide some insights into the processing of both wild and cultivated plants. Because of the importance of corn in the historic Puebloan diet, traditionally women had to spend many hours a day grinding corn into meal (figure 7.5). The task was not a minor one. An average Hopi family is estimated to have used about a quart of meal per day (Bartlett 1933), and more, of course, during ceremonial occasions when entertaining. A girl's dowry consisted of ground corn, prepared by her and her family in the three to six months preceding the marriage. Corn generally was ground three times to produce successively finer meals. Because of the large amounts of time this required, women often ground corn together, even having gatherings analogous to quilting bees.

The tools for corn grinding are the metate and mano. The *metate* is a large, flat or trough-shaped stone on which the corn to be ground is placed (figure 7.6), and the *mano* is the handstone used to grind the corn on the metate (figure 7.7). While today manos and metates are primarily corn-grinding tools, they are also used to grind other plants, pigments, sherds to be used as pottery

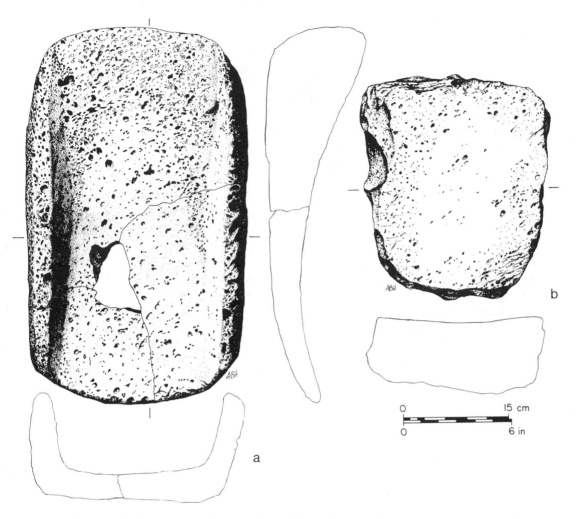

Figure 7.6 *Metates from Lizard Man Village: (a) trough metate, (b) grinding slab.*

temper, and clay. When grinding corn, the Hopi place their metates in sand-stone or wooden grinding bins that serve to catch and contain the ground meal. The metate is slanted at about 30 degrees to produce a comfortable grinding angle and situated about 45 cm (1.5 feet) from a wall to allow the woman to brace her feet while grinding (Bartlett 1933). Ethnographically, most households have at least three metates: one coarse, one medium and one fine grained. The mano used with a metate often corresponds to it in tex-ture. This tool kit allows a woman to begin processing corn on the coarse metate, then move on to the medium, and finally finish on the fine, producing a very fine cornmeal flour. Given the importance of metates and manos to a Hopi woman's daily work and to Hopi subsistence, it is not surprising that ritual accompanies the procurement of metates. Each year at the end of February or beginning of March, women journey to traditional source areas to quarry the sandstone for their metates, carrying it home on their backs.

At Lizard Man Village we discovered eleven whole metates, eighty-seven metate fragments, and a total of two hundred manos and mano pieces. The metates are primarily of basalt, probably because there is a lot of suitable basalt near the village, and basalt provides a good grinding surface. Two major types of metates can be identified. While twenty-one of the fragments were too incomplete to classify, a total of fifty-five trough metates and twenty-two grinding slabs were identified.

Trough metates (figure 7.6a) are distinguished by a distinct grinding-groove the width of the mano. Grinding on these proceeded with a repetitive, back-and-forth motion. The high sides of the trough metate kept the ground materials somewhat contained, and the results of the grinding were probably pushed off one end into a bowl or basket. By the Pueblo IV period (A.D. 1350–1500), the mealing bins and slab metates (figure 7.6b) used by historic Zuni and Hopi had pretty much replaced trough metates. A flat or "slab" metate used with a long mano stretching across its entire width was placed in a rectangular sandstone bin where the ground meal accumulated and was later collected. Theoretically, the use of the longer mano means an increase in efficiency and would have decreased the number of hours Pueblo women had to spend grinding corn. No mealing bins were found at Lizard Man Village, nor were any metates found in rows graded by coarseness, a pattern that may associated with the production of the fine flour needed to make piki and, thus, not a part of the Sinagua cooking regime. Most of metates found had been discarded into trash deposits or built into room walls after discard. As described previously, however, Room 2/3 had two complete metates on the roof, indicating that, as in historic times, roofs were important work areas. These two metates are illustrated in figure 7.6. The trough metate is fairly coarse-grained basalt, while the slab metate is of fine-grained basalt, perhaps indicating that the Sinagua of Lizard Man Village also ground their corn first on a coarse metate, then sometimes on a finer one to achieve the desired consistency.

For analysis I divided the manos into categories based on overall size and shape: (1) large convex, (2) large rectangular, (3) small rectangular, (4) large ovoid, (5) small ovoid, (6) large amorphous, and (7) small amorphous (figure 7.7a-g). Large, convex manos are rectangular in shape with convex transverse grinding surfaces, formed by use in a trough metate. Because I was interested in knowing what the manos had been used to grind, I examined all the whole manos under a microscope, looking for identifiable patterns of usewear. Lee Fratt, who has worked with ground stone from the pre-Hopi Homolovi sites, helped me to learn the technique and provided me with comparative specimens and color photomicrographs of a variety of wear types. At the moment, wear on basalt has not been as well studied as that on sandstone, making it impossible to give much precision to most wear identifications.

Both convex and large rectangular manos were apparently used to grind grains such as corn or amaranth, as were about half the small rectangular manos. The remaining small rectangular manos were used to grind a variety

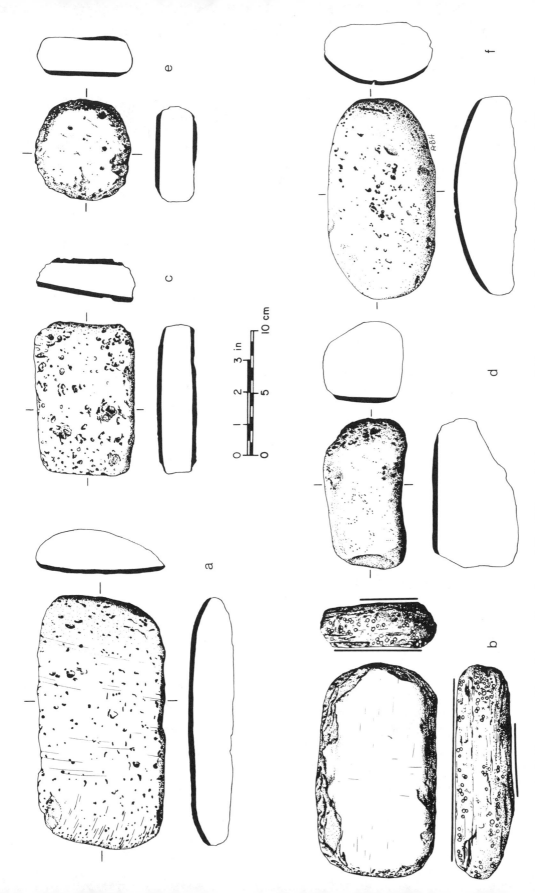

Figure 7.7 Manos and handstones from Lizard Man Village: (a) large convex, (b) large rectangular, (c) small rectangular, (d) small ovoid, (e) small amorphous, and (f) large ovoid.

of substances which I cannot identify, but which may have included soft plant parts, nuts, and pottery sherds. None of the amorphous manos were used to grind corn or were even used with any kind of metate. Thus, in archaeological parlance they are, strictly speaking, called *handstones* rather than manos. Handstones were used for tasks such as smoothing plastered walls, polishing floors, and processing hides. Like the amorphous manos, some of the ovoid manos are actually more accurately termed handstones. Others have been used with a metate to grind a variety of substances, both hard and soft. Although the time investment in grinding may not have been as great for the Sinagua as it was for the Hopi, the data from the Lizard Man Village manos shows a fairly large commitment to the grinding of corn or amaranth.

It would have been of great benefit for the Sinagua to have stored any agricultural surpluses that occurred during good years to provide a buffer against poor ones. Several of the pueblo rooms (2/3, 9, and 8) and one pithouse (Room 13/17) have associated storage pits. We also discovered one very large storage pit just to the north of the village in the area designated "Room" 24. When we discovered them, none of the pits still contained the remains of stored foods. All had been abandoned and used as garbage dumps. Ceramic vessels, basketry, and cloth and skin bags were also undoubtedly used for some types of storage. Large, thick jars which would have been hard to move and may well represent storage vessels that would have provided a storage space for grains that was secure from rodent pests. They probably doubled as water jars, conserving this valuable resource against times of drought. Despite some evidence for storage facilities, there is no evidence that the Lizard Man Villagers stored vast quantities of foodstuffs from year to year. Judging by their health, they may not always have had much in reserve.

Hunting

Hunting supplemented wild and domesticated plant foods and at times may have provided a significant portion of the diet. During historic Hopi times,

> We liked meat and ate almost any kind that we could get. The old people showed us how to make deadfalls to catch kangaroo rats, prairie dogs, porcupines, badgers, chipmunks, squirrels, and turtle doves. The men used heavy rock deadfalls for trapping coyotes, foxes, wildcats, and other large animals. Sometimes they went long distances to hunt bear and deer. Whenever they killed a large wild animal, they brought the carcass home, covered it with a wedding robe, smoked mountain tobacco before its nostrils, and asked for forgiveness. They also prayed to the godmother of wild animals to send us more game. They formed large parties on foot or horseback and hunted rabbits with dogs, clubs, and curved throwing sticks. We little boys made snares of horsehair to catch birds. I learned to catch bluebirds with a hair from a horse's tail set as a snare on the upper stem of a sunflower stalk, with a worm for bait. We also practiced at shooting at birds and small animals with bow and arrows. But we were told never to kill any creature that we did not intend to eat. (Talayesva 1942:54, 55)

We do not know whether the Sinagua, like the Hopi, performed rituals when they killed an animal, although the likelihood seems great. Similarly, like most groups that rely, in part, on hunting and gathering, it is probable that the Sinagua did not make a practice of killing animals that they did not intend to utilize. We can surmise that much of the Sinagua hunting was probably done with traps, but none of these survive at Lizard Man Village. Bows and arrows were also important hunting tools, as is demonstrated by the large number of whole and broken arrowheads—over 250 in all. None of the perishable portions of the bows or arrows survive at Lizard Man Village, but some have been recovered from dry contexts elsewhere in Sinagua territory.

Animal bones preserve better than plant remains. Their recovery requires only careful excavation and screening. An examination of these faunal materials is possible using modern, well-identified bones to compare with the ancient bones. My husband and collaborator, John Whittaker, has for years been in the process of obtaining comparative specimens. Frankly, some of the aromas associated with this occupation have not always made him popular around the house or in the Anthropology Department at Grinnell. Basically, the process entails collecting road kills (with all the appropriate permits, of course), cleaning the bones well, then labeling and storing them for future reference.

The collection stage has its problems, as when John collected a road kill the first day of a four-day field trip with students. By the end of the trip the students had become so desperate that their creative energies erupted in the epic ballad, "I Love It Because It's Dead," sung to the tune of the old Sesame Street favorite, Oscar's theme song, "I Love It Because It's Trash."

It is preparing the bones, however, that has caused the most strained relationships. Our backyard frequently harbors trash cans concealing rotting carcasses, and dead animals are staked out on our archaeological sites for the bugs to devour. Nevertheless, tensions rose when, after a stone-tool sheep butchering in our backyard (for a study on butchering marks being done by one of our friends, whose wife was smart enough not to allow him to conduct his experiments at home), John brought a partially rotted sheep skull into the house and proceeded to boil it in one of my best pans. The house reeked for days after, despite our best efforts to dispel the stench.

Regardless of the potential difficulties of obtaining a comparative faunal collection, animal bones are a valuable source of information about prehistoric diet. At Lizard Man Village we found the remains of over thirty different species of animals. Because one individual animal may be represented by anything from a single bone to an entire skeleton, a raw count of bones tells only part of the story. The minimum number of individuals represented in a faunal assemblage is estimated by the most common unique bone for each species. Thus, if there are four right femurs, two left femurs, six ribs and one right clavicle, the minimum number estimate will be four.

Rabbit, a common animal in the pinyon-juniper zone as well as a crop pest in cultivated areas, was probably the most frequently consumed meat. Both jackrabbit and cottontail were hunted. We know that historically Pueblo groups frequently captured rabbits communally, using nets and throwing sticks. The presence of rabbits of all ages in the Lizard Man Village faunal remains supports the notion that this might have been one of the ways that Sinagua hunted rabbits. We can tell that rabbits were often prepared by roasting, because about one-third of the rabbit tibiae (lower leg bones) were snapped off at the foot and burned in this region. This pattern would occur if the feet had been removed and the animal cooked over an open fire with the broken bone protruding from the fleshy leg. Interestingly, this is a less nutritious means of preparation than stewing.

Deer, fairly numerous in the Flagstaff area today, were also hunted, as were antelope. While deer and antelope remains are much less common than rabbit (160 total bones and a minimum of 33 individuals versus 2021 bones representing a minimum of 152 individuals), the amount of meat on a single deer carcass is so much greater than that on a rabbit that the caloric disparity may not be as great as the bone frequencies would initially suggest.

With the possible exception of turkey, which was only represented by seven bones and may have been hunted wild, dogs were the only domesticated animals at Lizard Man Village. Some dog bones are very difficult to distinguish from coyote. However, the teeth on one mandible are very crowded, which is one indication of domestication, and other teeth found singly are very worn, suggesting old domestic animals. It is not unlikely that much of the carnivore gnawing observed on other faunal remains is due to scavenging by domestic dogs. Dogs are a potential food source as well as hunters, scavengers, and companions. About 19 percent of the canid bones are burned, which may indicate that dogs were eaten (although the sample size is small, making this conclusion tentative).

Other mammals found at Lizard Man Village include fox, coyote, weasel, badger, skunk, squirrel, prairie dog, chipmunk, and gopher. These animals may have been eaten, hunted primarily for their pelts, or simply have been intrusive. The rodents present a particularly interesting problem for archaeologists. We know that historically pueblo groups ate rodents. Southwestern wood rats are the main ingredient of a dish described by Cushing:

> The rats were choked en route to our camp, and, perhaps a little too soon for their own comfort, thrown into a bed of embers, where, after roasting a few moments, they bloated up into oblong balls, became divested of their tails, legs, ears, whiskers, and all other irregularities, and when pulled from the fire, looked like roasted potatoes overdone. They were "shucked" in a twinkling—came out clean and white except for a greenish tendency of what were once their undersides—meat, bones, visceral contents, and all, and stirred into about a pint of salt and water. Thus concocted was the "rat-brine:" green in color, semi-fluid, and meaty in taste—for they made me eat some of it, I do *not* regret to say), and very aromatic in flavor, a quality which the rats derive from the trees in which they live and on the berries and leaves of which they feed. (Cushing 1920:599–600)

Nevertheless, many of the species found in the faunal remains live and, in fact, burrow on the site today. One season a gopher simultaneously amused and annoyed us by establishing residence immediately adjacent to one of the excavation units and popping out of tunnels in the walls of the trenches. This creates the suspicion that many of the bones may be intrusive, not associated with prehistoric human occupations at all. Sometimes it is easy to see that rodent bones are intrusive. We have found entire skeletons buried in the rodent burrow where the creature died. These can easily be sorted from the analysis. Another possible index of intrusiveness is the percentage of burnt bone. Only about 2 percent of the gopher bone is burnt, corroborating our hypothesis that much of the gopher bone may be intrusive. This 2 percent contrasts with the 10 to 15 percent burned bone for rabbits, deer, and antelope, all species which are likely to have been eaten. Prairie dogs and rock squirrels—both larger rodent species that are likely to be food sources but also are clearly resident on the site—show intermediate percentages of burning, about 7 percent.

Bird remains from quail, killdeer, morning dove, turkey, jay, owl, raven, crow, bluebird, and meadowlark as well as several unidentified species represent use for both food and feathers. All of the birds found are fairly common to the area today with the exception of the scaled quail, which has been found at other Sinagua sites in the area but had disappeared by the time Europeans arrived. It is a grassland species, so its presence probably is an indication of a less wooded environment during the occupation of Lizard Man Village.

Turkey and quail are the most common birds. No bird species is very well represented, perhaps because bird bones are small and are thus preserved and recovered less frequently and identified less reliably than bones from larger species. It seems likely that both the turkey and quail were hunted or trapped and eaten. Although it is possible that the turkeys were raised in the village, there is no concrete evidence for this, and the relative scarcity of turkey bones suggests otherwise. Other species may have been obtained for their feathers or for various types of ritual use. This seems particularly likely for species if large parts of a single individual are found together. The wing of a great horned owl found in Room 3, for instance, could have been a fan or part of a dance costume. Most of the bones of a meadowlark were found in the same room. If the bird had been eaten, the bones would probably have been scattered, so it was most likely plucked or skinned and the whole carcass discarded.

Using Isotopes to Obtain Information about Diet

Whenever humans ingest food, they incorporate the carbons from the foods they eat into their bones and teeth. Because categories of plants and animals have characteristic percentages of different carbon isotopes, the stable carbon isotope ratios of human bones will reflect dietary practices. For example, arid-climate semitropical grasses such as corn, amaranth and the chenopods contain high proportions of the ^{13}C isotope relative to the ^{12}C isotope and are termed C4 plants. The nitrogen isotopes ^{15}N and ^{14}N are also differentially concentrated as they enter the diet in proteins. The proportion of ^{15}N tends to increase as an individual eats more meat. Forensic pathologists Marc Krouse and Gill King submitted fifteen bone specimens from Elden Pueblo and Lizard Man Village for stable isotope analysis. They interpreted the results as demonstrating that cultigens (or other C4 plants) accounted for 50–70 percent of the human diet; animals eating C4 plants made up 10–15 percent of the diet; and C3 plants (most plants) accounted for the remainder. These percentages look similar to those of the agricultural Basketmaker and Pueblo populations on Cedar Mesa in the four-corners area and Mississippian corn agriculturalists in the Midwest. No differences in isotope proportions were observed between Lizard Man Village and the larger site of Elden Pueblo. This suggests, albeit on the basis of a very small sample, a fairly homogeneous subsistence pattern among Sinagua sites. The nitrogen isotope data did indicate that males may have eaten more meat than females, but again the sample size is very small and the data should not be overinterpreted.

Summary

The Sinagua subsistence pattern can best be described as a diversified adaptation to an environment marginal for cultivation. Agriculture provided storable crops, such as corn and beans, but was at the mercy of climatic conditions. By scattering field locations and locating secondary, temporary residences nearby, these conditions could be somewhat buffered. Hopefully, if the crops in one locale failed, those in another area would succeed. The use of a variety of wild plants and animals provided a further bit of insurance against starvation. Some wild crops, such as amaranth and pinyon, can provide reasonable quantities of storable food. Clearly, the Sinagua had considerable expertise in the maximal use of their environment. Nevertheless, as the analysis of Sinagua health in the previous chapter demonstrated, Sinagua subsistence was probably quite fragile.

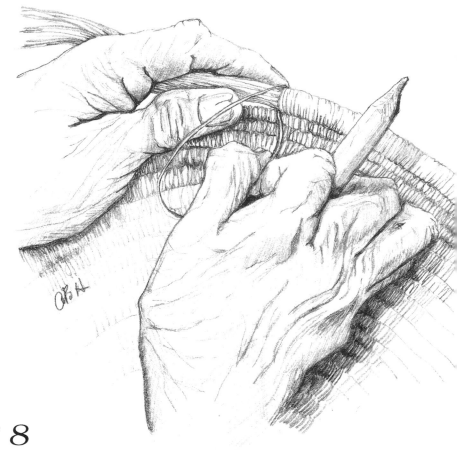

Chapter 8

THE ARTISANS OF LIZARD MAN VILLAGE

Knowledge about crafts was passed from generation to generation. In addition, creative individuals periodically made innovations that were adopted, or ideas were borrowed from neighboring groups. Thus, Sinagua technology shows continuity through time but cannot, by any stretch of the imagination, be described as stagnant. We know something about the actual processes for manufacture through analyses of the tools and the waste products of production, as well as the artifacts themselves. Historically and today Native Americans in the region still produce some, but not all, of the items found in prehistoric sites. Many of the crafts have also been replicated by archaeologists, professional artists, or hobbyists. For example, in addition to Pueblo artisans who produce ceramics derived from, but not identical to, prehistoric types, several potters specialize in replicas of prehistoric ceramics. Stone tools are also replicated for profit, and there is a growing community of amateur flintknappers as well, complete with newsletters, knapping meets, t-shirts, and bumper stickers ("When Atlatls Are Outlawed Only Outlaws Will Have Atlatls" and "Grind It, Bind It, Stick It In A Mammoth"). This chapter describes but a few of the many manufacturing activities that would have occurred in a Sinagua community such as Lizard Man Village.

Pottery

Sinagua ceramics, called Alameda Brown Wares by archaeologists, are primarily reddish brown. Most are plain wares, undecorated or enhanced only by an overall slip of reddish-brown clay. Often they are highly polished, and the bowls have shiny, black interiors. Despite being unpainted, Sinagua pots are often quite well-made and extremely beautiful (figure 8.1).

Ceramic Manufacturing Techniques

Experimentation combined with ethnographic data has informed us of the basic processes of Sinagua ceramic manufacture. The first steps are the collection and preparation of the clay. The choice of clay will affect the final color of the vessel. The clay may be prepared by picking out large impurities, sifting, grinding, aging, and kneading. Nonplastic inclusions or temper are routinely mixed with manufacturing clays. This opens up the texture of the clay and makes it dry more evenly, which decreases cracking. The post-eruptive Sinagua used primarily volcanic cinders and tuff (consolidated volcanic ash)

Figure 8.1 *An example of a Sinagua bowl. The interior is smudged and burnished and the exterior is burnished.*

as temper. The pottery tempered with cinders is called Sunset Brown or, if covered on the exterior with a slip of reddish clay dissolved in water, Sunset Red, while that tempered with tuff is called Angell Brown.

Next the vessel was formed. The Sinagua characteristically used a paddle-and-anvil technique. After a base had been formed using slabs and coils of clay, a stone anvil (figure 8.2a) was held inside the vessel, and the exterior was slapped with a wooden paddle to thin and shape the pot (figure 8.2b). Sometimes the use of the paddle and anvil can still be discerned by the presence of circular anvil indentations on the interior of a pot. Other vessels were smoothed with a sherd scraper (a more complete description appears later in this chapter) or a basalt cylinder. The smoothing marks are also still visible on the interiors of some pots, particularly on jar necks, where the paddle-and-anvil technique may have been used less often.

An alternative to paddle and anvil is coiling. Like the Hopi today, the Kayenta and Winslow, from whom the Sinagua obtained some pottery (see the section on exchange in the following chapter), differ from the Sinagua in favoring coiled pottery, which is built with a series of clay "snakes" and then smoothed and scraped to thin (figure 8.3). However, some Sinagua vessels are also made using a coiling technique, and some of these are *corrugated*. On corrugated vessels the original coils are smoothed on the inside to provide a stable, watertight vessel but are pinched, flattened or smeared on the outside of the vessel to produce a decorated surface. The Sinagua corrugated vessels are made of a reddish brown clay that is then pinched or impressed with the fingers (figure 8.4a,b). Not surprisingly, given their more extensive use of coiling, the Kayenta and Winslow made many more corrugated vessels than the Sinagua. A fair number of these, particularly the Tusayan Grey Wares of the Kayenta, made their way to the Sinagua area as trade goods.

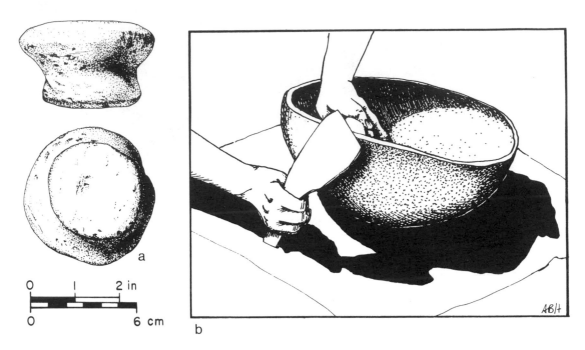

0   1   2 in

0   6 cm

a

b

Figure 8.2 *(a) Stone pottery anvil found at Lizard Man Village. (b) The use of a paddle and stone anvil.*

After the vessels were shaped and partially or fully dried, the exteriors of jars and both the interiors and exteriors of bowls were often *burnished* into a shiny polish by rubbing the surface with a smooth rock, termed a polishing pebble. Pots were fired in an open fire rather than a closed kiln, probably using wood for fuel. Today sheep dung is used, but, since the prehistoric pueblos lacked domestic animals with the exception of dogs and turkeys, dung would not have been as abundant. By allowing the exterior of vessels plenty of oxygen during the firing process, the Sinagua potters produced a reddish brown exterior. Interiors are usually a starkly contrasting black. These interiors were produced by inverting the vessels during firing to deny the interiors access to an oxygen supply, a process called *smudging*.

Smudging, burnishing, and clay slips provide the decoration for most Sinagua vessels. As mentioned previously, a few more are corrugated. Most of the painted ceramics found on Sinagua sites are trade wares, originally made by the Kayenta and Winslow. Only rarely are Sinagua ceramics painted as well as slipped (figure 8.4b and c). Coconino Red-on-buff is a particularly interesting example of a local painted type. Colton associated these with the red-on-buff pottery made by the Hohokam and suggested that they were an indication of Hohokam immigration. However, some archaeologists feel the designs actually look more similar to contemporary Kayenta and Winslow

Figure 8.3 *Hopi woman making coiled pottery ca. 1890–1900.* ▶

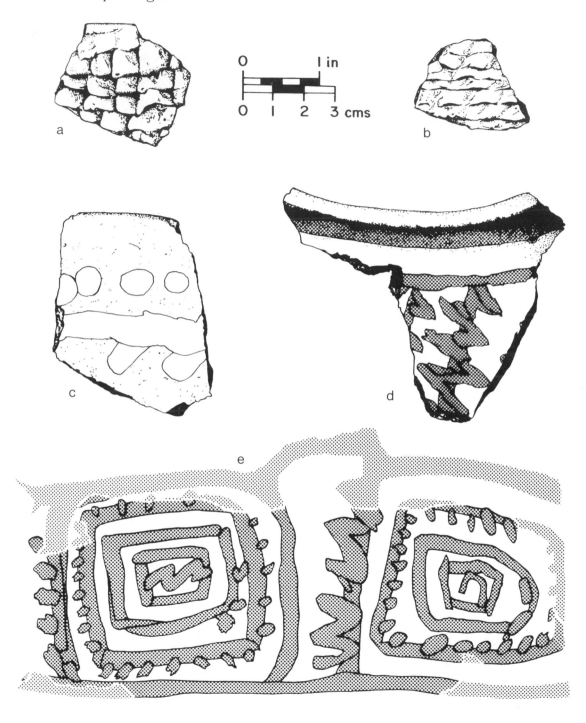

Figure 8.4 *Sinagua Pottery Types: (a) Elden Corrugated, (b) Sunset Corrugated, (c) Sunset White-on-red, (d-e) Coconino Red-on-buff.*

patterns than to those made by the Hohokam. A reasonable view, consistent with the evidence, is that they are a local reflection and adaptation of styles from both the Pueblos of the four-corners area and the Hohokam.

The tools and manufacturing debris the Lizard Man Villagers left behind show us that they made at least some of their own ceramics. Stone anvils, sherd scrapers, basalt cylinders, and polishing pebbles provide the basic tool kit for ceramic manufacture. Manos and metates may also have been used to grind clays and pigments. All of these are found at Lizard Man Village. Hunks of clay that have been tempered with cinders but not yet shaped into pottery, and cinder-tempered but unfired pottery sherds demonstrate the early phases of ceramic manufacture. In addition, a few of the sherds at Lizard Man Village show distinct manufacturing errors. All of the readily identifiable problems are the result of overfiring. Sherds are warped, crazed, and even show signs of vitrification (figure 8.5). Some of the vessels were probably still usable, but others may not have been, making it less likely that they were traded than that they were used at home or even simply discarded immediately after firing.

Today it is Pueblo women who manufacture the pottery, but, as with room construction, it is not now possible to be certain who the ceramic artisans were among the Sinagua. The cross-cultural study by Murdock and Provost mentioned earlier does not show a clear tendency for either gender to dominate in ceramic manufacture. Furthermore, in many societies the situation is complex, with men doing some of the production tasks and women doing others. Thus, while Southwesternists have usually assumed that ceramic manufacture was the realm of women because that was the case historically, the assertion should be accepted with caution.

Ceramic Repair, Reuse, and Recycling

The large quantities of pottery sherds on the surface of Lizard Man Village give mute testimony to the frequency with which pots were broken. Sometimes damaged vessels were simply discarded; other times they were repaired, reused, or recycled. Cracked ceramics were repaired by drilling paired holes on either side of the crack, then lacing cord through the holes to bind the crack together. Resin was sometimes then applied to seal the fissure and make the vessel waterproof again. At Lizard Man Village, we discovered two whole vessels with paired drill holes positioned along cracks (figure 8.6) and an additional 104 sherds with drill holes. An analysis of the drilled sherds shows that the villagers repaired imported pottery, particularly painted types, more frequently than locally-made wares. While only about 10 percent of the total sherds are from imports, about 42 percent of the sherds with repair holes are imported. The difference is caused exclusively by the painted imports. Plain imported wares such as Tusayan Corrugated or Deadmans Gray are repaired in about the same frequency as the local plain wares. The differential repair rates support our expectation that nonlocal painted wares were the more valued ceramic types.

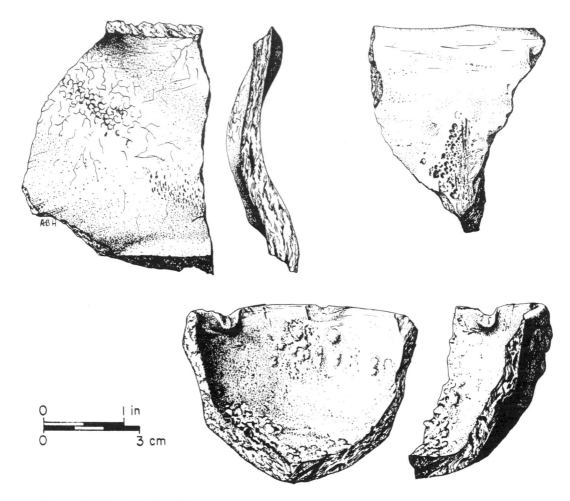

Figure 8.5 *Overfired and vitrified sherds showing warping, crazing, and bubbling.*

Broken pottery was also sometimes modified to produce new tools or ornaments. There are a variety of shapes, most of them fairly uncommon. We are not certain about the function of many of them, although some were probably game pieces and others are drilled to produce pendants. The most common types of recycled sherds are sherd disks, pottery fragments that have been ground into a circular shape (figure 8.7a-b). We found over 250 sherd disks at Lizard Man Village. Many of the disks are centrally drilled. Drilled sherd disks are simply and rapidly produced. First a suitable sherd is selected—large and with little curvature. Here also the Sinagua tended to choose imports over local wares, perhaps because of the desire to use sherds that were decorated. About 38 percent of the sherd disks from Lizard Man Village were produced on imported sherds, a figure consistent with the differential repair of nonlocal vessels.

Figure 8.6 *Vessel showing repair holes positioned along crack.*

First the sherd is roughly chipped into shape, then ground to finish. Hunks of sandstone can be used for this and other abrading tasks, and the site is littered with many scraps of sandstone that have been used as abraders. The central hole can be drilled using a stone drill, either worked by hand or rotated using a bowdrill (figure 8.8). Since it is difficult to make a perforation through the entire thickness of the sherd in one drilling operation, most of the drilled disks have been drilled biconically, first working from one side then completing the hole by turning the sherd over and drilling from the reverse. Production is easy. Even as a novice at this type of activity, it took me less than fifteen minutes to make a drilled sherd disk.

Undrilled sherd disks of various sizes may have been used as bases for the manufacture of pots, as potcovers or plates, or as gaming pieces. Games and gambling were common among Native Americans. Don Talayesva, the Hopi quoted earlier in the chapter on subsistence practices, recounted gambling with Navajo. At Lizard Man Village one man between forty and fifty years old was buried with two worn bone disks, probably once contained in a long-disintegrated pouch, under his left hip. These are interpreted as gaming pieces, perhaps used in some type of wagering activity, as are small shaped sherds (figure 8.7d–e) showing no signs of wear from tool use and often seemingly too small for most other uses.

The most common interpretation of drilled sherd disks is that they acted as flywheels on spindle whorls (discussed in more detail in the section on spinning below). It seems likely that they were used for a variety of functions including, but probably not limited to, flywheels for drills or spindles, buttons, and in games. An intriguing find was discovered at a site called Medicine Cave. A knotted buckskin thong about 8 cm (3 in.) long was discovered strung through the hole of a drilled sherd disk, then knotted again on the other side. The exact use is uncertain. Perhaps it was twirled as a game. At present the use of the drilled disks is somewhat ambiguous. Further experimentation with sherd

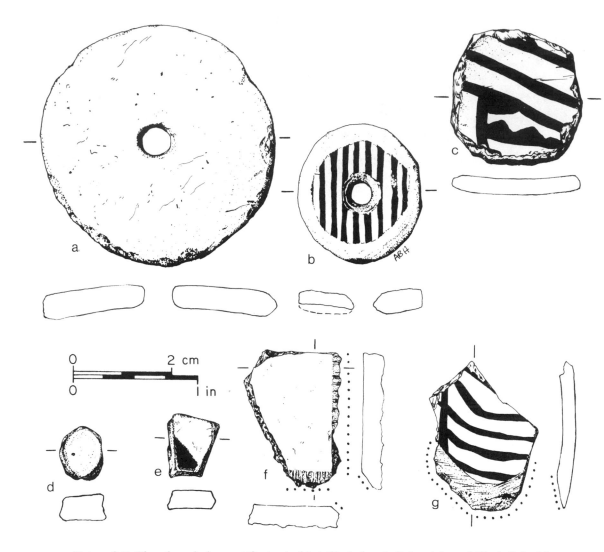

Figure 8.7 *Sherd and clay artifacts: (a-b) drilled sherd disks, (c) undrilled disk, (d-e) gaming pieces, (f) sherd scraper with steep edge wear, (g) utilized sherd with acute edge wear.*

disks is needed, particularly including observations of usewear.

Sherds are also potentially tools. Sherds used as pottery scrapers are common in the four-corners area and less common, but present, at Lizard Man Village. The relative paucity of pottery scrapers among the Sinagua may be due, in part, to the fact that the paddle-and-anvil technique requires less scraping and smoothing than coiling, and, in part, to Sinagua use of basalt cylinders for part of the necessary scraping. When the unmodified edge of a sherd is used to scrape a ceramic vessel, a steep usewear pattern is produced (figure 8.7f). Under the microscope striations running perpendicular to the edge of the sherd

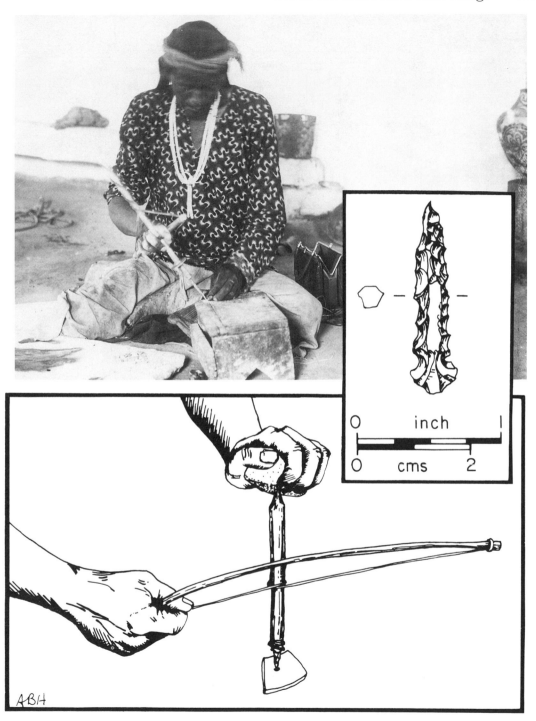

Figure 8.8 *Use of the bowdrill: Above, a Zuni man uses a bow drill. Below, a drawing of a bowdrill in use. Inset shows a close-up of a drill found at Lizard Man Village.*

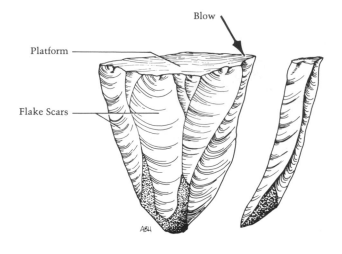

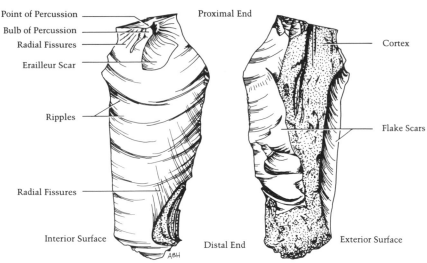

Figure 8.9 *Flake and core morphology and terminology.*

can be seen. A second distinct wear pattern was also observed at Lizard Man Village. Seven sherds had very acute edge angles (figure 8.7g). Under the microscope, we could see striations running parallel to the edge of the sherd. On the top face of the sherd the wear was very distinct. Depth of wear was less at the center, producing a curved pattern. Experimentation showed that similar wear could be produced by smoothing a ceramic vessel using side-to-side motions, but there is no guarantee that this is the activity that produced the sherds we found at Lizard Man Village.

Arrowheads and Other Chipped Stone Artifacts

While today pottery sherds are the most common artifact at Lizard Man Village and similar sites, artifacts made from chipped and ground stone are also common. The Lizard Man Villagers made a wide variety of tools by flaking pieces of chert, obsidian, and fine-grained basalt. Stone tool production is a reduction process. Stone is fractured by striking, and *flakes* are removed to leave a sharp edge and produce the desired form. Individual flakes often have sharp edges, and some are good cutting tools without further modification; others are just waste. All flakes have a recognizable morphology, including features such as striking platforms, bulbs of percussion, and ripples (figure 8.9). *Cores* are nodules of rock with scars from previous flake removals. Tools can be made on the core itself, by simply continuing the reduction process until the desired form is achieved (figure 8.10a), or on flakes (figure 8.10b-d). When smaller flakes are removed from a larger flake, this is called *retouch*. Most of the Lizard Man Village tools are made on flakes.

At Lizard Man Village we found over 250 *projectile points* or, as they are more commonly known, arrowheads (figure 8.10b–d). Projectile points are produced by initially striking flakes from a large core, probably using a hammerstone. These small, roughly spherical stones with the peck marks that occur as a result of striking other stones (figure 8.11a) are not uncommon at Lizard Man Village. The flake is then shaped and thinned using an antler tine in a technique called pressure flaking. Instead of actually hitting the flake, the tip of the antler is pressed against the edge of the flake to break off a smaller retouch flake from the reverse side. Ideally, this thins the point by producing a series of long, thin flake scars often running more-or-less parallel to one another. Flakes are removed from both sides of the tool, a procedure referred to as *bifacial working*.

The Lizard Man Villagers chose the best available materials for producing their projectile points. *Obsidian*, or volcanic glass, was the preferred material. Fully 70 percent of the projectile points are made of obsidian, despite the fact that obtaining obsidian required considerable effort. Furthermore, sources of high-quality obsidian were utilized in preference to closer low-quality sources. The closest source, Robinson Crater, is about twenty-four miles away, but the obsidian there is of poor quality and was eschewed in favor of the higher-quality obsidian from the Government Mountain source about thirty miles away and the even more distant Mt. Floyd source, some eighty miles away. Only one point was made from the close but poor-quality source at Robinson Crater, while 161 were produced of material from the slightly more distant but higher-quality Government Mountain source, and nineteen points were made from the very distant, high-quality Mt. Floyd source. Points not made of obsidian are generally made from varieties of *chert*, all available thirty to forty miles away in the bed of the Little Colorado River.

The abundance of projectile points found at Lizard Man Village is due to the importance of hunting using a bow and arrow (see chapter 7 for more information on hunting practices). Most of the projectile points at Lizard Man Village are small triangular points (figure 8.10b,c). Larger points (figure 8.10d) are probably somewhat older and may represent collection and, possibly, reuse of old points. Some of the older points may have had symbolic uses rather than being part of a tool kit. Ethnographically, projectile points were used as good-luck amulets against ghosts, lightning, and other dangers. At Lizard Man Village two points showed heavily worn edges and surfaces as if they had been carried around for some time, perhaps as charms. Another large old point was recovered from the burial of a young woman, and two were found at the bottom of postholes in pithouse rooms, perhaps placed there during dedicatory ceremonies or to protect the house from lightning strikes.

While projectile points are the most easily recognizable chipped-stone artifact to the layperson, they are only one of many tool types. Other chipped-stone tools include drills, bifaces, choppers, and scrapers. Drills (figure 8.8) often superficially resemble projectile points. They are similar in shape and are both bifacially worked. Drills are distinguished by their pointed tips with thick cross-sections, rather than the thin, flat profiles characteristic of projectile points. The edges of drills are usually heavily dulled by wear, and striations can sometimes be observed running around the tool perpendicular to the edges. These stone drills may have been hafted on a shaft and then twirled between the palms or used with a bow drill to perforate a wide variety of materials from shell and argillite to ceramics and wood. Choppers (figure 8.10a) were used for heavy cutting. Scrapers are basically flakes that have had small retouch flakes removed from one or more edges. The retouch is by definition *unifacial* and produces a steep edge. While experiments have shown that such an edge is indeed useful for scraping, the term itself is morphological and does not imply that archaeologists know this was the actual function of all tools given this name.

Not surprisingly, a reduction process such as flintknapping produces large quantities of refuse in the form of flakes that are too small to be useful, irregular stone fragments called *shatter*, and tools that were broken or spoiled by mistakes in working them. An analysis of this waste, or *debitage*, can yield information about the details of the manufacturing process. For example, by looking at the frequency of pieces including some of the weathered outer surface of the rock, called *cortex*, it is possible to determine whether whole rock nodules were brought back to the site to be worked there or whether the preliminary stages of the reduction process were performed at the quarry site. It is also possible to determine whether flakes were produced using a hard hammer such as a rock or a soft hammer such as an antler or piece of wood. Hard

Figure 8.10 *(a) Chopper, (b) long, unnotched, small triangular projectile point, (c) short, unnotched, small triangular projectile point, (d) long, serrated, small triangular projectile point, (e) short, serrated, small triangular projectile point, (f) short, corner-notched small triangular projectile point, (g) corner-notched large projectile point, (h) contracting stem large projectile point, (i) ovate Pinto point.*

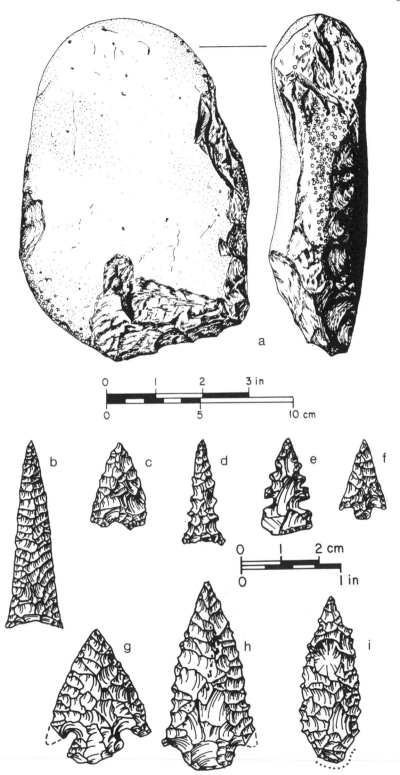

a

b   c   d   e   f

g   h   i

hammer flakes, which are usually struck from ordinary cores, generally have more distinct bulbs of percussion and larger striking platforms than soft hammer flakes. Soft hammer flakes, primarily resulting from biface production, are generally flatter and thinner than hard hammer flakes, and the striking platform usually has a small lip on the interior. The Lizard Man Village knapping debris is primarily hard hammer flakes, the result of fairly casual knapping. This is further reflected in the morphology of cores, which show a relatively unpatterned sequence of flake removal (figure 8.11b). Thirty-one percent of the chert and only 21 percent of the obsidian have cortical surfaces. This suggests that while both materials are being reduced from nodules at Lizard Man Village, the obsidian may be arriving in slightly more reduced form. The obsidian debitage is also a bit smaller than the chert debris. Less than 2 percent of the obsidian debitage measured over 4 cm (1.5 in.), in contrast to 6 percent of the chert. This could be the result of more initial processing at the quarry site or could be due to more intensive reuse of a more valuable material.

It is usually assumed that stone tools were made by men. This fits in well with our preconceived notions of gender roles but may, in fact, be a fallacious assumption. Certainly no one refutes the notion that both women and men (and children too) used stone tools. The technology for producing simple stone tools such as flakes or scrapers is quite simple. My husband John (who teaches flintknapping) says that in an hour or less he can easily teach someone to make flakes and modify them into scrapers. This may mean that most adults and older children knew the very basics of stone tool production and could, when convenient, just pick up a suitable rock and produce the needed flake or simple tool. Some individuals were undoubtedly much more proficient *knappers* than others, with a larger repertoire of techniques. Control of raw materials may be another limiting factor on who produced stone tools. We do not

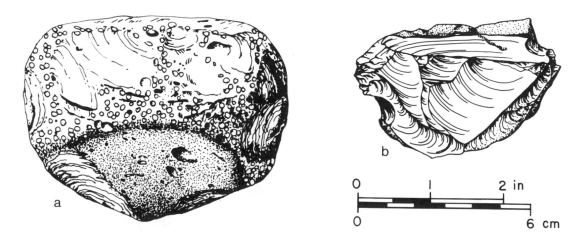

Figure 8.11 *(a) Hammerstone, (b) core.*

know how procurement of raw materials was organized or whether the materials were viewed as household or individual possessions. Nevertheless, low-quality materials in the form of fine-grained basalts were available locally, and it is not unlikely that knapping was widely practiced.

Making Arrows

The Sinagua would have made bows and arrow shafts in addition to the less perishable projectile points. Dry cave sites and cliff dwellings elsewhere in the Southwest provide some clues to the production of bows and arrows. At Lizard Man Village itself we found the tools necessary to produce bows and arrows, even though these artifacts themselves had long ago decayed.

Projectile points were probably often attached to a shaft with an intermediate foreshaft (figure 8.12). The foreshaft was slotted and the stone point attached with sinew or glue. The foreshaft, in turn, fit into a socket in the main shaft, which in the Southwest was often made of cane and usually feathered. The use of a foreshaft greatly increased the possibility that the hunter could salvage a portion of the arrow when a tip broke or an animal escaped with an arrow embedded in it.

Along with the knapping tools for making arrowpoints, we also find shaft straighteners for producing the rest of the arrow. These are lumps of soft stone with a polished groove (figure 8.13). Experiments have shown that a cane arrow

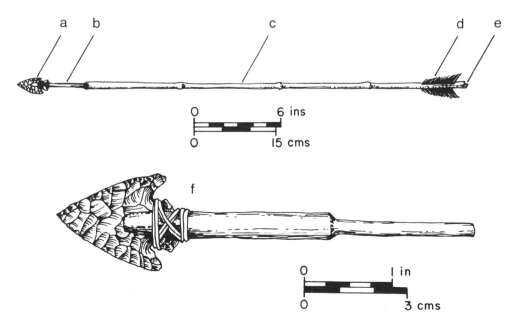

Figure 8.12 *Diagram of arrow showing use of a foreshaft to mount a projectile point: (a) point, (b) foreshaft, (c) main shaft, (d) fletching, (e) nock, (f) close-up of arrow and foreshaft.*

can be effectively smooth and straightened by rubbing and bending it in a heated shaft straightener. It is often assumed that most of the arrow production was done by males, while females were the ceramicists. One example of an arrow shaft straightener we found at Lizard Man Village seems to cast doubt on this perhaps-too-simplistic premise, as it combines a shaft straight- and a pottery anvil on the same tool.

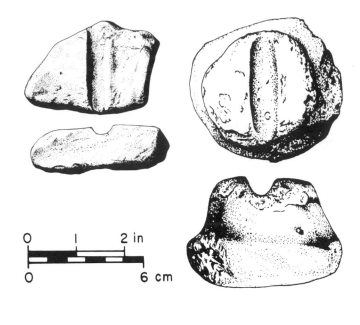

Figure 8.13 *Arrow shaft straighteners. The arrow shaft straightener to the right is made on a pottery anvil. This particular multi-purpose tool goes against traditional stereotypes of discrete gender roles.*

Spinning, Weaving, and Basketry

No woven fabrics or basketry were preserved at Lizard Man Village. We do know, however, that the villagers would have used both cloth and baskets, since both of these have been found at other Sinagua sites. Moreover, impressions of cloth were discovered inside one sherd that we excavated, and three had impressions of basketry (figure 8.14f). Tools found at the site suggest that the villagers not only used, but probably also made, both basketry and cloth.

Bone awls and needles would most likely have been used to make baskets, although they may have been used in weaving as well. The twelve needles we found are all manufactured from jackrabbit radii (figure 8.14a). A similar needle was found at Wupatki with a yucca-fiber thread attached. The needles all have fairly broad tips, so they would not have been suitable for sewing fine cloth or hides and were probably used as weaving tools or in the production of nets, baskets, clothing, or bags of coarse cloth. Cactus needles were probably used for finer work but would not survive well in this context. We discovered a total of twenty-one bone awls or awl pieces and an additional twenty-six fragments that could have been either awls or hairpins, but were most likely awls. Most of these are cut awls, produced by splitting large mammal bones, then grinding the tip to produce a point (figure 8.14b). Metapodial awls (figure 8.14c-e) are a special type of cut awl made from a split metapodial (the lower leg or cannon bone of a deer or antelope) with one of the distal condyles retained to produce a handhold. All but two of the nine metapodial awls from Lizard Man Village have a distinctive, very restricted tip that is particularly characteristic of basketry awls (figure 8.14c,e). Thus, despite the fact that both the baskets that were once used at Lizard Man Village and the debris from making them have long ago decayed, the tools that do survive testify to the craft.

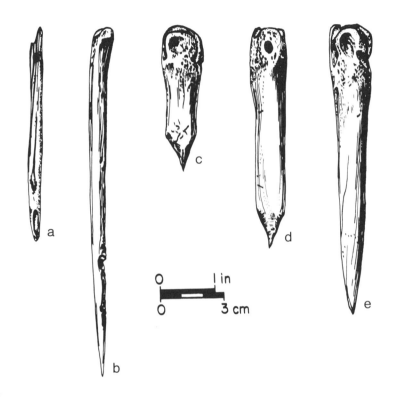

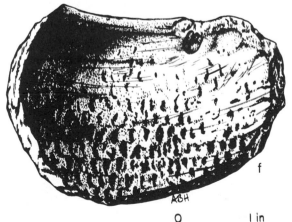

Figure 8.14 Basket-making tools and basketry impressions on pottery found at Lizard Man Village: (a) rabbit radius needle, (b) cut bone awl, (c-e) metapodial awls, (f) basketry impressions on sherd interior.

Cotton thread and probably cloth were additional Sinagua products. Cotton seeds are common in the floral remains at Lizard Man Village. Theoretically cotton could have been either grown or traded as bolls, preprocessed fiber, or thread. The presence of seeds suggests that at least some of the cotton was grown or acquired as bolls. Cotton was originally domesticated in Mesoamerica. The cotton grown in the Hopi area historically was an annual adapted to arid climes with short growing seasons. The Hopi harvested the bolls before they burst open, then dried them on rooftops. The first stage in processing is removal of the seeds. Hopi cotton, because of its fairly short fiber, can be ginned by hand fairly easily. This task was sometimes done by men but was also shared by women. Those seeds not needed for next year's planting can be popped and eaten. Next the men treated the cotton fibers by beating them lightly with switches to produce a fluffier, cleaner fiber and arranged the fibers into laps ready for spinning. Spinning was done with a hand spindle consisting of a shaft and a whorl (figure 8.15). The whorl acts as a flywheel, helping the spindle to maintain its velocity for a longer time.

At least some of the drilled sherd disks that we found could have been used as spindle whorls. Others had holes so off-center that they simply would not have functioned well as flywheels. In addition to the whorls, we discovered six flat molded disks that may have been spindle whorls, seven spool whorls and one bead whorl (figure 8.16). The use of the spool and bead whorls as spinning tools in Mexico is well-documented. In addition, several spinning kits including complete spindles have been discovered in dry contexts in the southwestern United States. Most of the whorls on complete spindles are of wood, horn, or cucurbit (squash) rind, although one sherd whorl is reported from Canyon Creek in eastern Arizona. The size and shape of the drilled sherd disks is very similar to those of the documented whorls, so the whorl interpretation seems not unlikely.

Figure 8.15 *Hopi man spinning, ca. 1917.*

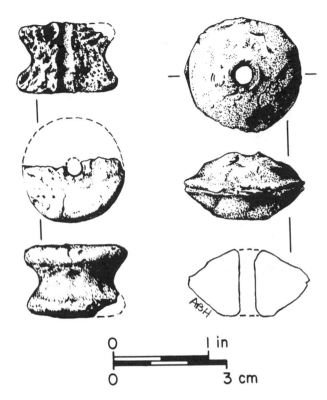

Figure 8.16 *Molded clay spoindle shorls.*

Several types of thread were spun in the prehistoric Southwest. In addition to cotton, yucca, apocynum (Indian hemp), cedar or juniper bark, human hair, animal fur, and feathers were all spun, either by hand or using a spindle. Yucca, which produces a fairly coarse fiber, was mainly used for sandals, bags, nets, belts, and aprons. Aponycum produces a somewhat softer yarn and was also used for blankets.

Archaeologists have attempted to discern the type of fiber spun by examining whorl characteristics. Mary Parsons studied spinning in contemporary Mexico and discovered that women spun heavier fiber (like the yucca) on large whorls, which have a greater moment of inertia, and cotton on smaller whorls. The variability in size of the Lizard Man Village whorls would suggest that the villagers were spinning some cotton, some intermediate fiber such as apocynum, and a small amount of a large fiber like yucca.

While cross-culturally both spinning and weaving tend to be women's duties, among the historic Puebloan groups of the Southwest men are the spinners and weavers. Again we have no concrete evidence that this gender division of labor was true in the prehistoric past. We are merely making an educated guess if we postulate that men were the weavers.

We found no evidence of looms or other weaving equipment at Lizard Man Village, although this does not mean that weaving was not done there. Weaving equipment tends to be of wood, making it perishable and hence found only in dry contexts. A fairly complete weaving and spinning kit was discovered at Antelope House in the Mesa Verde area. A vertical loom was probably used for weaving fabrics (figure 8.17). This could have been mounted to one of the ceiling beams and held taunt by a heavy basal beam or anchored to the floor via twig or string loops. This method of securing the loom produces a row of about five holes in the floor surface, usually running parallel to a wall.

Figure 8.17 *Hopi man weaving, ca. 1921.*

Jewelry

While the Lizard Man Villagers made little shell or turquoise jewelry, probably acquiring these as finished items rather than raw materials, they did make argillite jewelry. Argillite is a soft, easily workable stone, a claystone or shale. Since iron is the major impurity, argillite is normally a reddish color. Nevertheless, when Steve Williams, a geologist, examined the stone jewelry from Lizard Man Village using an Energy Dispersive X-Ray Spectrometer, he discovered that the chemical composition of most of the grey and black stone jewelry was identical to argillite. Thus, while most of the argillite jewelry is red, some is grey or black.

In addition to finished pieces of argillite jewelry, we found raw materials and all the stages of manufacture at Lizard Man Village. This includes unworked and very slightly worked raw material (37 pieces, over 160 grams) and a number of artifacts that have not yet been completed. My favorite is a small round pendant (figure 6.12p). The pendant had been ground into the desired shape. All that remained was to drill it for stringing. This was usually done by drilling holes from each side to meet in the middle forming a biconical perforation. A bow drill such as that shown in figure 8.8 might have been used for drilling. Unfortunately, these two holes did not meet and an afternoon's work was cast into the garbage, perhaps with whatever the ancient Sinagua used for an oath.

Argillite disk beads are made by grinding the argillite into slabs of the desired thickness, grooving the slabs into long strips, then square segments approximately the size of the bead. Stone drills are used to produce large holes and cactus spines to produce the almost microscopic holes of very small beads. Finally the beads are ground into shape by rolling the entire strand along a piece of sandstone to ensure a uniform size. The Sinagua also carved argillite into a variety of forms. Although jewelry items are most common, an argillite bowl was excavated at Kahorsho, a site very similar to Lizard Man Village. Pendants, beads, bracelets, rings, and noseplugs are all manufactured from argillite. Sometimes shell forms such as *Glycymeris* bracelets or rings are replicated in argillite.

Specialization

There is no evidence for specialists in any of the manufacturing activities discussed above. Neither the techniques needed nor the equipment required for any of the crafts are beyond the scope of an average household. Furthermore, both tools and manufacturing debris are scattered throughout the site rather than concentrated in specific locales. For none of the production activities discernable is the amount of manufacturing debris very great. This would suggest that manufacturing activities were sporadic, geared primarily to household needs, rather than toward production for exchange.

This is not to imply that some individuals were not better artisans than others or that, consequently, their products may not have been admired and even coveted. There may well have been considerable pride in workmanship and even sometimes a bit of rivalry. Certainly many of the artifacts we find are extremely well made, beyond just the basics needed for utilitarian functioning. To discuss the meaning of a craft to the artisan in a culture long extinct is speculative at best. Nevertheless, when one handles some of the beautiful objects made by the Sinagua and other ancient Puebloan peoples, one can not help but feel admiration and empathy for their art.

To say that there were no craft specialists among the Lizard Man Villagers is also not to imply that the villagers never exchanged their goods.

Ceramics, weaving, baskets, food, jewelry, and most other items undoubtedly circulated both within the village itself and between the village and other Sinagua and non-Sinagua villages. Sinagua villages like Lizard Man Village were basically self-sufficient in terms of the basic necessities. In addition to foodstuffs, they produced tools of all sorts including hoes, axes, and drills, pottery, cloth (or at the very least thread), and even small figurines that might have been toys. Nevertheless, they were tied via marriage, friendship, politics, and trade to a wider world outside the village.

Chapter 9

FAMILIES, COMMUNITIES, AND THE WIDER WORLD

Hopi society is organized around corporate kinship groups, which share a notion of common ancestry, a name, property, rights, and responsibilities. These groups are termed clans by anthropologists. According to legend, however, clans did not exist in the underworld where the Hopi originated. Tradition tells us that when the Hopi emerged into this world, they had a bilateral kinship system, one that more-or-less equally recognizes relatives from both the mother's and the father's sides and lacks *corporate groups* (Eggan 1994). The newly-emergent Hopi separated into bands, which diverged and wandered the Southwest before ultimately settling in the Hopi mesas. During their travels, the Hopi began to emphasize descent through the maternal line by prescribing that individuals marry outside their mother's clan and that men live with their wives' families after marriage. Particular clans acquired names that recorded events and reflected relationships to the natural world. Thus, when one band came upon a dead bear, they became Bear Clan. Through such tales about their past, the Hopi define their social world and recount the development of the present system of matrilineal clans and matrilocal residence.

According to this system, houses, land, and some ceremonial responsibilities are inherited through the female line. Because the Hopi also have a matrilocal residence pattern, women tend to remain in the households of their mothers after marriage, while men leave their natal families and move in with their wives. Thus, a household tends to be composed of a group of related women and their husbands and children. Because clans have primary responsibility for particular ceremonies, the major religious mentors for a man are his mother's brothers and other members of his mother's clan rather than his father. Men instruct their sisters' sons in ritual and are responsible for much of their upbringing. In many ways the mother's brother is the major authority figure. Sons and daughters live in the same household as their fathers, however, and fathers teach their sons life skills such as planting and tending crops. Often a child's relationship with its father and members of the father's family is close and affectionate. For a son, this may mean that he chooses to belong to the religious organization of his father's clan as well as his own.

The divorce rate is quite high among Hopi. This tends to be true of groups with matrilineal, matrilocal systems, perhaps because of a potentially awkward division of authority and residence. Men remain the political and religious authorities and are clan leaders as well. Nevertheless, in their own households they are not in a position of supreme authority. They are not a member of the clan with which they reside, they do not own the land they farm, and they are not the primary figures responsible for their own children's religious education. Their authority is more centered in the household(s) of their mother and sisters, where other men reside.

It was once hypothesized that matrilocality was generally associated with horticultural societies. This notion has been questioned on several grounds. Most important, cross-cultural statistics show that matrilocality and horticulture are no more highly associated than patrilocality and horticulture. An alternative thesis (Divale 1974) is that matrilocal residence confers an advantage when activities such as trade or war necessitate the absence of men from the village for long periods of time, leaving women alone. A matrilocal residence pattern ensures cooperation between co-residing women. It also makes it less likely that a group of men from one village will attack a neighboring community, since the men drawn from a single village will generally originate from a number of surrounding villages and still have mothers and sisters in those villages. Drawing a war party of related men from a number of villages produces the same result, since their wives and children are scattered. Thus, in locales where warfare is endemic, matrilocal residence tends to encourage peace among neighboring villages and concentrate conflict farther afield. Contrast this with a system of patrilocal residence. Under this system, if a group of related men is drawn from a single village, most of their relatives will be in the community of origin. It is only the relatives of their wives that tie them to surrounding communities, thus the reluctance to attack them may be much less. Matrilocal residence is often found among groups such as the Iroquois, where there was internal peace but considerable external aggression.

One of the desires of both Hopi tradition and anthropological research is to explore kinship systems. Although a specific time frame is lacking, Hopi tradition offers one description of changes in the kinship system, discussing both the origin of specific clans and of the matrilineal clan system in general. According to this perspective, the kinship system was certainly not static. If at one time the entire Puebloan region had a similar kinship system, the variability in Puebloan kinship seen by the time it was studied in the nineteenth and twentieth centuries provides anthropologists a further hint that considerable change may have occurred. Ethno-historic evidence shows that a number of Native American groups have experienced significant changes in their kinship systems, both due to changes in basic subsistence patterns and to contact with Europeans. In the Southeast matrilineal systems became more bilateral and patrilineal as groups encountered European missionaries and settlers. The Plains tribes adapted to profound changes in subsistence patterns by altering residence patterns, which ultimately had an effect on other aspects of the kinship system as well. The Crow, for example, were originally matrilineal, matrilocal farmers. When they moved west and began to hunt buffalo, however, residence changed to bilocal or patrilocal, perhaps because of changes in the gender division of labor. Women were the primary farmers and would have been key to the subsistence system when the Crow were horticulturalists, while men took the major role in buffalo hunting. Clearly archaeologists can not simply assume that because the modern Western Pueblos have a matrilineal, matrilocal kinship system, their prehistoric ancestors did as well.

Archaeological Interpretations of Family and Lineage

In a classic study, William Longacre (1970) attempted to determine the post-marital residence patterns at Carter Ranch Site, a Mogollon pueblo located in eastern Arizona and occupied between A.D. 1050 and 1200. Longacre theorized that, if women were the potters and taught their daughters ceramic techniques, pottery design elements would be most similar among groups of related women. It follows that if women scattered after marriage, as they would in a patrilocal residence system, design elements would be dispersed rather than clustered. On the other hand, if women remained in the same or nearby households, as they would in a matrilocal residence system, pottery design elements should be clustered (figure 9.1). The reverse should be true of artifacts manufactured by men. In a patrilocal system, styles transmitted through men should be clustered, while in a matrilocal system they should be scattered.

Longacre analyzed 175 pottery design elements from rooms at Carter Ranch. He found two clusters of design elements, each associated with a residential unit, and from this inferred that matrilocal residence was, in fact, typical of the prehistoric Mogollon. Analysis of grave goods from three clusters of burials provided further support for his hypothesis. Pottery design elements in the northern cluster of burials were similar to those in the northern residential unit, those in the southern burial cluster resembled the designs in the southern unit, and those in the central group of burials were mixed. The centrally-located burials also included more ceremonial items, so Longacre posited that they might represent higher-status individuals from both kin groups.

Longacre's analysis was intriguing as an attempt to discern social institutions not often researched by archaeologists, but his analysis has subsequently been criticized on several grounds. I will discuss two in some detail, primarily to demonstrate the dynamic nature of archaeological analysis and reanalysis. The first criticism relates to the formation processes discussed in chapter 3. Obviously, one of the basic assumptions of Longacre's analysis is that the pottery found in a dwelling was manufactured and used by the inhabitants of that dwelling. This would not necessarily be true of trash dumped into a room after its abandonment. Since even pottery sherds found in actual contact with floors are likely to be post-abandonment trash deposits, this implies that only whole vessels found on room floors should have been included in Longacre's analysis. Unfortunately, the Carter Ranch rooms did not include whole pots on floors, so Longacre was forced to used sherds instead. The assumption that the use of particular pottery designs will reflect familial ties has also been criticized. Longacre's model assumes both that mothers will teach daughters pottery making and that an individual's pottery will be most similar to the ceramics of the person from whom she learned. Even if we accept the notion that women were the potters (another potentially vulnerable assumption of the model), there was no ethnographic evidence that daughters' ceramics should be most similar to their mothers'.

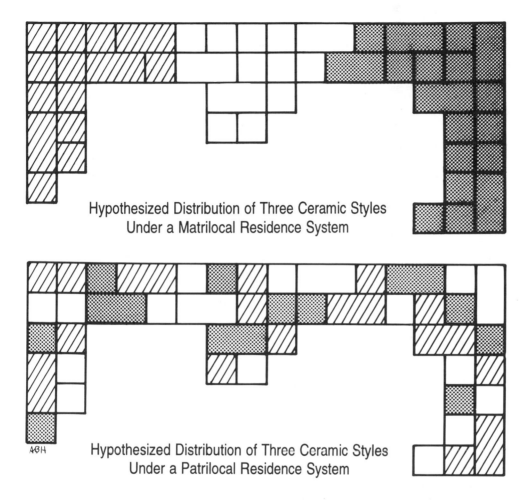

Figure 9.1 *Theoretical distribution of ceramic style elements in a matrilocal pueblo contrasted with the theoretical distribution for a patrilocal pueblo. For constructing this distribution, it was assumed that women made the pottery. Note that styles cluster in the matrilocal pueblo but are dispersed in the patrilocal pueblo.*

Inspired by the latter criticism, Longacre set out for the Philippines to do an ethnoarchaeological study of modern Kalinga potters. He chose the Kalinga because they still made and used traditional ceramics at the household level. Modern Pueblo potters, on the other hand, like most North Americans, use mainly plastic, metal, china, and glass for daily activities and produce ceramics primarily for the tourist and fine-art markets. It seemed likely that the commercial nature of Pueblo ceramics, and the fact that they are no longer made in many households, would have changed patterns of learning and style transmission. Longacre's study of Kalinga pottery is now a long-term project that has yielded insights on a wide variety of topics including his original concern with style transmission. Among the Kalinga, local work groups are important influences on the styles learned and produced by potters. Women, often neighbors as well as kin, get together and make pottery while chatting and watching children. The learning and emulation that takes place in these groups produces similarities in the use of design. This suggests that the patterns Longacre found in the Carter Ranch ceramics may reflect potters learning from others in a group, but the composition of the group cannot be assumed. While this finding casts some doubt on Longacre's initial method of studying matrilocality using archaeological data, it should not discourage us from attempting to find other ways of studying social systems archaeologically.

Another potential technique for studying postmarital residence patterns is examining the biological variability in the individuals buried at a site. This method assumes that individuals are buried at their place of residence rather than at their natal home, which may, of course, not be true, especially if their birth family resides nearby. In a matrilocal system the women of a village are more closely related and so should be more homogeneous in inherited physical traits than the men, who marry in from a number of kin groups. In a patrilocal system, the men should be more homogeneous. Walter Birkby, a forensic anthropologist at the University of Arizona, examined 163 adult skeletons from Grasshopper Pueblo, another thirteenth- and fourteenth-century Mogollon pueblo, recording information about inherited nonmetric skeletal characteristics such as the presence or absence of particular foramina (openings in the bone to allow the passage of nerves and blood vessels) and dental anomalies such as extra cusps. He concluded that at the site as a whole the skeletons of the women were more homogeneous than those of the men. This suggests that men were marrying into the village, which implies a matrilocal residence pattern.

At Lizard Man Village the number of burials is too small for this type of analysis to be very conclusive. It would be interesting it do some more complete nonmetric analyses of all the available Sinagua skeletal remains to determine whether intrasite variability tends to be greater for males than females, as we would expect with a matrilocal residence pattern. At Lizard Man Village many individuals were buried in abandoned and filled or partially-filled pithouses. This may simply be a matter of convenience, since soils in these areas would have been disturbed and therefore easier to dig. Alternatively, it may reflect a tendency to bury the dead in spots of particular relevance to a family, perhaps an earlier residence. Some nonmetric analyses of these burial grouping should also be of interest. In the future, DNA analysis also holds potential for discerning biological relationships, then translating this information into social patterns.

At the moment we do not know much about Sinagua kinship and family organization. Cross-culturally, the household tends to be the smallest basic unit of social organization. Definitions of what constitutes a household vary, however. We do not know whether small nuclear families comprised of parents and their children were the norm or whether a more extended family, including married siblings, children, and others was more common. Similarly, a bilateral kinship system with no corporate groups is a possibility, as are both matrilineal and patrilineal clan systems.

There is a tendency to use modern pueblo analogies and infer a matrilineal, matrilocal residence system as a best guess. This also implies clans with corporate ownership. Small hints that this assumption may be accurate come from studies of neighboring Pueblo groups like the Mogollon peoples previously described; from the ceremonial architecture that, like modern kivas, may have been communally built and maintained, perhaps by a clan; and from a couple of sites that appear to have several discrete cemetery areas, possibly indicating social units.

Villages and Communities

Most of the Sinagua villages contemporaneous with Lizard Man Village are small. Like Lizard Man Village, they would have been occupied by a group of some ten to twenty people, perhaps two to five families, probably organized simply on the basis of kinship. Several, such as Elden Pueblo and Wupatki (figures 9.2 and 9.3), are considerably larger, perhaps occupied by several hundred individuals. It is likely that they were large enough to have required social mechanisms beyond kinship to tie unrelated individuals together, adjudicate disputes, and ensure cooperation. These might have included religious groups, age grades, societies, or special leadership positions.

The size of villages such as Lizard Man Village may also be deceptive, since it is likely that groups of tiny units like Lizard Man Village functioned as larger communities. We have found no less than fourteen roughly contemporaneous small villages within approximately a twenty-minute walk from Lizard Man Village. Not all of them would have been occupied at any one moment in time. Nevertheless, the site distribution suggests that during the Angell-Winona through Elden phases (A.D. 1065–1250) this area of the pinyon-juniper forest supported a fairly dense scattering of small hamlets like Lizard Man Village. Undoubtedly, nearby settlements would have been linked by kinship, friendship, and exchange, and perhaps by social and religious organizations as well.

Sodalities, organizations which recruit members from outside the boundaries of kinship groups, may have functioned to unify both villages and multivillage communities. Among modern pueblos, religious societies and ceremonial dance groups are often under the leadership of clans but also recruit members from other kin groups. This provides linkages across kinship units.

In the Mogollon area of eastern Arizona at the site of Grasshopper Pueblo, J. Jefferson Reid and Stephanie Whittlesey (1997) feel they can identify membership in social or religious societies based on artifact sets found in burials. They suggest four male sodalities. *Glycymeris* shell pendants, bone hairpins, and *Conus* shell tinklers each indicate membership in a sodality. These artifacts, and thus membership in these societies, appear to be mutually exclusive. Membership in a fourth male society, indicated by clusters of arrows above the left shoulder, cross-cuts the other three societies. Women could belong to a

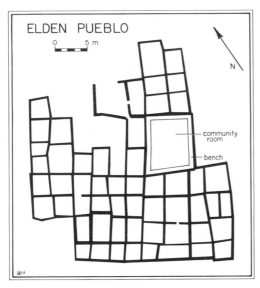

Figure 9.2 *Elden Pueblo: (a) photograph of the site showing the community room area, (b) site plan.*

society whose membership was indicated by *Conus* shell rings, and both men and women belonged to a group symbolized by *Glycymeris* shell bracelets. No similar phenomenon has been noted for the Sinagua; however, the research really has yet to be done. It is possible that a closer examination of patterns in the Sinagua data will reveal something similar. At present we have no concrete evidence of the existence of Sinagua sodalities, although architectural features such as the kivas, ball courts and community rooms would presumably be shared by fairly large groups of people and may suggest such organizations.

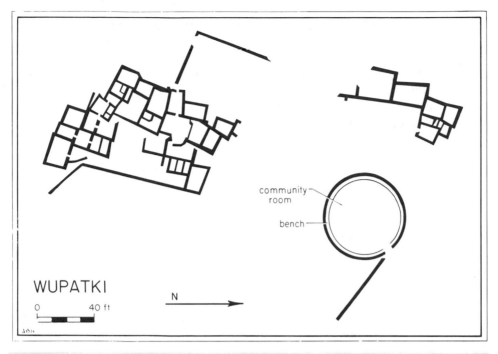

community
room

bench

WUPATKI

0   40 ft

N

Figure 9.3 *Wupatki Pueblo: Above, site plan; below, overall view.*

Religion

Religion ties communities together through shared beliefs, periodic communal ritual, and membership in religious organizations. Like all human societies, the Sinagua certainly had a system of religious beliefs and practices, but
we do not know the details of Sinagua religion.

The belief in *katsinas*, ancestor spirits that act as mediators with the gods and which today are an integral part of the traditional religions of the Hopi and other Puebloan groups, had probably not yet been introduced to the Pueblo area at the time Lizard Man Village was occupied. Katsina iconography on pottery and kiva walls and in rock art does not appear until the early 1300s (Adams 1991, 1994). In the Southwest this was a time of population movements, increasing settlement size, and the development of a settlement plan incorporating an enclosed plaza area or areas which contained a kiva or kivas. Adams argues that the present form of Puebloan religions provided a means for incorporating new populations into a community, and the mechanisms for successfully integrating them through cooperation and participation in a common ceremonial life.

Puebloan religion today emphasizes fertility, rain, and harmony. In addition, the ceremonies redistribute goods and reinforce community mores. During many of the religious ceremonies, katsina spirits visit the pueblos in the form of dancers. During the dances the katsinas can function as disciplinarians, whipping, frightening, and making fun of those who stray from community standards of behavior. It appears unlikely that katsinas danced at Lizard Man Village; nevertheless, the Sinagua certainly had religious beliefs that fulfilled many of the same integrative functions as Hopi and all other religions. In addition, the basic religious themes of fertility and harmony are so similar among all the modern Puebloan groups, and are so typical of agricultural societies in general, that we can logically expect them to have been important themes in Sinagua religion as well.

During the occupation of Lizard Man Village, Sinagua religion appears to have been centered in small semi-subterranean kiva-like structures and above-ground community rooms found at some sites. Additional aspects of religious ceremony probably took place in ball courts, open plaza areas, and perhaps in regular domestic structures as well.

The most frequently identified Sinagua ceremonial room is the kiva, which was described earlier in chapter 2. Hopi kivas, men's activity centers as well as the locus of religious ceremony, are identified by benches, ventilators, niches, *sipapus* (floor features symbolizing the hole through which The People climbed into this world from the underworld), ritual objects such as fetishes, eating implements, and artifacts associated with male activities such as weaving. Domestic refuse and artifacts associated with the activities of women, such as cooking or pottery making, tend to be lacking. By these criteria, the earliest securely identified Sinagua kiva is at the Pollack Site, an approximately forty-room pueblo occupied a bit later than Lizard Man Village. This room, a square pithouse with a flagstone floor, benches on two sides, and a hole in the appropriate position for a sipapu, is very reminiscent of kivas at the historic Hopi site of Awatovi.

A number of earlier sites, including Lizard Man Village, have rooms with many but not all of the features of Hopi kivas. The current norm is to use the presence of a bench as the hallmark of a kiva/ceremonial room. Using this criterion many Elden Phase (A.D. 1150–1250) sites, including some extremely small ones, boast at least one kiva. (In chapter 3, I tentatively identified Room 19 and one of the incarnations of Room 2 as ceremonial rooms.) However, a few sites—even some relatively larger ones—do not. Furthermore, most early sites, like our series of pithouse villages, lack discernable ceremonial facilities. How can we reconcile this with the notion that all communities have ritual and religious needs?

Part of the problem may be in our very definitions of ritual space. While for purposes of discussion anthropologists tend to dichotomize the sacred and profane, most of the world's cultures do not. Certainly, the Hopi kiva is not limited to religious activities, nor are religious activities limited to specifically-designated ceremonial structures. Homes, fields, plazas, and many natural areas are symbolically important and are a part of the ritual space. Furthermore, religion is integrated into domestic, agricultural, political, and other daily activities. Undoubtedly, this was true of the Sinagua as well. Many early kivas elsewhere in the Southwest have domestic features and refuse in juxtaposition to ceremonial.

Although we know nothing about the details of the activities for which they were constructed, community rooms are another type of structure that may have provided a space for religious activities and certainly served to integrate the members of a Sinagua community. These rooms are very large structures that could have accommodated a great number of people, allowing the inhabitants of a large village or a number of smaller ones to congregate. Indeed, community rooms tend to be found at the larger sites such as Elden Pueblo and Wupatki, mirroring the integrative needs of these communities. Morphologically, community rooms vary considerably. For example, the Wupatki community room (figure 9.2) is a circular benched structure measuring about 16 meters (53 feet) in diameter and located on the periphery of the community. At Elden Pueblo (figure 9.3) the community room, located on the eastern side of the massed room block, is a large 8.5 meter (28 feet) by 10.8 meter (35.3 feet) room, also with a bench. In contrast, at New Caves Pueblo the community room measures about 8.5 meters (28 feet) by 9.5 meters (31 feet) but lacks a bench.

Structures interpreted as ball courts are also found throughout the Sinagua area. A ball game with ceremonial import was played by both the Maya and the Aztecs and throughout much of Mesoamerica. Two teams played with a rubber ball weighing up to five kilograms (11 lbs.) on a large outdoor court with high masonry sidewalls. The exact size and form of the ball courts varied through both time and space in the Mesoamerican world, although most were elaborate constructions with associated temples. In the prehistoric Southwest both the Sinagua and Cohonina in the north and their more southerly neighbors, the Hohokam, constructed simpler, generally earthen, ball courts. According to the most recent analysis, the ball courts in the Northern Sinagua area appear early, even before the eruption of Sunset Crater, but are very rare in all time periods. The excavated and reconstructed ball court at Wupatki (figure 9.4) is an excellent example of a late ball court, and the only Southwestern example with formal masonry walls (although Cohonina ball courts often have stone boundaries). Although neither the exact use of the courts nor their cultural significance is certain, it is generally assumed that they were of ceremonial import. Because only a relatively small number of sites have ball courts, the activities centering around them may have been one of the types of occasions that drew many Sinagua to a single site and provided opportunities for contracting marriages, trading, and establishing and re-establishing social links. It is also possible that they helped to maintain trade and political connections between the Hohokam and Sinagua regions and with northern Mexico.

The very diversity of ritual spaces in different villages is of interest in and of itself. Some sites have identifiable ceremonial rooms analogous to kivas; others do not. Likewise, walled plazas, community rooms, and ball courts are found at only a few sites. Some ball courts are not even very securely associated with specific sites. If these facilities were each used for particular types of ceremonial activities, this may imply that no single village was religiously independent, that each relied on others for some aspects of ritual activity. Given the dispersed nature of Sinagua populations, this type of religious organization would make a lot of sense, since it would provide ample opportunities for integrating multiple sites into larger communities.

Figure 9.4 *Ball court at Wupatki.*

Establishing Links Through Exchange

The residents of Lizard Man Village would have interacted with both the occupants of neighboring Sinagua villages and with more distant peoples of diverse ethnic backgrounds, speaking other languages and observing different customs. We know from the distribution of artifacts that exchange of goods certainly took place; regional similarities in technology, style, and some social customs and beliefs indicate that ideas were exchanged as well.

From ethnographic examples, it is clear that trade occurs for a variety of reasons. Sometimes nonlocal goods are desired or needed. Shell, turquoise, and obsidian, for example, are not found in the Sinagua area. Sometimes foreign-made goods may be desired for their better craftsmanship, aesthetics, or simply for a diversity of style, even when a local variant is available. Temporary scarcities can also be alleviated through trade. Exchange can redistribute goods when conditions are temporarily better in one area than another and also serves to link groups, both locally and further afield. These linkages promote peace and stability in the area and provide an additional buffer in case of desperate conditions, since there may be the possibility of increasing the flow of needed goods or even seeking refuge with another group, if trade and social connections have been previously established.

The first and easiest step in reconstructing a prehistoric exchange system is simply mapping the distribution of nonlocal goods across space. A list of imports and their points of origin can be obtained by determining the source areas for as many of the artifacts found in the region as possible. The next step is to look for possible routes along which the goods may have traveled, and to attempt to reconstruct the social circumstances that facilitated or obstructed their movement. Did individuals go on expeditions to collect raw materials at their source? Were the sources of some raw materials controlled by particular groups and access to them restricted? Were there market towns? Were there full-time merchants? How much of the exchange was ritualized, conducted as a part of ceremonials or between ritual trading partners? These are but a few of the questions that interest us but tend to be very hard to answer.

As mentioned earlier, the easiest step in reconstructing exchange patterns is to identify nonlocal products and their probable source areas. Figure 9.5 depicts the likely movement of some of the identifiable nonlocal goods into the Sinagua area. Because ceramic styles tend to be characteristic of particular groups and are generally easily identifiable, their exchange is fairly well documented. About 10 percent of the pottery sherds found at Lizard Man Village are nonlocal types. Tusayan White Wares, Tsegi Orange Wares and Tusayan Grey Wares come from the Kayenta area; Little Colorado White Wares from the Winslow area; San Juan Red Wares from the Mesa Verde area; Prescott Grey Wares from the Prescott area; San Francisco Mountain Grey Wares from the Cohonina area; Chavez-Kinnikinnick and Diablo Brown from the Northern Sinagua to the east in the Anderson Mesa area; and Verde Brown and Wingfield Brown from the Southern Sinagua in the Verde Valley. As mentioned earlier, often the design elements used in contemporaneous painted ceramics are very

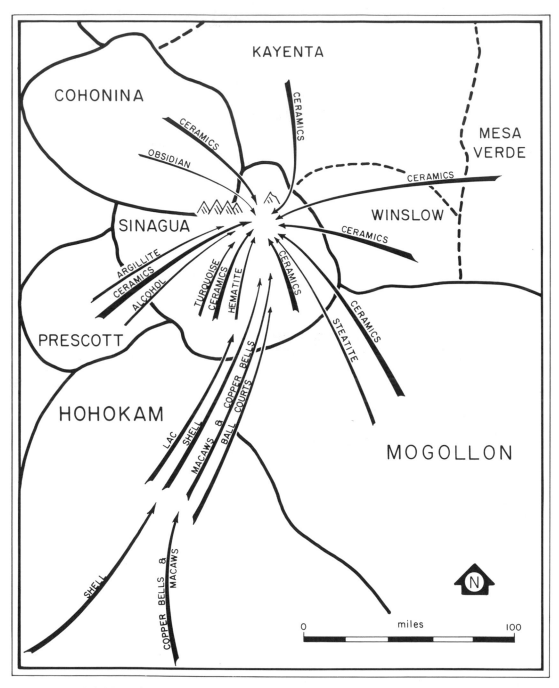

Figure 9.5 *Map showing the import of goods to the Sinagua.*

similar between adjacent regions, suggesting considerable communication and exchange of ideas as well as goods. It is primarily on the basis of differences in paste, temper, and painted designs that the different subgroups are identified.

When we find nonlocal ceramics, we cannot always assume that the vessel itself was the primary item being exchanged. Some of the vessels were probably traded as pots, while others were exchanged for the contents. For example, it has been suggested that pitting inside many of the Prescott jars is due to the effects of having been used to store an alcoholic beverage that might have been the real focus of exchange. This may be an especially attractive hypothesis, since these pots are undecorated and not discernibly better than anything made by the Sinagua; however, only chemical testing of residues can really determine what the vessels once contained. Other pottery probably originally transported food or other small items as well, but again more research is needed.

Shell was primarily obtained from the Gulf of California. Since there are no fresh water sources right at the Gulf, shells were probably collected on the beach, then taken a bit inland for preliminary processing, presumably by the local villagers. Shell processing sites with vast quantities of shell debris have, in fact, been discovered inland from the coast. Artifact blanks and some finished pieces were then traded north to the Hohokam who, according to some models, may themselves also have made collecting trips to the Gulf occasionally. The Hohokam are known as the master shell artisans of the Southwest. They crafted a variety of forms including *Glycymeris* shell bracelets, *Conus* tinklers, carved shell pendants, *Strombus* trumpets, and a variety of shell beads (figure 6.12). Particularly noteworthy are inlaid ornaments and shell etched with complex designs by using fermented *Sagauro* cactus-juice vinegar as an acid. The Sinagua appear to have obtained much of their shell from the Hohokam as finished ornaments. Nevertheless, the Sinagua also did some shell working, and several sites such as Winona Village and Wupatki have large numbers of unworked and worked shell fragments. Of the 615 pieces of shell we recovered at Lizard Man Village, only 14 are whole unmodified shells, 45 are unworked fragments and an additional 48 are worked fragments, some of which probably came from finished objects. This suggests some, but not extensive, shell working in the village and exchange in both finished and unworked shell.

It is possible to determine the exact source location of some minerals such as turquoise and argillite by comparing the trace mineral constituents of the artifact with the trace minerals in various sources. We could not afford to have sources determined for the few Lizard Man Village pieces of turquoise, although the variation in the colors of the stone suggests the possibility of several points of origin. Relatively nearby sources in Arizona are likely, but there are other possibilities such as the sources at Cerritos, New Mexico, an area that was the focus of a lively prehistoric turquoise trade. Mark Elson and James Gunderson, who are interested in the distribution of argillite, had six argillite pieces from Lizard Man Village analyzed and found that five of the six were from the Del Rio area, near present-day Prescott, Arizona. Argillite from this source has distinctive white flecks and spots. Since these are frequent in the unsourced argillite from Lizard Man Village, it seems safe to assume that most of the argillite used there was either obtained through collecting expeditions to the Prescott area or through exchange with populations from this region. While the turquoise, like the shell, seems to have primarily reached the village in finished form, the Lizard Man Village residents appear to have been making a fair amount of argillite jewelry themselves (see chapter 8).

Other imports found at Lizard Man Village include a variety of pigments: red hematite, possibly from the Oak Creek Canyon area; green malachite, often in rather impure form in conjunction with kaolinite, copper sulphate and other inclusions such as chlorite, azurite, and limonite from around Jerome, Arizona; blue azurite, like the malachite probably from the Jerome area; and yellow limonite and jarosite. Some of these may have been obtained in direct collecting expeditions, but most probably arrived at Lizard Man Village through networks of exchange.

A wide variety of perishable items was probably also imported to Lizard Man Village but not preserved. Feathers from macaws and other exotic birds were doubtless exchanged. A medicine bundle from the site of Medicine Cave contains such feathers. Feather blankets, basketry, cloth, alcohol, and foods— especially exotics such as nonlocal herbs, agave, and cactus fruit—may also have been traded. Copper bells and macaws, more exotic imports originating in Mexico, also occasionally made it to the Sinagua area, probably via the Hohokam. No copper bells or macaws were recovered in the Lizard Man Village excavations; however, Tse Tlani, a nearby site even smaller than Lizard Man Village, boasts a copper bell, as do the larger sites of Elden and Wupatki. Wupatki, which the Hopi believe is the last home of the Parrot Clan, has at least eleven parrot or macaw burials. Five of these bird burials come from a single room, identified on other grounds as a kiva. One bird had been buried at the foot of a child and had a prayer stick tied around its leg. All this suggests the religious and ceremonial import of parrots and macaws. The birds themselves originate in northern Mexico. The site of Casas Grandes (Paquime) in northern Mexico, which may have acted as a center for exchange activities with the prehistoric Southwest, has numerous pens for raising parrots and macaws.

Ideas moved as surely as goods. Many of them may not be visible in the archaeological record, but some influences on style, technology, or religion have left material traces. The regional similarities in ceramic designs and the ball courts discussed above are prime examples for this period. The katsinas and their associated beliefs are another, later instance of an exchange of ideas and beliefs over a broad area which had direct material consequences. Agricultural techniques and plant varieties, weaving, and other technologies spread in similar fashion.

Goods also circulated locally: through barter, as gifts, as a part of marriage exchanges, during ceremonials, and probably through gambling as well. Local exchange was probably very important for unifying the group and for providing a buffer against variability in crop yields. Local movement of goods is harder to document than long-distance exchange, although some successful studies show it is by no means impossible. Trace element or petrographic analyses of local ceramic clays and tempers can provide one means of studying the local as well as regional movement of goods. Both clays and the nonplastic inclusions used for temper often vary from place to place. Atomic absorption, instrumental neutron activation, x-ray fluorescence, inductively coupled spectrophotometry, and the electron microprobe have all been used to detect variability in the composition of clays and/or tempers. Ethnographic studies suggest that potters are unlikely to travel more than 5 to 8 km to obtain their raw materials, thus it can reasonably be assumed that vessels found at a distance from the source area for the clay or temper are probably trade wares. None of the available chemical techniques have been used to study Sinagua ceramic exchange yet, and we can provide no details about Lizard Man Village's trade relations with other nearby communities, but this research is part of our future plans.

If the residents of Lizard Man Village were obtaining goods from outside the village, they must have been exporting something. Possible exports include argillite jewelry, cloth or thread, pottery, and pinyon nuts. While both weaving implements and preserved cloth fragments from other sites show that the Sinagua wove cloth, there is no direct evidence of weaving activities at Lizard Man Village. However, we do know that they were growing cotton and, as discussed in the previous chapter, the numerous presumptive spindle whorls argue for the probability of spinning and weaving in the village. While Sinagua ceramics are found elsewhere as trade goods, for example in the Southern Sinagua regions of the Verde Valley and at some Cohonina and nearby Kayenta sites, they do not seem to have been as common a tradeware as the decorated red wares and white wares made by their neighbors. The Sinagua seem to have desired the decorated Kayenta wares, but plain Sinagua pottery apparently had less appeal for the Kayenta. Pinyon nuts, which are abundant in the pinyon-juniper zone where Lizard Man Village is located, are today a coveted food and might also have provided a trade resource for the Sinagua. Although we have no archaeological evidence for this, historically pinyon nuts were traded widely throughout California and the Southwest. Similarly, ethnographic analogies suggest that meat and hides might also have been exchanged.

Contexts of Exchange

It is likely that exchanges took place in a variety of social contexts, including bartering, ceremonials, gift giving, marriage, gambling, and the politics of war and peace. At religious events, goods may have been redistributed as part of the ceremony itself. At katsina dances today redistribution, particularly of food, is a part of the ceremony. In addition, individuals from both near and far may have used the occasion to conduct their own exchanges. Ritual exchanges, particularly at marriage, and gift giving also probably accounted for the movement of some goods, as did gambling. Raiding and spoils of war can also redistribute goods; but I would argue that the very dispersed settlement pattern of the northern Sinagua at this time, with many small villages and isolated dwellings in nondefensive locations, suggests a time of relatively peaceful conditions.

The Organization of Exchange

Ascertaining the mechanisms of exchange is considerably more complex than simply charting the movement of goods. There are two major competing models for the way in which trade might have been organized in the Sinagua area. One model suggests that elite members of society controlled at least a portion of the exchange system. These higher-status individuals would have presumably facilitated long-distance trade by coordinating exchanges with elites in other regions. Their own positions would have then been enhanced, since they would have been able to control the access of others to imports. There is little agreement about whether elites controlled most long-distance trade or just certain status goods such as turquoise, macaws, or shell.

The second model, which I argue here, posits that most trade among the Northern Sinagua was open to anyone and was organized casually, by a small group or conducted by individuals, rather than being institutionalized or controlled by a few. It was probably entrepreneurial to a certain extent in that a desired object was being obtained. However, trade also aimed at cementing ties between individuals and, hence, between the social groups to which they belonged.

The notion of individually rather than hierarchically organized trade is supported by two lines of archaeological evidence: (1) the distribution of imports is not what would be expected if items were being exchanged through trade centers, and (2) there are no sites with the kind of manufacturing debris that would indicate organized production for export.

If all individuals have more-or-less equal access to exchange, the quantity of an imported object in a village will vary with the number of residents of the village and the distance of the village from the source. If we assume that no one is a privileged elite, then the number of imports should increase in direct proportion to site size. For villages the same distance from a source, the relative frequency of an import should be the same no matter what the size of the village, although the absolute quantity of the import would be expected to increase with community size. Similarly, the relationship between distance from the source of the import and the relative frequency of the import should be a fairly predictable one. Distance is the critical variable, if exchange is between roughly equal communities. As distance from the source increases, the relative frequency of the import should decrease (figure 9.6a). Since under this model goods move from village to village rather than being distributed via central trade centers, Renfrew (1975) has called this mode of exchange "down-the-line" trade.

In contrast, in a community where some individuals coordinate exchange and/or have more access to imports because of their elite status, the presence of these privileged individuals should increase the average number of the im-

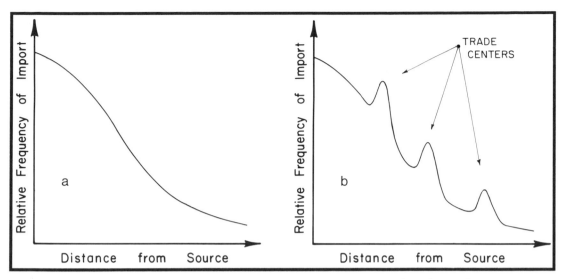

Figure 9.6 *Graph showing theoretical relationships between the relative frequency of an import at a site and the site's distance from its source under two possible systems of exchange: (a) down-the-line exchange, (b) exchange mediated through trade centers.*

ported items per person and therefore the relative frequency of the import. The very fact that a site functions as a trade center should also increase the relative frequency of imports at the site. In a sense, trade centers might be viewed as secondary source locales—distant from the original source, perhaps, but acting as an acquisition point for the communities around them. While the relative frequency of imports should still decrease overall as distance from the source increases, trade centers will have considerably larger frequencies of imports than other sites the same distance form the source (figure 9.6b). If the Northern Sinagua exchange system were organized by elites living at somewhat larger sites such as Elden or Wupatki, the expectation is that these sites would have a higher relative frequency of imports than predicted on the basis of their distance from the source.

Theoretically, this gives us an easy means for comparing the two models of exchange. Unfortunately, the archaeological reality is not nearly so simple. First, because different amounts of excavation have been undertaken at various sites, it is extremely important to discuss imports in terms of relative frequencies rather than absolute quantities. Unfortunately, for many sites published information does not allow the calculation of relative (or even in many cases absolute) frequencies. The need to deal in relative frequencies also makes it difficult to study distributions of rare artifacts. In the case of extremely rare objects a single find can curiously skew the relative frequencies. For example, finding two copper bells rather than one doubles the relative frequency. Nevertheless, most of us would be loath to put too much weight on such a scant sample. The archaeologist is also less likely to have found a rare artifact at a site that is less extensively excavated. Assume that the probability of finding a rare artifact type is one in one thousand for each ten square meters excavated and that the artifact is evenly dispersed across sites. As more and more square meters are excavated, the probability of finding one or more of the artifact type obviously increases. At most sites where little excavation has occurred the relative frequency of the artifact will be zero. Using this model, however, if extensive excavation has been undertaken, the probability of finding at least one of the item can be quite large. In our example, if one hundred of our hypothetical ten-square-meter units are excavated, the probability of finding at least one of the rare artifact type is now approximately one in ten, rather than one in one thousand. Clearly, rare artifacts are more likely to be found at sites with extensive excavation. To an extent, this statistical phenomenon automatically discriminates against all smaller sites, since their excavation possibilities are limited by their size.

Variability in excavation techniques also makes it hard to compare sites. Whether or not excavated fill was screened is particularly critical. The earliest excavators did not screen any of their dirt. In the 1930s at Winona and Ridge Ruin, however, McGregor utilized screens. This is at least partly responsible for the fact that these sites appear relatively rich in small finds such as shell, argillite and turquoise. Even into the 1970s, however, many excavations, most notably some of those associated with road construction projects, still did not routinely screen. Small "exotics" such as beads are doubtless underestimated for all of these sites.

An additional difficulty is in sorting out the artifacts from burials and those from trashy fill deposits. A single necklace in a burial can produce more beads than the fill in an entire site. This occurs both because the number of beads lost or thrown away is presumably fairly low as a percentage of beads in use (if indeed these are valued items) and because the recovery rate for small isolated beads is doubtless lower than for those found in any kind of cluster and hence excavated with more attention, care, and possibly the use of finer screens. Because extensively excavated sites often produce more burials, the probability of discovering any specific burial good becomes greater. I would argue that for comparability burial artifacts and fill artifacts need to be analyzed separately. However, this is rarely possible from published reports.

Because they are common, large in size (and hence found in quantity even when screens have not been used) and more frequently found in trash deposits than in burials, pottery sherds are probably the easiest import to investigate quantitatively. The Sinagua ceramic evidence supports the model of a more casually organized, egalitarian trade system. Nonlocal sherds, for example, are found in very similar quantities at villages like Lizard Man Village and at larger communities in the same area. Only at sites very near the boundaries to other culture areas do the percentages of ceramic imports significantly diverge. McGuire and Downum (1982) looked at the number of Kayenta imports in the Sinagua and Hohokam areas as a function of site location and site size. They concluded that distance from the Kayenta region rather than site size accounted for the variability in the relative frequency of this import. This is the pattern expected for Renfrew's down-the-line trade (figure 9.6a).

Smaller items such as shell are much harder to assess for the reasons outlined above. McGuire and Downum also attempted an analysis of the distribution of shell. For this import they concluded that the frequency of shell imports varied with site size rather than distance from the source, using the Hohokam site of Snaketown as the origin point for shell. Their research provides some tentative support for a trade-center model of exchange. The general pattern of the shell artifacts is somewhat suspect, however, because of the lack of a relationship between distance and the relative frequency of shell imports. Even if large sites are acting as centers for the redistribution of shell, those large sites near source areas should have more shell than larger sites farther away. Interestingly, their largest site, Gila Butte, was also the closest to Snaketown. Oddly, it did not have a particularly high relative frequency of shell. Some of the problems of dealing with previously excavated materials and with small and somewhat rare items may be at the heart of the matter. The sixth largest site, Ridge Ruin, located some 115 air miles from Snaketown, has by far the highest proportion of shell artifacts. It is possible that this is partially due to the extensive use of screens at Ridge Ruin and partially to the discovery of a particularly rich burial. Furthermore, all of the extremely small sites had moderate to small proportions of shell. Again, this is not unexpected with a relatively rare artifact type.

The paucity of manufacturing debris at Northern Sinagua sites also supports the non-hierarchical exchange model. If trading were done on a large scale and coordinated by elites, one would expect centralized manufacture and storage of some trade goods. At Casas Grandes in northern Mexico, clearly a trading center, there were over a million pieces of shell. On a much less impressive scale, more than three thousand pieces of shell manufacturing debris were recovered at Snaketown, a Hohokam center. While it is hard to produce an absolute figure indicating how much debris should result from specialized manufacturing for exchange, it is clear that the sparse quantity of unworked and partially worked shell pieces from Lizard Man Village (a total of forty-four pieces) is inadequate. A few Sinagua sites such as Wupatki and Ridge Ruin have produced substantially greater quantities of manufacturing debris from shell working, and were certainly the locations of some manufacture, but none come close to yielding the quantities of debris found at sites like Casas Grandes or even Snaketown. The same appears to be true of the manufacture of other items such as *lithics*, ground stone, bone tools, and thread. In no case are overwhelmingly large quantities of manufacturing debris or production equipment or facilities evident.

Individuals and, to some extent, even villages may have specialized in the production of certain items. Lizard Man Village, Kahorsho, and Winona-Ridge Ruin all manufactured argillite items; but Tse Tlani, Two Kivas, and Wupatki do not appear to have done so. Wupatki, on the other hand, had larger quantities of unworked and fragmentary shell. Stanislawski (1963) counted approximately a hundred *Cardium* shells, twenty-eight *Haliotis* and smaller numbers of several other genera. At Winona and Ridge Ruin McGregor (1941) also found shell at all stages of the production process and proposed that at least some manufacturing was occurring. Village specialization would help maintain vigorous local trade networks and social connections. When everyone in the area has access to essentially the same resources, one way of assuring interaction is to produce specialties. This does not mean that all or most adults of the appropriate gender are not capable of producing a particular item, simply that some make one item well and exchange it, while others produce something else. Nor does it mean that the individuals participating in the exchanges are by any means full- or even part-time specialists. The quantity of items produced by an individual or even a village would probably be quite small, and exchange would be on a limited scale.

Clusters of individuals in a village producing similar items would also facilitate the acquisition of nonlocal raw materials and might result in a tendency for some individuals and villages to have closer ties with particular culture areas. Thus, villages where some individuals were producing argillite jewelry might have closer ties with the Prescott area from which they were obtaining their argillite, and villages where there were artisans working in shell might have closer ties to the Hohokam. This could be tested by comparing the frequency of imports; however the comparative data is not available at this time.

The volume of exchange in the Sinagua area is well within that which could easily have operated on an individual basis. Let's assume that each household owned an average of two hundred pots, which is probably a high estimate. With approximately 10 percent nonlocal wares at the site, this number assumes a household inventory of approximately twenty imported vessels. Even given breakage over time, this would imply that a household would be exchanging only a few ceramics in any given year. Even if the total volume of exchange is increased by counting shell, obsidian, and other nonlocal items, the actual number of objects acquired by any one household annually was probably not great. Ethnographic studies clearly show that a low volume of exchange can easily be handled through individual initiatives.

Longacre's study of Kalinga potters provides data that shed some light on this issue. Michael Graves (1991), originally one of Longacre's doctoral students, has shown that fairly large quantities of even heavy and awkward items like ceramics can be exchanged by individual entrepreneurs with no institutional infrastructure. In the Kalinga village of Dangtalan the eighteen to twenty households actively marketing pottery traded an average of about twelve vessels a year, with the most active household exchanging around thirty-three a year over the four-year period for which data were collected. Women simply loaded pots on their backs and set off to barter, usually for rice or beans.

The historic Hopi traded in a similar fashion. People would take goods to be traded to another pueblo and hold an informal market in the plaza. They would be received as relatives by members of their own or an equivalent clan, who would give them a place to stay and enhance the social aspects of the trip.

Similar mechanisms of exchange were probably common among the Sinagua. While some exchange probably took place when individuals or small groups of relatives and friends went on trading ventures, some also occurred when outsiders visited Lizard Man Village. These foreigners may have been specialized part- or full-time traders from more hierarchically organized cultures like the Hohokam or just entrepreneurial individuals. It is possible that some of these foreigners remained in the area, perhaps marrying locals and establishing trade outposts. This is one possible explanation for pithouses found at sites like Winona that are very similar to those found in the Hohokam area.

Obviously, the issue of how trade was organized is directly relevant to the question of hierarchies. The model I have proposed does not assume any significant degree of social stratification. The alternative model relies on a hierarchy of leadership positions and assumes that the regulation of exchange is one of the functions of elites. Ultimately, more comprehensive issues of social organization must be resolved before the organization of exchange can be effectively described.

Chapter 10

EGALITARIAN OR STRATIFIED

The Current Debate about Social Organization

A rapid survey of contemporary newspapers will reveal a lack of consensus about interpretations of current events, even when the rough outlines of the facts are agreed upon. Political agendas and belief systems structure notions of reality. It should not be at all surprising that Hopi, Zuni, Navajo, New Age, and archaeological interpretations of the past differ or that consensus is lacking even within each of these groups. Within the academic discipline of archaeology, the evidence can often be read in multiple, sometimes contradictory, ways. For the Sinagua area and the Southwest in general, one of the major issues that has recently generated controversy is the amount of social stratification present. Early interpretations of the Sinagua and other prehistoric Southwestern Pueblo groups were heavily based on analogies with the Hopi, and, thus, used an egalitarian model of social organization. However, this has been and is being challenged.

To say a society is egalitarian is not to imply that all individuals are identical or even that they are all equal. Clearly, some people will have larger families, be healthier, smarter, more popular, or more skilled. Some may even take on special leadership roles. Furthermore, in all societies age and gender are important organizational principles with distinct implications for the types of roles available to the individual. What an egalitarian society does imply is that all individuals have more-or-less equal access to basic resources. Leaders in egalitarian societies tend to be relatively powerless, leading by example and inspiration rather than coercion. Social control is primarily through mechanisms such as public opinion, ridicule, and accusations of witchcraft, rather than through more formal legal systems. While there can be considerable movement of goods, most transactions are *reciprocal exchanges* between individuals. Much of the social glue is provided by kinship; further integration may be provided by sodalities such as age grades, religious organizations or warrior societies. Critical to the notion of egalitarian societies is that position is not inherited.

By the early 1980s a considerable number of archaeologists in the Southwest were arguing for a more hierarchical, stratified social organization in past pueblos than in historic times (Cordell 1989, Feinman 1989, Upham 1987, 1989, Wilcox 1981), perhaps the equivalent of what the cultural anthropologist Service (1962) has termed a chiefdom—a society with inherited positions entailing prestige, some actual coercive power, and differential access to resources. In chiefdoms exchange on an individual basis persists, but some flow of goods is controlled by elites, often through redistributive mechanisms in which a central individual or group gathers items, then disperses them. In part, these archaeologists were reacting negatively to what they considered excessive reliance on ethnographic analogies to the modern Pueblos. They pointed out that considerable changes in social organization in the Southwest may have occurred due to the depopulation and disruption wrought by European contact and conquest.

It is clear that there is some, and perhaps in some areas considerable, cultural continuity between the historic and prehistoric pueblos. Nevertheless, given the time that has occurred since the Sinagua occupied communities such as Lizard Man Village, cultural change is a surety. This means that, while analogies with modern groups can be used to suggest hypotheses about the past, they cannot be directly used to demonstrate any specific features of prehistoric social organization. The investigators arguing for complexity are certainly correct in asserting that it is the archaeological evidence that must testify to the social organization of prehistoric groups, rather than simplistic analogies with modern descendants.

Archaeologically, more hierarchical social, political, and economic organization is usually argued on the basis of (1) differential expenditures in burials, (2) patterns of site hierarchy, (3) indications of the existence of redistribution, and (4) labor-intensive public works that would have required leaders to coordinate. I believe I can show that the archaeological evidence does not support a highly stratified model of social organization in the Sinagua region during the time that Lizard Man Village was occupied. It is my opinion that in the Sinagua area and much of the prehistoric Southwest a basically egalitarian organization was the rule. After discussing and refuting more hierarchical models, I will propose an egalitarian model of Sinagua social organization that seems compatible with the evidence from Lizard Man Village and other contemporary Northern Sinagua sites.

How Burials Reflect Status

In addition to fulfilling religious necessities for the afterlife, the ceremony that marks the transition from life to death often also reaffirms the deceased's identity and relationships with others. Thus, burials provide a potential source of information about personal status. Patterns in grave treatment and goods can yield clues to religious beliefs, gender roles, and the degree and type of economic and social differentiation.

In chiefdom-level societies some individuals have greater access to prestige, power, and resources than others. At least some of these positions of authority are inherited. Such ascribed positions are often denoted by considerable pomp and ceremony. Sumptuary rules may, for example, restrict certain attire to chiefs or their families. Symbols of power such as staffs, thrones, or special jewelry may indicate particular positions of power and prestige. Some individuals will have enhanced access to some or all resources. This may mean a better diet, more lavish clothing, and/or a larger or fancier residence.

Sumptuary rules and differential access to resources may be mirrored in the treatment of individuals after their death. Thus, staffs, sumptuous costumes, and insignia of prestige and power may be buried with leaders. The mere presence of a unique object or costume does not automatically signal a powerful individual, however. Some roles may entail special attire and symbols but not carry real power or authority. Traditionally, archaeologists have assumed that greater investments in mortuary treatment indicate greater status. This implies that in relatively egalitarian societies, where variability in burials will be due to factors such as age, gender, cause of death, and personal accomplishments, the variation in expenditures will be relatively minor. In contrast, lavish expenditures for some individuals should indicate the high status of the person being interred. Ethnographic evidence demonstrates that the relationship between burial variability and social hierarchy is fairly strong, but not invariable. Some stratified societies ignore burial as an avenue for displaying status in favor of other alternatives. Thus, the degree of stratification may be underestimated in these cases. The other danger is in overestimating the variability in status. In most societies, even egalitarian ones, some variability in burials occurs. Therefore, the mere existence of variability, even variability that has implications for cost, cannot be seen as an indication of hierarchy. On the contrary, it is necessary to show the presence of extreme variation in expenditures and bi- and tri-modality in the distribution of burial treatment in order to make an effective case for social hierarchy.

In addition to simply identifying variation in status, archaeologists also often attempt to differentiate between ascribed and achieved status by examining the distribution of variability in burials. Theoretically, in societies with ascribed status, high-status burial goods and methods should be used for all the members of an elite family and should thus be found with bodies of all ages and sexes. In societies with only achieved-status positions, only older individuals should be given high-status burials.

The Sinagua practiced both cremation and inhumation. Burial customs changed some through time, and cremations seem to be more common in earlier time periods than inhumations. Some of the difference in burial treatment may also be due to ethnic differences. While we found some scattered fragments of cremated bone at Lizard Man Village, no intact cremations were discovered. As mentioned previously, the burials from Lizard Man Village are all rather late. We found no burials which can be assigned to the Angell-Winona Phase. Perhaps the scattered fragments of cremated bone represent these burials, and we simply did not find the main burial area for the early occupation of the village. The small sample of burials from Lizard Man Village restricts their potential as a source of data, if they are examined in isolation. In order to see patterns in burial practices that might reflect social organization, a large number of burials is needed.

John Hohman (1992) has completed the only comprehensive analysis of Sinagua burials to date. He looked at all of the burials available to him in 1992, some 592 burials from over thirty sites spanning the entire range of Northern Sinagua occupation. Since most of the data are from the Angell-Winona through Elden Phases (A.D. 1065–1250—the occupation period for Lizard Man Village, as well), his analysis concentrated on this time span. On the basis of the distribution of number of items per burial, Hohman argued for an increasingly hierarchical social structure between the Angell-Winona and Elden Phases. Obviously, simply counting the number of items in a burial has problems. It is unlikely that all goods were equally valued or had the same meaning when placed in a grave. Nevertheless, Hohman's analysis is the best we have at the moment, so we will examine his distributions (figure 10.1) and his interpretations of them. He views the distribution of goods in Angell-Winona burials (figure 10.1a) as bimodal, reflecting a two-tiered hierarchy of status. Of the five burials with the most grave goods, four were male, although the burial with the most goods belonged to an older woman. Three of the high-status male burials included artifacts that Hohman classified as religious, and, on this basis, Hohman proposes that during the Angell-Winona Phase some men (and perhaps occasional women) were able to achieve high status, perhaps through religious activities. This is consistent with the interpretation of the Northern Sinagua as egalitarian during the Angell-Winona Phase.

By the Elden Phase (figure 10.1c,d) Hohman interprets Northern Sinagua social organization to be considerably more hierarchical. Despite the fact that the Early Elden Phase burial goods distribution (where he puts the Lizard Man Village burials) (figure 10.1c) looks almost identical to the Angell-Winona distribution (figure 10.1a), he suggests the Early Elden Phase distribution is trimodal. One group is composed of burials including zero to three offerings, the second with four to six, and the third with seven or more offerings. The Late Elden Phase distribution is also interpreted as tri-modal, with groups defined as having zero to six, seven to twelve, and over fourteen offerings. Each group is equated with a status level. Hohman further suggests that the highest-status group can be further subdivided into one group with fourteen to eighteen offerings and a second with nineteen or more. The highest-status burials belong to males who are interred with religious goods. Hohman also claims to identify a "wealthy merchant class who control various trade items and/or the production of rare or exotic goods"(Hohman 1992:340). Ascribed status is inferred by the fact that some children are buried with fairly large numbers of goods.

The most obvious problem with Hohman's analysis is that his curves simply do not display the patterns of modality that he claims. The Angell-Winona and Early Elden distributions are the most similar in shape, despite the fact that he sees the former as bi-modal and the latter as tri-modal. All of the distributions are, in fact, simply extremely right-skewed distributions rather than either bi- or tri-modal. It may be due to the similarity in sample sizes that the Angell-Winona and Early Elden (figure 10.1a and c) distributions seem most similar to one another. Likewise the Padre and Late Elden distributions, which have larger sample sizes, are alike in including more extreme outliers. Given similar underlying distributions, one would expect fewer extreme outliers in small samples than in larger ones. This is merely another variant of the problem of finding rare items in sites with very limited excavation and raises the possibility that much of what we are interpreting (or overinterpreting) is simply sample bias.

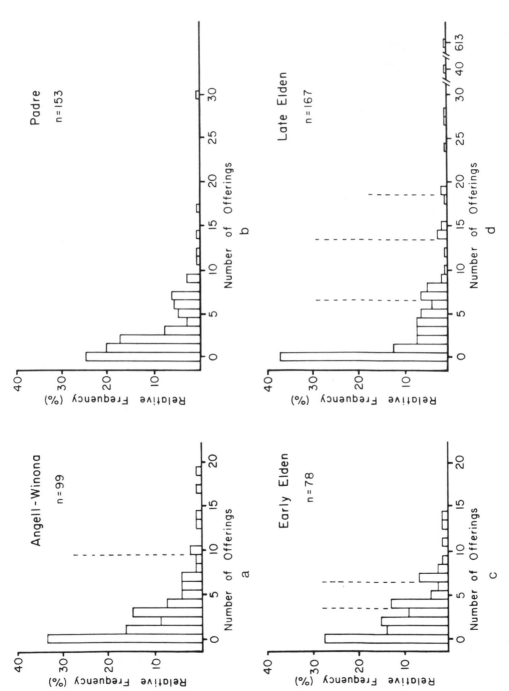

Figure 10.1 Hohman's histograms of the distributions of number of burial offerings by phase from earliest to latest: (a) Angell-Winona Phase, (b) Padre Phase, (c) Early Elden Phase, (d) Late Elden Phase.

A more reasonable interpretation of the skewed distributions character-istic of Sinagua burial goods is that there is a continuum of statuses. This does not obviate the notion that some individuals were more important than others or were buried with more goods for other reasons. For example, the "magician" burial (figure 1.5) described earlier, which may be the richest burial in the Southwest, was found in a Late Elden Phase context at the site of Ridge Ruin. Undoubtedly this individual was important and, given the nature of the items buried with him, his status was at least partially due to his religious position. Egalitarian societies, of course, may have religious societies and religious lead-ers. If the "magician" was just one of many religious leaders in the region with-out real coercive power or special access to resources, as might be expected in a relatively egalitarian society, why was he buried with so much more para-phernalia than other similar men? Southwestern ethnography may provide a clue. In many Puebloan groups, only personally-owned religious items were buried with an individual; however, when the last member of a religious society died, all the ceremonial goods were interred with the body. Perhaps this is what happened in the case of the "magician."

Site Hierarchies

One of the most important characteristics of a chiefdom is a decision-making hierarchy. Instead of a single level of leaders, usually centered within the vil-lage or band, a greater territory is united by several hierarchically-ranked leadership positions. Archaeologically, site hierarchies are expected to mirror the decision-making hierarchy. If some types of decisions require the author-ity of a chief or council, the location of the decision-making authorities becomes a center. One might expect this center to be larger than the sur-rounding sites it serves. Given the presence of elites, it might also have richer burials, more symbols of leadership and "elite" items, and perhaps more ostentatious residential architecture.

Proponents of a hierarchical model of Sinagua social organization (Gratz and Pilles 1979, Plog 1989, Pilles 1996) have suggested that by the Elden Phase, Northern Sinagua sites can be divided into a four-tiered hierarchy. At the bottom are very small, temporary and special-purpose sites like field houses. At the top are larger primary sites with specialized communal archi-tectural features such as walled plazas, community rooms, and associated ball courts, which would have required communal labor to construct and would have functioned to integrate large numbers of people. According to this model, the primary sites tend to occupy prominent locations and include a Hohokam-type pithouse, which might have been the residence of a trader from the south. Primary sites, since they would have functioned as redistributive cen-ters and residences for elites, should also have the higher percentages of trade goods and other exotics discussed in the previous chapter. In Peter Pilles' most recent exposition of these hierarchies (Pilles 1996), Chavez Pass (Nuvakwewtaqa), Juniper Terrace, Ridge Ruin, Wupatki (figure 9.3), Old

Caves Pueblo, and New Caves Pueblo are cited as the primary sites for the Northern Sinagua area (figure 1.1). Elden Pueblo (figure 9.2) is not mentioned, despite its large size. I can think of no good reason, but perhaps it is in part modesty, since Pilles has been excavating at Elden for many years.

As provocative as the hierarchical model is, it does not stand up well to scrutiny. First of all, none of the Northern Sinagua Elden Phase sites is really all that large. Table 10.1 lists some of the excavated Northern Sinagua sites. It includes a few smaller sites and most of the better known and larger ones. Even the very largest sites are only in the fifty- to one-hundred-room range. When only contemporaneously occupied rooms are counted (an impossible task at the moment, since the relevant data simply does not exist for most of these sites), the sizes would doubtless be reduced even further. Remember that at Lizard Man Village we were able to identify twenty-five rooms but concluded that no more than a maximum of eight were ever occupied simultaneously. Furthermore, a number of the presumed Elden Phase (A.D. 1150–1250) centers may, in fact, be somewhat later than the Elden Phase, belonging to the subsequent Turkey Hill (A.D. 1250–1300) Phase. During these later phases, as I will discuss in the next chapter, the Sinagua were abandoning small sites in favor of a few larger ones; thus some large sites may be late agglomerations rather than early redistributive or elite centers.

The paucity of large sites in the Sinagua area is illustrated by the fact that, when Peter Pilles was asked to compile a list of Sinagua sites with more than sixty rooms (by no means a gargantuan community by today's standards!) for a conference and subsequent volume on the Pueblo III Period (A.D. 1150–1350) (Adler 1996), he had to redefine the notion of a large site to include those with twenty or more rooms. Twenty rooms is a small village of no more than a dozen or so households. In general a community of this size should not require a very elaborate leadership structure.

Secondly, a perusal of table 10.1 also reveals that not all the so-called primary sites have the full array of architectural features that the proponents of hierarchy would predict. Nor are these architectural features by any means exclusive to primary sites. Community rooms, kivas, walled plazas, ridge-top locations, and Hohokam-style pithouses are all found at small sites as well as larger ones. Ball courts are sometimes not even very clearly associated with specific sites.

We have already discussed the "magician" burial from Ridge Ruin. This site, despite having an extremely impressive burial, is quite small, with only about nineteen pueblo rooms. It is classed as a primary site because it has a walled plaza, is located on a ridge, and is near two ball courts. Its primary claim to inclusion in the primary-site category, however, appears to be the "magician" burial. Two Kivas, which has a very similar location and layout but lacks such an impressive burial, is not listed as a primary site. Wupatki Pueblo, probably the most impressive site on the list, is located on the boundary between Kayenta and Sinagua territory. Some (Wilcox 1996, for example) would call this site Kayenta rather than Sinagua. Nevertheless, the presence of many Sinagua artifact types plus Sinagua features such as a ball court argue

Table 10.1 **Comparative Data for Excavated Northern Sinagua Sites**

Site Name	NA number	Pithouses Rooms	Pueblo Rooms	Room Blocks	Excavated Rooms (all)	Other
Juniper Terrace	1814	3	16 to 20 (59)	2	16	Walled plaza. One of pithouses = kiva. one = "Hohokam." Ball court ca. 400m east.
Three Courts Pueblo	618	3	6	1	9	Walled plaza. Pithouse X = "Hohokam," ball court .3 miles SE.
Ridge Ruin	1785	5	19 (30)	1	7	Walled plaza. Two ball courts. "Magician" burial.
Winona Village	several	20+	3	1	23	Ball court. "Hohokam" pithouse. Discrete trash mounds.
Two Kivas	700	2 to 4	14 to 19	1	10 to 13	Walled plazas. Two large, shallow rooms = community rooms? Two pithouses = kivas? Two stories in part.
Lizard Man Village	17957	15	8	2	21	Two benched rooms = kivas.
Turkey Hill Pueblo	660	1	22+ (35)	1?	23?	Two stories in part.
Old Caves Pueblo	72	?	70 to 80 (55)	1?	a few	Possible walled plaza or community room. Ball court below site.
New Caves Pueblo	several	?	50 to 100 (34)	4 to 8	a few	Walled plazas. 2-3 possible community rooms. Ball court ca. 100 m. west.
Elden Pueblo	142	5?	60 to 70 (65)	1	37+	Community room. Prepared surface plaza.
Wupatki	405	0?	70+ (102)	2+	37+	Walled plaza? Ball court. Community room. Three stories in part.
Fortress Hills Pueblo	6612	2 to 4	5	1	6	Pithouse - kiva?
Kahorsho	10937	10	5	1	15	
Turkey Tank Fort	113	0	4	2	3	Walls blocking access.
Pendant Pueblo	7449	1	3	1	3	Ramada.
Rincon Pueblo	7432	0	3	1	3	Two ramadas.
Tse Tlani	8752	4	3	1	7	
Wilson Pueblo	1139	1	5	1	6	Wing walls.
Hibbard Pueblo	1140	0	4	1	4	
Spur Site	8756	0	16	2	5	
Sunset Pueblo	16387	0	34(22)	1?	1	
Beals Saddle Site	7350	1	5	1	5	Benched room = kiva.
2131 at Winona	2131	0	3	1	3	

Numbers in parentheses are Pilles' (1996) estimate of number of Pueblo III (A.D. 1150–1300) rooms.

for its inclusion in the Sinagua culture area. Wupatki is clearly an impressive site as Sinagua sites go. Today a national monument, it includes a central room block which is three stories high in places, a large community room, and a ball court. Juniper Terrace is also a good-sized site that includes a large central plaza. The ceramics at the site include the Sinagua Alameda Brown Wares, but also a high percentage of Cohonina Grey Wares, and it is possible that this is a Cohonina site rather than Sinagua. Alternatively, the population may be a mixture from the two groups. The occupation of Juniper Terrace probably ended about A.D. 1300, a bit later than the end of the Elden Phase. Old Caves and New Caves Pueblos are also both large sites for the area, perhaps numbering as many as a hundred rooms. Both are located at the top of cinder cones and include caveate rooms (hence the names). Both are also located fairly near ball courts, although it is likely that the ball courts pre-date their occupations, and both have community rooms. Both are also fairly late, probably dating primarily to the end of the Elden Phase and into the subsequent Turkey Hill Phase. Likewise, although Chavez Pass (Nuvak-wewtaqa) is eventually extremely large, the bulk of the site is also quite late. Pilles (1996) estimates only about twenty occupied rooms in each of three room-block areas prior to A.D. 1300. Thus, while there is certainly variation in the size and layout of Northern Sinagua communities during the Elden Phase, it is hard to envision a real system of hierarchies. There is simply not enough variability in size nor a great enough correlation between size and either location or layout. At most one might argue that a few sites are somewhat larger than their neighbors' sites.

"Hohokam-style" pithouses are listed as one attribute of primary sites and are often interpreted as traders' dwellings. Personally, I remain unconvinced. Hohokam pithouses are, as the name implies, dwellings that seem fairly Hohokam in style. Ideally, they also include significant quantities of Hohokam artifacts. The so-called Hohokam pithouse at Winona Village has a number of "Hohokam-derived" ceramic vessels, but all are of local manufacture; none are actual Hohokam imports. The only actual items from the Hohokam region found associated with the pithouse are shell ornaments, fairly common artifacts at many Sinagua sites which do, indeed, probably originate in the Hohokam region. The pithouses at two other sites, Juniper Terrace and Three Courts Pueblo, also have few or no possible Hohokam goods and may even predate the rest of the village. Note that Three Courts Pueblo is not currently seen as a primary site, despite its "Hohokam" pithouse, while several of the proposed primary sites such as Ridge Ruin do not even have a possible Hohokam pithouse. The explanation for this type of variability in pithouse design has yet to be conclusively determined, but there is currently no evidence that they were the residences of elite Hohokam traders.

Finally, the artifactual evidence does not support the notion that the slightly larger sites are acting as political or economic centers during the Elden Phase. As discussed earlier, if some sites are, in fact, the residences of elites who, to an extent, control redistribution and exchange, they should have a higher frequency of imports, exotic goods, and artifacts used as status markers than other sites. Interestingly, the proportion of imported ceramics appears to be about the same at Lizard Man Village as at so-called primary sites in the same region, a finding inconsistent with the notion that these communities were acting as trading centers.

Lizard Man Village produced a number of what are usually termed status goods, including the painted fiber armband, a fragment of a carved bone hairpin, at least two nose plugs, and pieces of turquoise cut into tiny slabs to be used as parts of a mosaic, perhaps to decorate jewelry or a wooden staff. Other small sites have produced rare artifacts as well. As mentioned previously, one of the few copper bells found in a Northern Sinagua site is from Tse Tlani, an even smaller site than Lizard Man Village. A carved argillite bowl, the largest argillite artifact from the region of which I am aware, was found at Kahorsho. It is true that some rare artifacts such as macaws and Hohokam cut shell have not yet been found at small sites. This may well simply be due to the sampling bias against small sites referred to earlier, however.

Evidence for Redistribution

Communal storage facilities are one possible indication of *redistribution*. Their absence, however, does not assure that no redistribution took place. Redistributive systems may have circulated items rapidly, redistributing them almost immediately after collection, thus eliminating the need for communal storage. Alternatively, small valuables such as turquoise and shell may have been the primary items obtained through redistribution. Again, the need for large storage areas is eliminated. Another characteristic of redistributive systems should be an uneven distribution of redistributed items across sites. Presumably individuals residing in redistributive centers would have greater access to redistributed goods, especially if the centers were the residences of elites. For the Elden Phase Sinagua, like the residents of Lizard Man Village, there is no evidence of communal storage, nor, as discussed above, is there evidence that the residents of any villages had enhanced access to resources.

Public Works

Public architecture that would require vast amounts of labor to construct has also been used to argue for strong leadership roles, based on the idea that people will not spend large amounts of time on communal projects unless some coercion is applied or incentives are very strong. While in extreme cases such as the pyramids this may be true, many fairly impressive projects can be achieved using volunteer labor, motivated by religious or other considerations rather than coercion and using part-time, temporary, or special-purpose leaders to coordinate the effort.

There are certainly some features at Elden Phase sites that might have required considerable amounts of labor and perhaps some community cooperation to construct. These include ball courts, community rooms, and walled plazas. Kivas presumably would be communally used and might have been village labor projects. The key question here is whether any of these constructions would have required intensive, long-term, or coercive leadership. I suspect but cannot prove that the answer is a resounding no. The issue is the easiest to dismiss for kivas. These structures are very similar to living quarters and should not have required much more labor to build than an ordinary dwelling. Walled plazas also should not have required inordinate amounts of labor, as the walls tend not to be very high. Although the rocks used to construct them are sometimes quite large and heavy, this is also true of some of the stones used in private houses. Since the basalt bedrock is quite close to the surface at some of the sites where these occur, it is possible that some construction of the walls was really effort expended to clear central surfaces. The community rooms and ball courts undoubtedly required the most construction labor of any Sinagua structures. Yet, even this effort must not have been great enough to require a real leadership structure. The earliest ball courts appear to be pre-eruptive and thus date long before anyone posits a hierarchical leadership structure.

Overview of the Egalitarian Model

In brief, the archaeological evidence does not convincingly support the idea that the Sinagua were hierarchically organized during the time that Lizard Man Village was occupied. A more egalitarian model is more consistent with the available data. In fact, I argue that a basically egalitarian social structure is one of the keys to the Sinagua's success in populating the Flagstaff area so completely and for such a long time. It is, of course, necessary to realize that this is simply a model which attempts to explain Northern Sinagua social and economic organization. Like all models, it cannot be proven, merely supported. Like all models, it only awaits new evidence and analysis for revision.

The Angell-Winona through Elden Phase Sinagua, like their ancestors before them and most of their neighbors in the Southwest, had a diversified subsistence economy, growing a variety of crops including corn, beans, and squash. They supplemented agricultural products with a wide range of wild animals and gathered plants. The agricultural activities of the Lizard Man villagers are shown by the carbonized remains of plants, tools such as hoes, and the remains of field systems. Use-wear analysis of manos corroborates the emphasis on corn and other seeds. As in historic times, one common method of preparation apparently entailed grinding the grains into meal.

Nevertheless, the Northern Sinagua environment is marginal for corn agriculture, and populations experienced periodic stress due to crop failures. Around Flagstaff rainfall is scarce, streams and springs are generally absent, and the growing season is short, making agricultural productivity uncertain. During the Angell-Winona through Elden Phases (A.D. 1065–1250), the environment was similar to that of today, although there was some variability within the period. Pollen and tree-rings suggest that shortly after the eruption of Sunset Crater the climate was more optimal both in terms of moisture and temperature. By the Elden Phase (A.D. 1150–1250) conditions were becoming cooler and drier, which would have had an adverse effect on the agricultural regime. Stress on the agricultural system may be reflected in the smaller size of corn cobs during the Elden Phase. Skeletal materials from Lizard Man Village also show stress and the likelihood of periodic food shortages. High infant mortality rates and low life expectancies, small body size, and nutritional conditions such as *cribra orbitalia* and tooth enamel hypoplasias testify that life for the Lizard Man villagers was often difficult. Since environmental conditions would indicate the likelihood of periodic crop failures, the fact that almost all of the villagers had some skeletal evidence of periodic stress is of particular interest to this theory.

A number of measures were undertaken in order to buffer environmental fluctuations. These included (a) using specially adapted crop types and a variety of water conservation techniques, (b) dispersing field locations, (c) utilizing nonagricultural foods in addition to crops, (d) minimizing population agglomeration, and (e) maximizing individual and group social networks through exchange, ceremony, and possibly marriage.

The Sinagua, like the modern Hopi and Zuni, probably used specially adapted crop varieties and a variety of techniques such as check dams, deep planting, and wide spacing of plants within fields to optimize their chances of success. Small site size and dispersed field locations allowed them to effectively utilize sparse agricultural resources. Field houses provided a place to stay when it was necessary to remain near widely scattered fields to plant, harvest, or scare away birds and other pests. The use of a variety of crops and the dispersion of fields buffered environmental variability to an extent. The weather in the Flagstaff area is often very localized; sometimes rain will fall on one site and not on another only a mile or two away. Augmenting agricultural produce with a wide variety of wild plants and animals further provided an environmental buffer. Moving village locations periodically may have decreased the effects of long-term overuse on immediate resources (for example, allowing wood to be replenished). Infestations of rodents and insects may have also been avoided in this manner. Furthermore, this movement would have familiarized individuals with different areas and allowed them to establish and maintain scattered fields.

Social as well as environmental buffers were essential. Despite their small size, Sinagua villages like Lizard Man Village were largely self-sufficient, producing a full range of goods including food, ceramics, thread, stone tools, and ornaments. While we can not demonstrate it, it is likely that individual households were also able to produce their basic subsistence requirements. This lack of specialists would allow very small villages to remain autonomous and village size to be very flexible and responsive to local conditions. While capable of being self-sufficient, villages were linked into social networks by shared beliefs and values, religion, and trade. Most sites have some type of religious facilities, but their exact nature varies. Lizard Man Village with its kiva may have been the scene for certain ceremonies, while the walled plaza area of Ridge

Ruin was used for others in a ceremonial cycle that incorporated neighboring villages into a single community. Ties between Sinagua villages were probably enhanced by exchange, friendship, and intermarriage. Trade with neighboring groups, well documented by numerous imports, not only allowed access to desired exotics but probably cemented relations with these groups, allowing a certain amount of intermarriage and providing even more of a buffer against lean years for both groups.

Cooperation and flexibility were the keys to survival. Because villages—and probably to a large extent even households—were self-sufficient, movement between groups and to new regions was possible in times of stress. Instead of an emphasis on institutional solutions or an accumulation of resources by favored groups, the optimal organization was egalitarian and cooperative. A social system where both individuals and villages were relatively similar and equal allowed maximum flexibility, but groups were loosely knit by kin ties and shared material culture, beliefs, and rituals, and probably intra-group exchange.

Ultimately this adaptation, because it relied heavily on a dispersed settlement pattern, worked well only when the region was peaceful. In the succeeding Turkey Hill Phase, which we are now investigating at New Caves (one of the aforementioned "primary" sites), people move into a few larger sites and small sites disappear. This may be due to defensive requirements in an increasingly hostile regional social environment. It is shortly after this that the Sinagua abandon the Flagstaff area altogether.

Chapter 11

LIZARD MAN VILLAGE— ABANDONED, BUT NOT FORGOTTEN

The Sinagua occupied Lizard Man Village and other communities in the Flagstaff area for over two hundred years. Life was not always easy, but people were satisfied enough with their existence that they did not leave the area. They loved and revered the peaks, the volcanic craters, and the pinyon-juniper forests. The landscape was the locus of numerous stories of their ancestors and their gods. They knew their surroundings intimately and understood them well.

By the early 1300s, however, the Sinagua abandoned the Flagstaff area, first moving southeast to the Anderson Mesa region to sites like Chavez Pass (Nuvakwewtaqa), then probably on to the Homolovi villages and the Hopi Mesas to the east and north. Why did the Sinagua desert the region, forsaking their home ground and venturing into new territories?

The most frequent explanation is environmental change. As we discussed earlier, the climate was becoming cooler and drier in the mid-1200s. This is a phenomenon found throughout the Southwest and is a common explanation for abandonments. Droughts occurred in the Southwest toward the end of the thirteenth century, coincident with the abandonment of many areas and the coalescence of populations in the most favorable locales—those with the most reliable sources of water. Some explanations also propose that groups like the Sinagua were part of the ecological problem themselves. In particular, the use of wood to make fires and construct dwellings may have caused deforestation with resulting soil erosion. We have no direct evidence of this at Lizard Man Village, although some pollen data indicates a somewhat more open, grassy vegetation than currently exists. Populations may have been dispersed enough to have avoided much ecological damage.

Coincident with the abandonment of sites and of whole regions is the agglomeration of populations into larger settlements and probably some ensuing increases in social complexity and hierarchy. Explanations of this phenomenon have stressed the need to settle in specific locales because of the availability of scarce resources, religious or social reasons for preferring more sizable communities, and the advantages of greater organization for effective use of resources. In the Flagstaff area, since populations do not coalesce in the most environmentally favorable locales, the first explanation does not work. The second is idiosyncratic and therefore hard to assess. I suggest that the third may be the main reason for the tendency toward larger community size and that the major advantage is defensive.

I do not eschew the notion that ecological problems were at least a significant part of the story. Nevertheless, the pattern of abandonments appears to be a bit more complex in the Flagstaff area than a search for locations with better subsistence resources. Warfare may be the missing element in the picture. We suggest that by the mid-1200s the political situation in the Flagstaff area had deteriorated. Peace had been replaced by conflict, and the previous adaptation which relied on small, dispersed and relatively indefensible villages was no longer possible.

By the late 1200s, the Sinagua had largely deserted hamlets like Lizard Man Village in favor of larger settlements, such as New Caves Pueblo. Given dispersed agricultural resources and a reliance on hunting and gathering to supplement the agricultural regime, these larger communities do not appear to be as effective an adaptation to the natural environment as the small settlements.

New Caves Pueblo is located on O'Neil Crater, an extinct cinder cone (figure 11.1). Its location is beautiful; the views are spectacular. Nevertheless, there is no water, and agriculture would be difficult on the cinder slopes. None of them appear to be terraced for farming, so we assume that the Sinagua farmed the flats below. All food and water would have had to be carried up a very long and steep ascent. On the top it is very windy. Sometimes in hot weather the breeze seems a godsend. Other times, as it picks up and distributes dust and makes papers fly, it is considerably less pleasant. In the winter the crater is exposed and cold. Several of the dwellings at New Caves have walls built adjacent to or around the rooms to combat the problem by acting as windscreens. Lightning may also have been a danger to the occupants of New

Figure 11.1 *O'Neil Crater, the location of New Caves Pueblo. The site runs from the crest on the left through the saddle, where a community room and walled plaza are located, to a more sparsely populated area on the crest to the right. A small pueblo is also located on the bench to the front of the crater, clearly visible because of the paucity of trees.*

Caves. The location is high and exposed, and we have observed several rocks that have been struck by lightning.

Despite the disadvantages of its location, a large number of people decided to move to New Caves Pueblo. It is much larger than Lizard Man Village, with more than one hundred rooms situated in several small clusters. Some of the rooms are constructed in natural caves along the interior face of the crater. In addition to living spaces and a large community room, the site boasts a walled plaza at the very center of the community. A ball court is nearby (a few minutes walk from the crater) but appears to have been abandoned prior to the occupation of New Caves Pueblo. At the top of one section of the crater, in the least accessible portion of the site, the structures are bordered on one side by cliffs and enclosed on the other by walls. The advantage of living in a community like New Caves Pueblo may be defense. In addition to the obvious advantages of size for security, New Caves is located in an easily defensible location which is augmented by the construction of enclosing walls.

There is considerable controversy over the extent to which the prehistoric pueblos were warlike. Archaeological evidence for warfare, especially if it is primarily on a fairly small scale with an emphasis on raiding, is sparse. We know from studies of Europe that only when texts become available does the prevalence of war become apparent. Because conflict is notoriously difficult to detect, we may well be underestimating the importance of war in the prehistoric Southwest. Normally casualties were probably fairly slight, so mass burials would not be expected. Most individuals who die as a result of war do not show identifiable skeletal injuries. On the other hand, an isolated individual with a projectile point embedded in a bone may have been the victim of murder or an internal dispute. Weaponry is often indistinguishable from tools (an axe), hard to identify (an unmodified stone used as a missle), or made of perishable materials (throwing sticks). Battles or the movement of warriors leaves little trace on the landscape, and that which is left tends to be scattered and difficult to interpret. The isolated possession dropped by a warrior is not only hard to find but impossible to identify as the belonging of an intruder. A more likely explanation, given the volume of exchange in the prehistoric Southwest, is that it is a trade good. Even the burning of a village is ambiguous, as there are numerous possible causes for a fire. The best evidence of warfare may be fortified communities. Even here it is hard to prove that a site location, tower, or wall was defensive rather than simply delineating a social group or demarking territory.

Haas and Creamer (1996) have recently argued quite convincingly that warfare might have been endemic thoughout the northern Southwest by the end of the thirteenth century. Many sites, including many of the popular tourist destinations like Betatakin, several sites at Hovenweep, and a number of the Mesa Verde pueblos, are located in defensible positions throughout the Southwest at this time. Furthermore, many of these sites have features that seem designed to enhance the ability of the community to protect themselves from attack—for example, blocking walls, convoluted entries, and watchtowers. Haas and Creamer conducted surveys of the Klethla and Kayenta Valleys specifically to test the notion that the thirteenth century was a period of warfare in the Kayenta area. Survey crews examined a large number of defensible locations in addition to a control sample of nondefensible areas.

> It got so that one of the best indicators of site location was when the survey crews were unable to find an access route to the top of a particular topographic feature. In each such case, a second effort revealed a skinny crack in the rock or steep trail up the cliff side, and a pueblo on top invariably dating to A.D. 1250–1300. (Haas and Creamer 1996:208)

Thus, the location of sites in both these valleys lends support to the hypothesis that the thirteenth century was not a time of peace in the Kayenta region. The location of sites like New Caves Pueblo that were founded in the late Elden and Turkey Hill Phases lends support to the hypothesis that by the end of the thirteenth century the Northern Sinagua area also may no longer have been peaceful.

The modern Hopi, while often viewed as essentially peaceful, historically had warrior societies and were successfully recruited in large numbers to the Spanish military. Clearly, by contact times the Hopi were well adapted to a situation where war was common and defense was important. It is not certain, however, when this situation began. Surely warrior societies can be formed fairly quickly, if needed. It is likely that residence patterns would have changed more slowly. The use of a matrilocal, postmarital residence system among modern groups may also be an indication of a more violent past with considerable long-distance warfare, although a very indirect one.

Thus, I suggest that Lizard Man Village and similar communities were initially abandoned not in a search for places with a more secure agricultural base in the face of declining environmental conditions, but in a search for increased security in a region that had become increasingly prone to war. This interpretation does not imply that the natural environment was not an important factor. Indeed, it is possible that the root cause of the social disruptions occurring at this period was a decreasing resource base. I propose, however, that warfare is the most urgent reason for the agglomeration of populations in primarily defensive locations immediately after the abandonment of sites such as Lizard Man Village.

The change from a dispersed to a more agglomerated settlement pattern was probably an unwise one in the Flagstaff area, however, and quickly exacerbated the Sinagua's problems. As I argued earlier, the ecology of the area favors a dispersed settlement pattern and an extremely flexible subsistence strategy, including the use of a wide variety of both domesticated and wild plants and animals and incorporating numerous social buffers as well. Divergence from this pattern probably led to a less stable subsistence regime, which caused the complete abandonment of the region.

Directions for Future Research

Research is never completed. While theories can be disproven by contradictory evidence, they are never securely proven, merely more completely supported. It is the nature of interesting theories and models that they suggest areas for further research. New hypotheses are generated, and new data is collected and analyzed to test them. Such is the continuing dynamic of research in archaeology and other sciences.

After the excavations at Lizard Man Village were completed, we spent one season investigating a similar nearby village, Fortress Hills Pueblo, to verify that Lizard Man Village was indeed typical of small Angell-Winona through Elden Phase villages. As I mentioned earlier, we are currently excavating the site of New Caves Pueblo. We chose this site because we felt that in order to understand Lizard Man Village and its place in Sinagua history we needed to understand the largest site in its vicinity. When we began to excavate at New Caves, we felt it would be contemporary to Lizard Man Village but would have have been occupied somewhat longer. We have now sampled from several areas of the site. Our preliminary assessment is that this larger community was primarily occupied after the abandonment of Lizard Man Village, and the length of occupation was fairly short. We have two more areas of the site that we would like to sample; then our work at New Caves is completed. The site has been extensively pot-hunted over the years, so it is by no means pristine in condition. Nevertheless, we would like to ensure that considerable portions of all components of the site are left unexcavated, available for investigation by future investigators who may have more techniques at their disposal than we do.

We are also continuing to survey the area around Lizard Man Village, Fortress Hills Pueblo, and New Caves. More survey is certainly needed to delineate not only those areas which were occupied in given time periods, but also to show which were abandoned or only sparsely used. More excavation, particularly in single-period sites, will also help refine our knowledge of Sinagua subsistence patterns and lifestyles. More detailed dating information will help us refine our chronologies so that we can more accurately determine which sites are contemporary and more reliably reconstruct exact sequences of events.

The possible agendas for future research are almost limitless. More specific and detailed information about climate would help evaluate the likelihood of successful crops. To date not nearly enough work has been done analyzing either floral or faunal remains. It would be useful to have data on differences in subsistence patterns, both through time and between large and small sites. Even as I write, Andrea Hunter and her students at Northern Arizona University are working on further analysis of floral remains.

Several additional pet projects of mine spring to mind. A much more complete analysis of Sinagua burials needs to be undertaken in order to provide information about the ways variability in mortuary ritual may have been a reflection of age, gender, ethnic affiliation, or social status. More analysis of exchange patterns is also a critical research project. To date not enough use has been made of the chemical techniques that would allow us to trace local and long-distance exchange networks.

While I have tended to juxtapose Native American and archaeological explanations and goals throughout the book, I see the relationship between the two as potentially symbiotic. Ethnohistory and ethnography provide a rich source of knowledge and hypotheses for archaeologists. Analogously, archaeologists can potentially answer questions of interest to some Native American groups. For example, attempts could be made to trace affinities between different Puebloan groups and to further document the movement of clans as they settled in different regions of the Southwest before ending up in their current pueblos.

Conclusion

It is important for an archaeologist to have imagination and empathy. It is not sufficient to see the past merely as a collection of abstract concepts. While we can never see the faces of the individuals who inhabited Lizard Man Village and similar sites, it is important to remember that they too were once people with the full array of experiences and emotions, and to try to hear the distant echos of their voices, no matter how faint.

Imagination is not enough, however. Archaeology cannot be merely speculation, no matter how attractive or romantic. The past has already occurred, and we cannot change it; we can simply try to understand it. For this we must rely on the interpretation of the material record of the past, historic documents, ethnohistoric accounts, experiments, and ethnographic analogy. The techniques for interpretation are scientific in nature but broad in scope.

Glossary

absolute dating dating techniques that yield a specific calendar date or a date range

arbitrary level a horizontal excavation unit based on an absolute measurement, rather than visible soil differences

archaeomagnetic dating an absolute dating technique based on a knowledge of changes in the earth's magnetic pole through time

artifact any object manufactured, modified, or used by humans, usually refers to movable objects in contrast to features which are not moveable

attribute any characteristic of an object, such as color, length, or material

bifacial tool a stone tool flaked on both faces

burnish polish applied to a ceramic by rubbing the surface of the vessel

chert a sedimentary silicious rock suitable for making stone tools

context the spatial or temporal position of an artifact in relation to other artifacts or features, the location in space, time, and cultural affiliation

core nodule of rock with scars from previous flake removals

corporate group a social group whose existence has continuity through time independent of individual members and which holds common rights to property of a material or non-material nature

corrugated pottery ceramics finished by retaining the coiled structure and modifying the coils using techniques such as pinching or scraping

cortex the external surface of a nodule of rock

datum a stable reference point with respect to which a site is mapped

debitage manufacturing debris, used most often with lithics

de facto refuse objects simply abandoned, rather than actually discarded

dendrochronology an absolute dating technique based on the comparison of tree-rings from archaeological specimens to a known sequence of tree-ring variation through time

diaphysis the shaft of a long bone, separated from the epiphyses by growing tissue which fuses at maturity

epiphysis the articular end of the long bone, separated from the diaphyses by growing tissue which fuses at maturity

feature an immobile trace of human occupation or manufacture, such as a hearth, pit, or ash stain

field house a small, temporary dwelling located near fields and occupied at certain times of the agricultural cycle

flake a piece of rock removed from a core and showing regular features including a striking platform and bulb of percussion

flotation a technique for separating carbonized plant remains from the dirt matrix by utilizing the fact that carbon floats in water

formation processes natural or cultural phenomena that are important in the production of archaeological sites

handstone a stone held in the hand and used for grinding, but not used in conjunction with a *metate* (in contrast to a *mano*)

hypoplasias linear irregularities in the teeth caused by the interruption of growth

in situ in the place of original deposition

isotopes variants of the same element that differ in atomic number, for example C^{13} and C^{14}

kiva Hopi word denoting a room, usually subterranean and with features such as benches, niches, and a *sipapu*, that is used for ceremonial purposes and as an area for weaving and other primarily male activities (The term is generalized by archaeologists to denote prehistoric rooms with a similar morphology interpreted as wholly or partially ceremonial in function.)

knapper an individual who makes flaked stone tools

law of superposition the principle that states that overlaying deposits are later than the layers underneath them

level in stratigraphy a layer or horizontal deposit

lithics chipped stone artifacts and debitage

mano a hand-held stone used for grinding, presumably in conjunction with a *metate*

metate the basal stone used for grinding in conjunction with a *mano*

midden an area used for the deposition of garbage

natural levels stratigraphic units recognized by color, texture, or other differences in the deposits

obsidian volcanic glass

pithouse a semi-subterranean or subterranean dwelling

plumb bob   a weight used for leveling

point provenience   the exact location in three dimensional space of an artifact or feature

porotic hyperostosis   pitted bone that occurs in anemic individuals

primary refuse   refuse left at the place of use

profile   a drawing of a stratigraphic section showing soil layers, features, and architecture

projectile points   pointed bifacial stone tools, including arrowheads and spear points

provenience   in a site, the position of an artifact or feature; more generally, information about location, cultural affiliation, or context

pubic symphysis   the area where the pelvic bones meet at the midline

pueblo   a Spanish word meaning village, used to refer to historic and prehistoric villages in the Southwest with clustered masonry or adobe architecture

radiometric dating   absolute dating technique based on the measurement of levels of unstable isotopes and relying on a knowledge of the rate of decay of the isotope

reciprocal exchange   transfers of goods or services between individuals or groups with no mechanism of central control; exchanges are generally fairly balanced and mutually beneficial

redistribution   the collection of goods or services and their reallocation by a central individual, group, or institution

relative dating   dating techniques that yield an order of occurrence, rather than specific calendar dates

retouch   a small flake resulting from shaping or sharpening the edge of a tool

secondary refuse   garbage deposited away from its location of use

seriation   a relative dating technique based on the notion that styles change slowly and systematically through time

shatter   irregular fragments of stone that are part of the debris from stone tool making

sipapu   a hole in the floor of a *kiva* symbolizing the place of emergence of the ancestors from the underworld

slip   a thin solution of clay applied to a ceramic vessel before firing, often to alter the color of the vessel

smudging   producing a black surface on a ceramic vessel by firing it in an atmosphere with carbon smoke and little oxygen

sodality   organizations which recruit members from outside the boundaries of kinship groups

stratigraphic levels   a sequence of sedimentary layers

stratigraphy   the vertical sequence of layers

sutures   places where bones articulate directly, often in an interlocked fashion, frequently used to refer to the junctures of skull bones

temper   nonplastic inclusions added to clay to make the drying process more even and reduce cracking, the amount and type of temper also affect the properties of the finished vessel

type   a category based on within-group similarities and between-group differences, used to classify artifacts; for ceramics the smallest unit of classification, having both temporal and cultural implications

unifacial tool   a stone tool flaked on only one face

ware   a group of pottery types which are technologically similar

References

Adams, E. Charles. 1991. *The Origin and Development of the Pueblo Katsina Cult.* Tucson: University of Arizona Press.

_____. 1994. The Katsina Cult: A Western Pueblo Perspective. In *Kachinas in the Pueblo World*, edited by Polly Schaafsma, pp. 35–46. Albuquerque: University of New Mexico Press.

Adler, Michael A., ed. 1996. *The Prehistoric Pueblo World A.D. 1150–1350.* Tucson: University of Arizona Press.

Bartlett, K. 1933. Pueblo Milling Stones of the Flagstaff Region and Their Relation to Others in the Southwest. *Museum of Northern Arizona Bulletin No. 7*, Flagstaff.

Berlin, G., David E. Salas, and Phil R. Geib. 1990. A Prehistoric Agricultural Site in the Ashfall Zone of Sunset Crater, Arizona. *Journal of Field Archaeology* 17(1): 1–16.

Bradfield, Maitland. 1971. *The Changing Pattern of Hopi Agriculture.* London: Royal Anthropological Institute of Great Britain and Ireland.

Breternitz, David A. 1966. An Appraisal of Tree-Ring Dated Pottery in the Southwest. *Anthropological Papers of the University of Arizona*, No. 10, Tucson.

Brothwell, D. R. 1972. *Digging Up Bones: The Excavation, Treatment and Study of Human Skeletal Remains.* London: British Museum.

Brown, Barton McCaul. 1987. Population Estimation from Floor Area: A Restudy of "Naroll's Constant." *Behavior Science Research* 21:1–49.

Colton, Harold S. 1932. A Possible Hopi Tradition of the Eruption of Sunset Crater. *Museum Notes, Museum of Northern Arizona* 5(4): 23.

Colton, Harold S. 1946. *The Sinagua: A Summary of the Archaeology of the Region of Flagstaff, Arizona. Museum of Northern Arizona Bulletin 22.* Flagstaff: Northern Arizona Society of Science and Art.

_____. 1960. *Black Sand: Prehistory in Northern Arizona.* Albuquerque: University of New Mexico Press.

Cordell, Linda S. 1989. History and Theory in Reconstructing Southwestern Sociopolitical Organization. In *The Sociopolitical Structure of Prehistoric Southwestern Societies*, edited by Steadman Upham, Kent G. Lightfoot, and Roberta Jewett, pp. 33–54. Boulder: Westview Press.

Cushing, Frank Hamilton. 1920. *Zuni Breadstuff.* Indian Notes and Monographs No. 8, Museum of the American Indian, Heye Foundation, New York. Originally published 1884–1885 in *The Millstone.*

Dean, Jeffery. 1970. Aspects of Tsegi Phase Social Organization: A Trial Reconstruction. In *Reconstructing Prehistoric Pueblo Societies*, edited by William A. Longacre, pp. 140–74. Albuquerque: University of New Mexico Press.

Divale, William T. 1974. Migration, External Warfare, and Matrilocal Residence. *Behavior Science Research* 9:74–133.

Eggan, Fred. 1994. The Hopi Indians with Special Reference to Their Cosmology or World-View. In *Kachinas in the Pueblo World*, edited by Polly Schaafsma, pp. 7–16. Albuquerque: University of New Mexico Press.

Feinman, Gary M. 1989. Structuring Debate and Debating Structure: A Mesoamerican Perspective on Prehistoric Social Organization in the American Southwest. In *The Sociopolitical Structure of Prehistoric Southwestern Societies*, edited by Steadman Upham, Kent G. Lightfoot, and Roberta Jewett, pp. 55–75. Boulder: Westview Press.

Flannery, Kent. 1982. The Golden Marshalltown: A Parable for the Archaeology of the 1980s. *American Anthropologist* 84:265–78.

Gilman, Patricia A. 1987. Architecture as Artifact: Pit Structures and Pueblos in the American Southwest. *American Antiquity* 52: 538–64.

Gratz, Kathleen E. and Peter J. Pilles, Jr. 1979. Sinagua Settlement Patterns and Organizational Models: A Trial Survey. Paper Presented at the 50th Annual Meeting of the Southwestern Anthropological Association, Santa Barbara, Available from the Museum of Northern Arizona, Flagstaff.

Graves, Michael W. 1991. Pottery Production and Distribution Among the Kalinga: A Study of Household and Regional Organization and Differentiation. In *Ceramic Ethnoarchaeology*, edited by William A. Longacre, pp. 112–43. Tucson: University of Arizona Press.

Haas, Jonathan and Winifred Creamer. 1996. The Role of Warfare in the Pueblo III Period. In *The Prehistoric Pueblo World A.D. 1150–1350*, edited by Michael A. Adler, pp. 205–13. Tucson: University of Arizona Press.

Hill, James N. 1968. Broken K Pueblo: Patterns of Form and Function. In *New Perspectives in Archeology*, edited by Sally R. Binford and Lewis R. Binford, pp. 103–42. Chicago: Aldine Publishing Company.

Hohmann, John C. 1992. *Through the Mirror of Death: A View of Prehistoric Social Complexity in Central Arizona.* Arizona State University Ph.D. Dissertation. Available through University of Michigan Microfilms.

Hole, Frank, Kent V. Flannery, and James A. Neely. 1969. Prehistory and Human Ecology of the Deh Luran Plain: An Early Village Sequence from Khuzistan, Iran. *University of Michigan Memoirs of the Museum of Anthropology.* No. 1, Ann Arbor.

Hunter, Andrea A. 1994. Native, Cultivated, and Domesticated Plant Use by the Lizard Man Villagers. Manuscript available from the Museum of Northern Arizona, Flagstaff.

Kamp. K. A. 1995. A Use-Wear Analysis of the Function of Basalt Cylinders. *Kiva* 61(2): 109–19.

Kent, K. P. 1983. *Prehistoric Textiles of the Southwest*. Albuquerque: University of New Mexico Press.

Longacre, William A. 1970. *Archaeology as Anthropology: A Case Study*. Tucson: University of Arizona Press.

Malotki, Ekkehart. 1987. *Earthfire: A Hopi Legend of the Sunset Crater Eruption*. Flagstaff: Northland Press.

Maule, S. H. 1963. Corn Growing at Wupatki. *Plateau* 36(1): 29–32.

McGregor, John C. 1941. *Winona and Ridge Ruin*. Museum of Northern Arizona Bulletin No. 18, Flagstaff.

_____. 1943. Burial of an Early American Magician. *Proceedings of the American Philosophical Society* 86(2): 270–98.

McGuire, Randall H. and Christian E. Downum. 1982. A Preliminary Consideration of Desert-Mountain Trade. In *Mogollon Archaeology: Proceedings of the 1980 Mogollon Conference*, edited by P. H. Beckett, pp. 111–22. Ramona, CA: Acoma Books.

Mindeleff, Victor 1891. A Study of Pueblo Architecture in Tusayan and Cibola. *Eighth Annual Report of the Bureau of American Ethnology 1886–1887*, pp. 13–228, Washington. Reprinted in 1981.

Mullett, G. M. 1987. *Spider Woman Stories: Legends of the Hopi Indians*. Tucson: University of Arizona Press.

Murdock, George and Caterina Provost. 1973. Factors in the Division of Labor by Sex: A Cross-Cultural Analysis. *Ethnology* 12:203–25.

Naroll, Raoul. 1962. Floor Area and Settlement Population. *American Antiquity* 27:587–589.

Nequatewa, Edmund. 1993. *Born a Chief: The Nineteenth Century Hopi Boyhood of Edmund Nequatewa*, as told to Alfred F. Whiting and edited by P. David Seaman. Tucson: University of Arizona Press.

Pilles, Peter, J., Jr. 1996. The Pueblo III Period along the Mogollon Rim: the Honanki, Elden, and Turkey Hill Phases of the Sinagua. In *The Prehistoric Pueblo World A.D. 1150–1350*, edited by Michael A. Adler, pp. 59–72. Tucson: University of Arizona Press.

Plog, Fred. 1989. The Sinagua and Their Relations. In *Dynamics of Southwestern Prehistory*, edited by G. Gummerman and L. Cordell, pp. 263–92. Washington, DC: Smithsonian Institution Press.

Rathje, William L. 1978. Archaeological Ethnography . . . Because Sometimes It Is Better to Give Than To Receive. In *Explorations in Ethnoarchaeology*, edited by Richard A. Gould, pp. 49–75. Albuquerque: University of New Mexico Press.

Redman, Charles. 1974. *Archaeological Sampling Strategies*. Addison Wesley Module 55.

Reid, Jefferson and Stephanie Whittlesey. 1997. *The Archaeology of Ancient Arizona*. Tucson: University of Arizona Press.

Renfrew, Colin. 1975. Trade as Action at a Distance: Questions of Integration and Communication. In *Ancient Civilization and Trade*, edited by Jeremy A. Sabloff and C. C. Lamberg-Karlovsky, pp. 3–59. Albuquerque: University of New Mexico Press.

Schiffer, Michael B. 1976. *Behavioral Archaeology.* New York: Academic Press.

_____. 1987. Formation processes of the archaeological record. Albuquerque: University of New Mexico Press.

Service, Elman. 1962. *Primitive Social Organization: An Evolutionary Perspective.* New York: Random House.

Stanislowski, M. B. 1963. *Wupatki Pueblo: A Study in Fusion and Change in Sinagua.* University of Arizona Ph.D. Dissertation. Available from University of Michigan Microfilms.

Talayesva, Don C. 1942. *Sun Chief: the Autobiography of a Hopi Indian.* Edited by Leo Simmons. New Haven: Yale University Press.

Upham, Steadman. 1987. The Tyranny of Ethnographic Analogy in Southwestern Archaeology. In *Coasts, Plains, and Deserts: Essays in Honor of Reynold Ruppe,* edited by S. W. Gaines, pp. 265–81. Anthropological Research Papers 38, Arizona State University, Tempe.

_____. 1989. East Meets West: Hierarchy and Elites in Pueblo Society. In *The Sociopolitical Structure of Prehistoric Southwestern Societies,* edited by Steadman Upham, Kent G. Lightfoot, and Roberta Jewett, pp. 77–102. Boulder: Westview Press.

Varien, M. D. 1984. *Honkey House: The Replication of Three Anasazi Surface Structures.* Unpublished M.A., Department of Anthropology, University of Texas, Austin.

Voth, Henry R. 1905. *The Traditions of the Hopi.* Chicago: Field Columbian Publication 96.

Whittaker, J. C. and K. A. Kamp. 1992. Sinagua Painted Armbands. *Kiva* 58(2):177–87.

Wilcox, David R. 1981. Changing Perspectives on the Protohistoric Pueblos, A.D. 1450–1700. In *The Protohistoric Period in the American Southwest, A.D. 1450–1700,* edited by W. D. Lipe and Michelle Hegmon, pp. 89–111. Occasional Papers of the Crow Canyon Archaeological Center No. 1.

_____. 1996. Pueblo III People and Polity in Relational Context. In *The Prehistoric Pueblo World A.D. 1150–1350,* edited by Michael A. Adler, pp. 241–54. Tucson: University of Arizona Press.

Wilson, John Philip. 1969. *The Sinagua and Their Neighbors.* Unpublished Ph.D. Dissertation. Harvard University, Cambridge.

Suggested Reading

Sinagua:

Fish, P. R., P. J. Pilles, and S. K. Fish. 1980. Colonies, Traders, and Traits: The Hohokam in the North. In *Current Issues in Hohokam Prehistory*, edited by D. Doyel and F. Plog, pp. 151–75. Arizona State University Anthropological Research Papers, vol. 23.

Describes the connections between Hohokam and Sinagua.

Kamp, K. A. and J. C. Whittaker. 1997. *Surviving Adversity: The Sinagua of Lizard Man Village*. University of Utah Anthropological Papers, No. 120, Salt Lake City.

Provides a detailed description of the data and model described in this book.

Pilles, Peter J., Jr. 1987. Hisatsinom: The Ancient People. In *Earthfire*, pp. 105–20. Flagstaff: Northland Press.

Provides a short readable synopsis of Sinagua prehistory.

Pilles, Peter J., Jr. 1996. The Pueblo III Period Along the Mogollon Rim: The Honanki, Elden, and Turkey Hill Phases. In *The Prehistoric Pueblo World A.D. 1150–1350*, edited by Michael A. Adler, pp. 59–72. Tucson: University of Arizona Press.

The most recent explanation of the thesis that the Sinagua were hierarchically organized.

The Prehistoric Southwest:

Adams, E. Charles. 1991. *The Origin and Development of the Pueblo Katsina Cult.* Tucson: University of Arizona Press.

A detailed scholarly discussion of the evidence concerning the meaning and origins of katsina-based religion.

Adler, Michael A. 1996. *The Prehistoric Pueblo World A.D. 1150–1350.* Tucson: University of Arizona Press.

A collection of descriptions of the Puebloan Southwest during the time Lizard Man Village was occupied. Especially interesting is the article on warfare by Haas and Creamer.

Cheek, Lawrence. 1994. *Ancient Peoples of the Southwest A.D. 1250.* Phoenix, AZ: Arizona Highways Book.

A survey of the prehistoric southwest with gorgeous pictures.

Ferguson, William M. and Arthur H. Rohn. 1987. *Anasazi Ruins of the Southwest in Color.* Albuquerque: University of New Mexico Press.

General overview of the prehistory of the Anasazi region with detailed descriptions, pictures, and maps of relevant archaeological sites.

Haury, E. W. 1976. *The Hohokam: Desert Farmers and Craftsmen.* Tucson: University of Arizona Press.

The classic volume on the Hohokam by the foremost Hohokam scholar.

Longacre, William A. 1970. *Archaeology as Anthropology: A Case Study.* Tucson: University of Arizona Press.

The classic attempt to demonstrate matrilocal residence archaeologically.

Merbs, C. F. and R. J. Miller, eds. 1985. *Health and disease in the Prehistoric Southwest.* Arizona State Anthropological Research Paper No. 34, Arizona State, Tempe.

Provides a good overview of studies on prehistoric health.

Minnis, Paul E. and Charles L. Redman. 1990. *Perspectives on Southwestern Prehistory.* Boulder: Westview Press.

A wide variety of professional articles on the Prehistoric Southwest.

Reid, Jefferson and Stephanie Whittlesey. 1997. *The Archaeology of Ancient Arizona.* Tucson: University of Arizona Press.

A synthesis of Arizona archaeology from the Paleo-Indian hunter-gatherers to the Spanish contact period.

Ethnographies:

Connelly, John C. 1979. Hopi Social Organization. In *Handbook of North American Indians, vol. 9, Southwest,* edited by A. Ortiz, pp. 539–53. Washington, DC: Smithsonian Institution Press.

A short, concise description of the Hopi.

Dozier, Edward P. 1983. *The Pueblo Indians of North America.* Prospect Heights, IL: Waveland Press.

A readable synopsis of Pueblo culture.

Dozier, Edward P. 1970. Making Inferences from the Present to the Past. In *Reconstructing Prehistoric Pueblo Societies,* edited by William A. Longacre, pp. 202–13. Albuquerque: University of New Mexico Press.

A discussion of the relevance of modern Puebloan groups for the archaeologist.

Eggan, Fred. 1950. *Social Organization of the Western Pueblos.* Chicago: University of Chicago Press.

A bit tough-going in spots, but the classic treatise.

Eggan, Fred. 1994. The Hopi Indians with Special Reference to Their Cosmology or World-View. In *Kachinas in the Pueblo World,* edited by Polly Schaafsma, pp. 7–16. Albuquerque: University of New Mexico Press.

Very short and readable.

Malotki, Ekkehart. 1987. *Earthfire: A Hopi Legend of the Sunset Crater Eruption.* Flagstaff: Northland Press.

A longer, more detailed version of the Hopi story of the eruption of Sunset Crater presented in chapter 1 of this book, with excellent cultural annotations and glossary.

Mullett, G. M. 1987. *Spider Woman Stories: Legends of the Hopi Indians.* Tucson: University of Arizona Press.

More chance to delve into some of the Hopi tradition via their oral literature.

Stories—Autobiography, Biography, and Fictional Archaeology:

Bandelier, Adolf F. 1972. *The Delight Makers: A Novel of Prehistoric Pueblo Indians.* New York: Harcourt, Brace, and Company. (Originally published in 1890.)

A full-length novel of the prehistoric Southwest written by the early archaeologist for whom Bandelier National Monument is named.

Nequatewa, Edmund. 1993. *Born a Chief: The Nineteenth Century Hopi Boyhood of Edmund Nequatewa,* as told to Alfred F. Whiting and edited by P. David Seaman. Tucson: University of Arizona Press.

The amusing and enlightening story of the first twenty years of Edmund Nequatewa, who was born in the Hopi village of Shipaulovi in 1880.

Roscoe, Will. 1991. *The Zuni Man-Woman*. Albuquerque: University of New Mexico Press.

A discussion of alternative gender roles centering on the life of We'wha, a Zuni berdache.

Sekaquaptewa, Helen. 1969. *Me and Mine*. Edited by Louise Udall. Tucson: University of Arizona Press.

A glimpse at the life of a Hopi woman at the turn of the century.

Talayesva, Don C. 1942. *Sun Chief: the Autobiography of a Hopi Indian*. Edited by Leo Simmons. New Haven: Yale University Press.

The amusing story of Don Talayesva's life, quoted extensively here.

Prehistoric Southwestern Crafts:

Dittert, Alfred E., Jr. and Fred Plog. 1980. *Generations in Clay: Pueblo Pottery of the American Southwest*. Northland Press: Flagstaff.

An attractively illustrated synopsis of modern and prehistoric pottery styles and techniques.

Guthe, Carl E. 1925. *Pueblo Pottery Making: A Study at the Village of San Ildefonso*. New Haven: Yale University Press.

A very early and thorough description of ceramic techniques.

Jernigan, E. Wesley. 1978. *Jewelry of the Prehistoric Southwest*. Santa Fe New Mexico: School of American Research Press.

A comprehensive overview of prehistoric Southwestern jewelry.

Kent, K. P. 1983. *Prehistoric Textiles of the Southwest*. Albuquerque: University of New Mexico Press.

The best reference on prehistoric weaving by the main expert in the field.

Mills, Barbara J. and Patricia L. Crown, eds. 1995. *Ceramic Production in the American Southwest*. Tucson: University of Arizona Press.

A collection of the most recent scholarly writing.

Whittaker, John C. 1994. *Flintknapping: Making and Understanding Stone Tools*. Austin: University of Texas Press.

A how-to book that also discusses the archaeological interpretation of stone tools.

Archaeological Methodology:

Aitken, J. J. 1990. *Science-based Dating in Archaeology*. New York: Longman.

Bass, William M. 1987. *Human Osteology: A Laboratory and Field Manual, 3rd edition*. Columbia, MO: Missouri Archaeological Society Special Publication No. 2.

Binford, Sally R. and Lewis R. Binford, eds. 1968. *New Perspectives in Archaeology*. Chicago: Aldine Publishing Co.

This volume is the classic of "New Archaeology," a 1960s and 1970s movement that stressed archaeology's connections to anthropology and its scientific basis. It still merits reading for the many ground-breaking articles within.

Coles, John. 1979. *Experimental Archaeology*. New York: Academic Press.

About the only brief, readable book on experimental archaeology currently in press.

Gero, Joan M. and Margaret W. Conkey, eds. 1991. *Engendering Archaeology: Women and Prehistory*. Cambridge, MA: Basil Blackwell.

A collection of articles ranging freely across time and space, but united by the theme of gender.

Gould, Richard A. 1978. *Explorations in Ethnoarchaeology*. Albuquerque: University of New Mexico Press.

Klein, Richard G. and Kathryn Cruz-Uribe. 1984. *The Analysis of Animal Bones from Archaeological Sites*. Chicago: University of Chicago Press

Kramer, Carol, ed. 1979. *Ethnoarchaeology: Implications of Ethnography for Archaeology*. New York: Columbia University Press.

Redman, Charles. 1974. *Archaeological Sampling Strategies*. Addison Wesley Module 55.

This is the most readable account of archaeological sampling strategies that I have come across.

Renfrew, Colin and Paul Bahn. 1996. *Archaeology: Theories, Methods, and Practice*. New York: Thames and Hudson.

Sutton, Mark Q. and Brooke S. Arkush. 1996. *Archaeological Laboratory Methods: An Introduction*. Dubuque, IA: Kendall Hunt Publishing.

Thomas, David Hurst. 1974. *Predicting the Past: An Introduction to Anthropological Archaeology*. New York: Holt, Rinehart, Winston, Inc.

Ubelaker, Douglas H. 1984. *Human Skeletal Remains: Excavation, Analysis, Interpretation, revised edition*. Washington, DC: Taraxacum.

Note: These selections only scratch the surface of the vast popular and professional literature.

Index